P. G. Wodehouse and Hollywood

P. G. Wodehouse and Hollywood

Screenwriting, Satires and Adaptations

BRIAN TAVES

with a foreword by RICHARD BRIERS

McFarland & Company, Inc., Publishers
Jefferson, North Carolina, and London

Also by Brian Taves
and from McFarland

Talbot Mundy, Philosopher of Adventure: A Critical Biography (2005)

Other Works by Brian Taves

The Jules Verne Encyclopedia

Robert Florey, the French Expressionist

The Romance of Adventure: The Genre of Historical Adventure Movies

***Frontispiece:* Ray Noble, Constance Collier, Wodehouse, Fred Astaire, and Reginald Gardiner on the set of *A Damsel in Distress* (1937).**

Library of Congress Cataloguing-in-Publication Data

Taves, Brian, 1959–
P. G. Wodehouse and Hollywood : screenwriting, satires and adaptations / Brian Taves ; with a foreword by Richard Briers.
p. cm.
Includes bibliographical references and index.

ISBN 0-7864-2288-2 (softcover : 50# alkaline paper) ∞

1. Wodehouse, P. G. (Pelham Grenville), 1881–1975 — Criticism and interpretation. 2. Wodehouse, P. G. (Pelham Grenville), 1881–1975 — Film and video adaptations. I. Title.
PR6045.O53Z865 2006
823'.912 — dc22 2006001518

British Library cataloguing data are available

On the cover: Robert Montgomery and Eric Blore in *Piccadilly Jim*, 1936; background art by Sarah Sanders

Manufactured in the United States of America

McFarland & Company, Inc., Publishers
Box 611, Jefferson, North Carolina 28640
www.mcfarlandpub.com

For Barbara Graber —
in Bertie Wooster's words,
"my good aunt and deserving aunt" —
with much gratitude

Contents

Foreword
by Richard Briers

It is, I believe, quite common for a person who is asked to introduce a book to at least be acquainted with its author. But not in this case. In my professional career I have met many people, some frequently, some only once, but Brian Taves has, as far as I recall, never swum into my ken.

But I am not proud. I say to myself, as would any member of the acting profession, it is sufficient that he knows me! And the reason he knows me, it seems, is that I am that rare individual: one lucky enough to have performed work written by Wodehouse in cinema, television and radio.

In 2004, two most authoritative and well-researched books about P. G. Wodehouse hit the bookshelves: the biography *Wodehouse: A Life* by Robert McCrum, and *The Complete Lyrics of P. G. Wodehouse* by Barry Day. I wouldn't have thought there was room for another completely new work, but like productions of *Hamlet*, it was not long before the next one appeared.

P. G. Wodehouse and Hollywood: Screenwriting, Satires and Adaptations is the first serious look at Wodehouse's contribution to the recorded media. Brian Taves, who cleverly found himself a niche in the Motion Picture/Broadcasting/Recorded Sound Division at the Library of Congress, has created a reference source that needs to be treated with care by those who love Wodehouse, for two reasons. First, as he explains with great thoroughness, by no means all the work to which Wodehouse gave his name (and it seems that in some cases he may not have done so wittingly) is of a very high standard, and you may take umbrage at the producers, directors and stars involved and want to throw things. But secondly, a significant part of the better work has been lost, and you may gnash your teeth at the loss.

My own favorite contribution to recorded Wodehouse was the series of radio programs that had the generic title *What Ho, Jeeves!* and started in the late 1970s. Michael Hordern played Jeeves to my Bertie, and the supporting cast included such wonderful players, too many of them now gone, as Paul Eddington, John le Mesurier, Ronald Fraser, David Jason,

Jonathan Cecil, Miriam Margolyes and Joan Sanderson. Even Percy Edwards found a role as Bartholomew, the Aberdeen terrier. The recordings were very hard work, but we loved the results.

The first Wodehouse in which I performed on screen was a 1962 film, *The Girl on the Boat*. It was released on video a few years ago as part of a Norman Wisdom celebration, and all I will say is that I looked very young. In contrast, perhaps, to my representation of Gally Threepwood in the BBC TV film of *Heavy Weather*, shown on Christmas Eve, 1995. But enough, I mustn't give away the plot. Read on — you'll find all you want to know about the silent adaptations, Wodehouse's spell as Hollywood screenwriter, his stories satirizing Hollywood, the coming of radio and television, recordings and developments since his death in 1975.

Richard Briers (left) as Galahad Threepwood with Peter O'Toole as Lord Emsworth in *Heavy Weather* (1995).

And when you have read the book you might just find that you know Brian Taves— a little — as well.

Preface

I first conceived this study of P. G. Wodehouse's Hollywood works in the early 1980s, gathering relevant data while completing my Ph.D. in cinema-television critical studies at the University of Southern California. While at the American Film Institute, and after beginning my career in the Library of Congress, I continued accumulating information. The preparation of a 1999 tribute to Wodehouse on film and television at the Library, together with presentations before each night's screening, gave me the opportunity to begin to organize my material. With the encouragement of newfound friends at the Wodehouse Society, I gave an address on Wodehouse and Hollywood at the group's 2001 Philadelphia convention. Beginning in 2000, I authored more than a dozen articles on various aspects of the subject in the journals of the American and British Wodehouse organizations. I gradually realized that the topic required going beyond the length possible in even a series of articles and demanded book-length treatment.

An important part of such a book would be the supplementary information. There are two appendices, one of Wodehouse's writing about Hollywood, and a complete filmography of all the motion picture and television works to which he contributed or that adapted his stories. Rather than simply abbreviating series information, I have included each episode, especially significant when each one is based on various stories by an author. I realized that it was especially important to note the sources for the adaptations of Wodehouse. In many cases, providing this information in a manner useful to readers in different countries presented unexpected complexities and challenges, because the original stories were often issued under several titles or collected in different anthologies in the United States and England. To maximize the usefulness of such information, I have given each original magazine appearance, along with the initial hardcover publication, for both countries.

Derek Keevil's early *Jeeves and Wooster* television series website opened my eyes to the necessity for explaining such related topics as the distinctions between British and American broadcasts. Combing my off-air tapes of every episode shown in the United States provided a surprise by revealing that the whole series had not been played in this country.

The collection of the Margaret Herrick Library at the Academy of Motion Picture Arts and Sciences filled gaps on Wodehouse's screenwriting as well as other bits of the puzzle of his Hollywood sojourn. I also saw the films preserved at the British Film Institute during a trip to England. Rare video titles were borrowed from Eddie Brandt's Saturday Matinee, where Claire Brandt combed the stills archive for illustrations.

I am grateful for assistance from Norman Murphy, David Landman, Curtis Armstrong, Luke McKernan, and W.C. Caywood. Margaret Compton provided a number of citations of which I was not previously aware.

Most of all, my thanks go to the internationally renowned Wodehouse scholar Tony Ring for many corrections and providing information, especially during a visit to his home for research. He also responded to my request and arranged the preface by that most noted of Wodehouse actors, Richard Briers, who for more than 30 years has definitively enacted many of the author's famous characters in movies, radio, and television.

As Bertie Wooster might say, I've been dashed fortunate, don't you think, Jeeves?

Introduction

Pelham Grenville "Plum" Wodehouse (1881–1975) has been part of film and television history in a number of ways in the course of some 150 movies and television productions. His 70-plus novels and even more numerous short stories have been made into many movie and television productions. Wodehouse was also a prolific lyricist, and adapter and originator of plays, and much of this stage work has appeared on screen. He spent two sojourns in Hollywood as a scriptwriter, which in turn led to a dozen novels, short stories, and autobiographical memoirs concentrating on Hollywood settings or characters.

Many writers have reflected one or two of these strands. For instance, some whose work was adapted for the screen also worked as scriptwriters, especially during Hollywood's studio era. However, few also wrote about the industry and covered all three bases. F. Scott Fitzgerald most prominently comes to mind, but his writing about Hollywood was considerably more limited. Wodehouse, by contrast, composed Hollywood stories over a span of 45 years, with all the transformations in the cinematic world during that time. When he concluded his literary portrait of Hollywood and filmmakers, his view had shifted to accommodate his own experiences with the changes that had occurred in the business.

Some might argue that a dramatic portrait such as Fitzgerald's Monroe Stahr from *The Last Tycoon* is inevitably the literary superior of Wodehouse's satires of such fictional moguls as Jacob Z. Schnellenhamer and Ivor Llewellyn. I would counter that for anyone familiar with Wodehouse's creations, his alternate Hollywood is the equal of any portrait, comedic or dramatic. Wodehouse's fictional Hollywood reveals that he understood the mechanics and the frailties of the industry as well as anyone. Moreover, his satire was keen and pointed, exposing the actual structure of the filmmaking process itself.

He observed not only the making of feature films of his stories, but shorts and series as well. He was swept along with the rise of a new medium, television, which was even more suited to his stories than movies. Wodehouse lived to see television develop its many forms, from single programs to series, and find new ways to adapt his work. And that shift surely altered his own conception of the medium, as over time it proved increasingly amenable to his brand of storytelling.

Of his own composing for the screen, Wodehouse spoke with undue humility to contemporary interviewers, mentioning only a few of the projects he labored over during the first of his two stints as a Hollywood screenwriter. This reticence has since been emulated by many neglectful biographers, and the full extent of his activities has been hitherto overlooked. Moreover, both times Wodehouse worked at the studios (1930–31 and 1936–37), he became involved with minor contretemps that were the result of the same sort of errors of judgment to which he fell victim during World War II. A review here of this latter portion of his life has been necessitated by the fact that Wodehouse became involved with the German film industry during his wartime stay in Berlin.

His work was adapted for the screen in a variety of countries, and outside of England and the United States his stories were notably popular in Sweden and Germany. He dealt with the arrangements of rights even when uninvolved in the adaptation itself. Wodehouse made appearances on television, and his life has been turned into documentary and drama.

Almost as important as another medium of adaptation are radio plays. The most significant of these are covered here, for in many cases they have proven the ideal medium for relating his stories, allowing his dialogue and narration to be spoken in their original form. Beyond this, the audio world has become increasingly vital in another way: more and more, the Wodehouse stories are not just read with the eyes, but heard, in spoken versions in which a single voice interprets his written word.

There is a further layer of intertextuality in Wodehouse's relation to the theater, his second career. Throughout his writing, Wodehouse's plays frequently became novels and vice versa, and he compared his literary style to making a musical comedy of life. He imagined his stories in theatrical terms and did his best prose writing after his stage experience. When screen versions of his work appeared, and when he went to Hollywood, it was with the background of both having had stories adapted for the proscenium arch and writing directly for it. Indeed, Wodehouse's single instance of transforming one of his own novels for the screen involved one he had also assisted in bringing to the stage, *A Damsel in Distress.*

This study seeks to interweave these diverse strands and following a general chronological outline, reveals Wodehouse's increasingly complex interactions with all these media. Various sections highlight the emphases that appeared at different times in his career, from adaptations, to screenwriting, to Hollywood satires.

I

The Silents

Pelham Grenville Wodehouse was born in Guildford, Surrey, England, on October 15, 1881. As the third of four brothers, family income did not offer the opportunity for a university education after he finished private schools at age 19. Young Wodehouse knew he wanted to write, but was urged toward a career in banking. After two years, already writing extensively for magazines and with his first book appearing, he was able to quit the day job in 1902.

Long before motion pictures began to figure in Wodehouse's mind, he had become active in the stage. Contributing the book or lyrics to more than 50 shows, Wodehouse's stage work was primarily in collaboration, or as an adaptation. Many foreign plays that made the transition to the English-speaking theater did so largely due to his skill. Several were adapted from the Hungarian, Wodehouse using a translation, with the original usually serving primarily as a source for the plot. In chapter 3 of his theatrical autobiography, *Bring on the Girls*, he says, "You know what stinkers these Hungarian books are. I had to invent practically a new story." Some of these adaptations eventually made their way to the screen, such as *Candle-Light*; *Good Morning, Bill*; and *Arthur*.

From 1915 through 1928 Wodehouse was involved in writing the lyrics, and sometimes the book, for some 18 musical comedies produced on the London and New York stage, nearly all of them highly successful. As he wrote in chapter 18 of his autobiography, *Over Seventy*, "For years scarcely a day passed whose low descending sun did not see me at my desk trying to find some rhyme for 'June' that would not be 'soon,' 'moon,' 'tune,' or 'spoon.'" In the summer of 1916 he first combined with his frequent collaborators, Jerome Kern and Guy Bolton. George Gershwin would be a less frequent collaborator. Typically Kern would provide the music, Wodehouse the lyrics, and Bolton the book. Their work helped to establish the new form of the American musical comedy, defined by its strong book, amusing dialogue, and lyrics that enhanced characterization or furthered the plot, and which could be performed on a small scale with limited sets and musicians. Wodehouse's lyrics were compared with those of W.S.

Gilbert and Oscar Hammerstein II, and had a warmth and sincerity beneath the apparent frivolity, summoning an aura of idealized happiness no less than in his prose.

Decades later the musical legacy of these years would be celebrated in two widely divergent films. In 1945, production began on a fictionalized biography of Kern featuring many of his songs. Kern died late in the year. The movie, one of Metro-Goldwyn-Mayer's top productions, was titled *Till the Clouds Roll By* and released in 1946. A number of Kern's associates were prominently mentioned, but Wodehouse was not, although three of his songs were performed. He later recalled that he received £1,000 per lyric, but in fact per a contract of February 13, 1946, he was paid $6,000 by Loews for the nonexclusive rights to "Leave it to Jane," "Cleopatterer," "The Sun Shines Brighter," "The Land Where the Good Songs Go," "Bill," and exclusive rights to "Till the Clouds Roll By."[1]

Many of the same achievements were related, but from Wodehouse's perspective, in *Wodehouse on Broadway*, a 90-minute Plymouth Theatre Royal production broadcast by the BBC in 1989, written and produced by Tony Staveacre and directed by Keith Cheetham. Unlike the heaviness of *Till the Clouds Roll By*, with its somber, unenlightening, and highly fictive tone, *Wodehouse on Broadway* was vastly superior. While a sprightly revue of 20 of his songs, *Wodehouse on Broadway* also placed them in a context that told of their creation. The biography and music weave together effortlessly, the songs not only presenting highlights of his work, but also commenting on the mood and development of Wodehouse's career. For instance, "Napoleon" is sung after mentioning producer Erlanger's own Napoleonic size and behavior.

Wodehouse on Broadway is narrated by the character of Guy Bolton and structured around the friendship between the two men, but it only partly captures the contrast in their characters that made their compatibility so surprising. Wodehouse appears not only in dialogue but direct address, and the script effectively weaves together many of his autobiographical anecdotes. The two not only observe performances of their work but sing it themselves, a combination surprisingly unobtrusive—and an indication of the success of merging the audience with the principals in their theatrical world.

While the recording is a taped performance of a stage production, visual effects, photographs, film projections of early New York, and period scenes help to convey the time and place. *Wodehouse on Broadway* is well staged, and although adhering generally to long shot and proscenium limits, occasionally breaks out of them. There is a willingness to surprise the audience, as when the performers from *The Rose of China*, a theatrical failure, are peremptorily dragged from the stage before finishing their number.

The outline is provided by the 1953 Bolton-Wodehouse joint reminiscence, liberally fictionalized, which they titled *Bring on the Girls.* The story begins in England, where the young Wodehouse first met Kern in 1906; they resumed the collaboration a decade later when Wodehouse arrived in the United States and they were joined by Bolton. *Wodehouse on Broadway* chronicles encounters with such individuals as Henry Savage, Marion Davies, the Gershwins, and the end of the collaboration with Kern. Wodehouse's strong affection for his alma mater, Dulwich College, is conveyed, his general disengagement from the world around him, and in the only major misstep, an excessively personal portrayal of his marriage to Ethel. *Wodehouse on Broadway* has a very strong viewpoint, and is certainly an interpretation, an enactment rather than a documentary, despite its generally factual tone; that is its strength, as long as it is accepted as such.

Wodehouse was living and writing in both England and America, selling stories to magazines in both countries. In the summer of 1914, he met a widow, Mrs. Ethel Rowley, who had a nine-year-old daughter, Leonora, in an English boarding school. He began a whirlwind courtship. When a check from Munsey's brought him $2,000 for *Their Mutual Child* (filmed six years later), it seemed enough of a prospect on which to marry. Bad eyesight caused him to be rejected for military service, so he remained in New York.[2] Subsequently he adopted his stepdaughter, Leonora, whom he came to idolize.

By the end of 1914, Wodehouse believed he had sold a book of short stories, *The Man Upstairs*, published in London by Methuen at the beginning of the year, to the Famous Players film company. The sale was to fetch at least $2,000, but his agent at the time proved incompetent and the result was a fiasco. Wodehouse had hoped that a series of films would strengthen his position with print editors.[3]

The first feature film from a Wodehouse source was made the same year, when *A Gentleman of Leisure* was produced, based on the 1911 play Wodehouse coauthored with John Stapleton from his 1910 novel titled *The Intrusion of Jimmy* in the United States. The play had been reprised in 1913 in Chicago under the title *A Thief for a Night.*

Henry Woodruff was originally slated to star in the film, but because of his illness, Wallace Eddinger took the role that had been played on the stage by Douglas Fairbanks and John Barrymore. A theater star in his first film, Eddinger is an unlikely romantic lead, bearing a strong resemblance to the up-and-coming cowboy star Hoot Gibson.

"My pearls have been stolen!" ***A Gentleman of Leisure*** **(1915), from left: Gertrude Kellar, Sydney Deane, Wallace Eddinger, and Carol Hollaway.**

A Gentleman of Leisure was produced by Jesse L. Lasky Feature Play Company for Paramount and released in January 1915. It was directed by George Melford, supervised by Cecil B. DeMille, with the scenario by William C. DeMille. Preserved at the Library of Congress, the movie is surprisingly faithful to the source, particularly considering the limitations of the 75-minute running time and the reliance on intertitles for exposition and dialogue. It includes most of Wodehouse's major incidents and characters, such as the shipboard meeting, the criminal break-in, outsmarting the crook, and the theft and exchange of the diamonds. From the standpoint of fidelity, *A Gentleman of Leisure* could not be better, but as a film it is not quite as skillful, although overall a commendable effort.

The collaboration with Stapleton proved an unusually acrimonious one for Wodehouse. In a letter of December 2, 1914, Wodehouse noted that he found that rights to moving pictures were so new a part of the entertainment scene that it was uncertain whether they were covered in his theater contracts. When Stapleton dramatized the book, he received two-thirds of the proceeds. When filmmakers wanted to put the story on the screen, the question arose whether it was to be derived from the book or the play.[4] By October 1914, Stapleton was disputing Wodehouse's right to sell the movie rights, and it became a test case with the Authors' League.[5]

On November 23, 1914, the rights to any silent presentation of the play, "and theme thereof" (presumably thus encompassing the novel), on screen were bought by the Jesse L. Lasky Feature Play Co. for 5 percent of the sales of the film. Stapleton was to receive $500 for providing a scenario for the movie, while he and Wodehouse were to receive a $500 advance apiece against the coming profits from the film. The contract had an unusual provision that the movie had to be in release by July 1, 1915, or $500 in penalties and another $500 would be paid to the authors every six months until the movie was in theaters—a sign of the strong negotiating position for the property. Wodehouse anticipated his share as up to £1,000. However, the play's producer then took legal action against Lasky, claiming that he had first claim on the film sales.[6]

A Gentleman of Leisure was remade in 1923, this time starring Jack Holt and directed by Joseph Henabery from Anthony Coldeway's less faithful adaptation. A new contract between Stapleton and Famous Players–Lasky was signed on November 13, 1923, and he was to receive $5,000 for the rights to the play, along with its source, *The Intrusion of Jimmy*. Rights were to remain with the buyer when copyright was renewed. Wodehouse's

A Gentleman of Leisure (1923) with Jack Holt as Robert Pitt (left).

name resurfaces when, on October 30, 1925, he and Stapleton jointly sold, for $750, all except film rights to the play to the Kane and Thatcher Holding Corp.[7]

Wodehouse was gaining fame in other ways. By 1915 his first serial, *Something New*, was bought by the *Saturday Evening Post* for $3,500, and in coming decades he would become accustomed to receiving up to ten times that amount from the magazine for a novel. By the end of the 1910s, Wodehouse stories and novels had gained a sufficient high profile that they became obvious candidates for filmic treatment. Wodehouse's British agent was setting prices for the movie rights to his stories.[8]

After *A Gentleman of Leisure*, a number of additional Wodehouse silent films were made in the United States and England, but unfortunately most of these are no longer extant. The same year, 1915, a Wodehouse short story was filmed as an American two-reeler from Essanay, *Rule Sixty-Three*, described by a reviewer as "cold reason attempting to get the better of Dan Cupid and suffering ignominious defeat.[9] Essanay also produced the next Wodehouse feature, *Uneasy Money* (1918), from a 1916 novel, and the movie was Essanay's first venture in a strategy to produce "Ultra Features" at various times. The story concerned an Englishman who inherits an American millionaire's fortune for improving his golf game, and decides to return it to the family.

The two-reel short *Stick Around* (1920), produced by A.J. Van Beuren, was a satire of musical conventions and based on the 1915 story "Bill the Bloodhound." Ernest Truex starred as a man who falls in love with one of the chorus who refuses to marry him. He follows her in preposterous disguise until a mouse up his pant leg makes him win the laughs of an audience, and the girl's affection. At the time, Truex was a neighbor and golfing buddy of Wodehouse, living in Great Neck among the Broadway-literati enclave, and he and Wodehouse considered a stage collaboration as well.[10]

In America, Wodehouse novels filmed included *A Damsel in Distress* (1919), *The Prince and Betty* (1919), *Piccadilly Jim* (1920), *Their Mutual Child* (1920) (from the novel known as *The Coming of Bill* in England), and *The Small Bachelor* (1927). Wodehouse's work for the theater was also brought to the silent screen: *Oh, Boy!* (1919) and *Oh, Lady, Lady* (1920), both from a book and lyrics by Wodehouse and Guy Bolton; *Sally* (1925), from the Ziegfeld musical by Bolton and Kern with lyrics by Wodehouse; and *Oh, Kay!* (1928), from the play by Bolton and Wodehouse.

Oh, Lady, Lady was produced by Realart Pictures, adapted by Edith Kennedy, with Major Maurice Campbell directing stars Bebe Daniels and Harrison Ford. Based on a Princess Theater show, it was Wodehouse's personal favorite.[11] In *Oh, Lady, Lady*, a man feared that a former sweetheart,

Bebe Daniels (center) and Harrison Ford (left) in *Oh, Lady, Lady*.

now an actress, wanted to scandalize his wedding, when in fact her intentions were good and she had fallen for his best man. Wodehouse turned the play into a novel, *The Small Bachelor*, from which the movie of the same title was made. In it, a prospective mother-in-law tries to foil her daughter's wedding, but true love triumphs.

The prices for Wodehouse material ascended rapidly over the decade, as revealed in copyright assignments. When Essanay bought the rights to *Uneasy Money* on January 14, 1918, $1,500 was paid; Wodehouse had earned $5,000 from the sale of serial rights to the *Saturday Evening Post*.[12] Nine years later, on February 27, 1927, when Universal bought all motion picture rights to *The Small Bachelor* in perpetuity, the sale brought $15,000. The American Play Company acted as agent for both deals.[13]

Strangely, the Owen Moore Film Corporation bought the rights to both *Piccadilly Jim* and *Love Among the Chickens* on July 19, 1921, although the movie *Piccadilly Jim* was already released by the end of 1919.[14] $8,000 was paid for the rights to *Piccadilly Jim*, $500 more than Wodehouse received for the sale of the novel to the *Saturday Evening Post*.[15] Wesley Ruggles directed Moore in the lead of *Piccadilly Jim*, using the streets and the subways of New York City as locations.

By contrast, the film rights to *Love Among the Chickens* brought $4,000, but this Stanley Featherstonehaugh Ukridge novel was never made. Wodehouse found that in order to release the rights he had to pay $250 to a crooked agent who had pocketed the serial sales proceeds and copyrighted the book in his own, rather than Wodehouse's, name.[16] Wodehouse was also involved in a stage version of *Love Among the Chickens*, collaborating with Rudolf Lothar; it was adapted by Herman Bernstein. The novel was first published in England in June 1906 and in the United States in May 1909, before being entirely rewritten for English publication in June 1921.

Several filmmakers were involved in multiple Wodehouse cinema productions during these years. Albert Capellani's first film was *Oh, Boy!*, which he produced, directed, and adapted; he also produced *A Damsel in Distress*. Both starred June Caprice, Creighton Hale (who had been in the stage production of *Oh, Boy!*), and William H. Thompson. The film of *Oh, Boy!* began by showing Capellani as an orchestra leader before an audience awaiting the curtain coming up on a musical comedy. A marriage is kept secret because of family opposition, and finally overcome by threatening to reveal their accidental drunken escapades. *Oh, Boy!* had originally cost $29,000 to produce but became the biggest hit Bolton, Wodehouse, and Kern ever wrote for the Princess Theater, leaving it sold out for months, with tickets scalped at the then-unheard-of price of $50.[17]

Jesse D. Hampton produced *The Prince and Betty*, with Robert Thornby directing the adaptation by Fred Myton, which starred William Desmond and Mary Thurman. Hampton paid Wodehouse $825 for the rights in a contract signed on April 15, 1919, with the provision that the author's name was to appear large enough to be read in the billing.[18] The source novel had a peculiar publication history, published in three different versions, originally as *Psmith, Journalist*, then in two different versions in the United States and England as *The Prince and Betty* in 1912, along with different serial versions of each. Finally, after the film, Wodehouse rewrote the book again nearly two decades later as *A Prince for Hire*, the only time he turned out a new version of one of his books after it was filmed. Ironically, the film is faithful to none of these sources, concentrating on the Ruritanian portion, involving a man whose prospects in the eyes of the woman he loves only worsen as a result of his change in status from penniless to the heir of the crown of a European gambling principality. A year later, Hampton produced *Their Mutual Child*, with George L. Cox directing an adaptation by Daniel F. Whitcomb, relating how "the tie that binds" initially separates, and ultimately unites, a husband and wife.

Two of the stage shows adapted to film starred Colleen Moore: *Sally*

Colleen Moore in *Sally* (1925).

and *Oh, Kay!*. The 1925 film version of *Sally* was from the play by Bolton, Kern, Clifford Grey, and Wodehouse. Descended from an original draft entitled *The Little Thing* in 1916, *Sally* was finally staged by Florenz Ziegfeld in 1920 as a vehicle for star Marilyn Miller, but Wodehouse was away while Bolton and Kern redrafted their original play; the result used little of the Wodehouse material. The silent movie script was adapted by June Mathis and directed by Alfred E. Green for First National Pictures, and starred Moore with Lloyd Hughes and Leon Errol.

The rights to *Oh, Kay!* had been sold to Elsie Janis on December 15, 1927. It was adapted for film by Carey Wilson and directed by Mervyn

Colleen Moore, Lawrence Gray, and Alan Hale in *Oh, Kay!*

LeRoy for First National Pictures, and starred Moore with Lawrence Gray and Alan Hale. A man and woman, each to be married separately the next day, meet when her yacht is damaged in the storm and she goes ashore at the deserted mansion where he is spending a last night. To elude a detective, she poses as his wife, while a bootlegger who is on the lam impersonates the butler. The original play, *Oh, Kay!*, had been an enormous success, uniting Wodehouse with George and Ira Gershwin, with whom he would collaborate on future stage and screen productions. On *Oh, Kay!*, Wodehouse assisted with the lyrics and anglicized them for the London production, while also collaborating on the libretto with Guy Bolton.

By 1919, Wodehouse was the subject of the first of two series of comedy shorts. The first series was made from Wodehouse's Reggie Pepper stories in 1919. Among the titles were *Making Good with Mother* and *Cutting Out Venus*, starring Lawrence Grossmith and Charles Coleman, and directed by Lawrence C. Windom. A Bertie Wooster prototype, Pepper was given a manservant who was a reformed burglar named "Jeeves."[19]

In 1924, six half-hour comedy shorts were made by Stoll Picture Productions Ltd. in England of Wodehouse's golf stories. These have recently

A poster for *Sally* (1925).

been restored, and three have been made available together on video: *Rodney Fails to Qualify*, *Chester Forgets Himself*, and *The Long Hole* (retitled *The Moving Hazard* in its reissue). The other titles in the series are *The Clicking of Cuthbert*, *Ordeal by Golf* and *The Magic Plus Fours*.

Produced by Andrew P. Wilson, the series was generally faithful to the stories and used some of the Wodehouse language in the intertitles. However, frequently major new subplots and gags were added, including a mischievous caddie played by midget Harry Beasley, possibly the source of Wodehouse's later jokes in "The Nodder" about child stars actually being midgets. The regular inserts of Beasley's antics interrupt the progression of the Wodehouse plot. The framing device of the Oldest Member was deleted, leaving Beasley as the only regular in the series, and he became advertised as the star of the series. His centrality was indicated by such introductions as "The eternal caddie, a student of form and language," before cutting to a shot of him holding racing forms.

This is the beginning of *The Clicking of Cuthbert*, which was not only the first of the films but the series title. *The Clicking of Cuthbert* effectively echoed Wodehouse's dichotomy between popular characters (and by extension, their literary taste) and the supposed refinement of the cultural elite — which he represents through the golfers and literary circles, respectively. Cuthbert (Peter Haddon) fails to impress Adeline (Helena Pickard), who prefers the poet Raymond Parsloe Devine (Peter Upcher). Her view is changed when visiting Russian novelist Vladimir Brusiloff (Moore Marriott), author of *The Sewers of Fate*, proffers a withering critique on Devine. Brusiloff would rather exchange golf yarns with Cuthbert. Despite the facts that Brusiloff is less caricatured than in the story and that the film diminishes his passion for the game by claiming he defeated his golf competitors in Russia by killing them, the adaptation renders the key theme of the story. Not until three segments of the 1970s *Wodehouse Playhouse* anthology on television were any of the golf stories again brought to the screen.

Amidst the plethora of silent comedic Wodehouse adaptations is the most distinctive of all Wodehouse pictures, *Der Goldene Schmetterling*, preserved by the British Film Institute. This Sacha-Film production was made in 1926 and directed by Michael Curtiz shortly before his departure for Hollywood. Starring an international cast, made in Austria and coproduced by German and Danish companies, the film was partly shot on location in England. It was distributed in England by Stoll, the company behind the Wodehouse golf shorts, in a form abbreviated to five reels. There it was titled *The Golden Butterfly*, but despite the title resemblance it was unrelated to the play *The Golden Moth* by Fred Thompson and Wodehouse, with which the film has sometimes been incorrectly connected. Instead, *The Golden Butterfly* was adapted from the 1915 short story "The Making of Mac's." (In the United States the movie had minimal release and was retitled *The Road to Happiness.*)

The slightly humorous tone of the original disappeared from the adaptation. The narrator of the original, the colloquial English waiter Uncle Bill, whose language, asides, and rendering of the tale provides much of the amusement, becomes only a secondary character, with the telling shifted to an omniscient perspective. As a result, even in its shortened English release form, *The Golden Butterfly*, with its intensely Germanic characterizations, acting, and costumes, becomes an example of *kammerspiele*, an intimate human drama with minimal number of players and embellishment, concentrating on artistic visuals and intensity of presentation.

At MacFarland's Restaurant, Andy (Nils Asther), leaves to study at Cambridge, but must quit to take over the family business upon the death of his father. One day, playboy Teddy Abernon (Jack Trevor) comes into the restaurant, and quickly becomes smitten with Lillian Winston (Lili Damita), the cashier and sweetheart of Andy. Despite the old waiter Uncle Bill (Charles Platen) telling Andy he is too strict, he becomes jealous of Teddy's flirtations with Lillian, especially when he learns she has been studying dancing to appear on a stage chorus. Bored with her job as a cashier, the monotony compels her to accept even such a man as Teddy.

Lillian becomes a star, dressing extravagantly, but Andy rebuffs Lillian's attempts at a reconciliation, and Teddy proposes marriage to her while others compete for her favor. She brings theatrical companions to MacFarland's, making it a fashionable, thriving establishment. Old customers miss enjoying the food in quiet, and Andy pretends not to see her. When Lillian and Teddy celebrate their engagement, Andy is dejected, realizing he has lost her. However, she too is sad, recognizing she cannot marry Teddy because she still loves Andy even though she believes he does not care for her.

On stage, in a surreal sequence evoking some of the most bizarre moments in 1920s German expressionist cinema, Lillian does an exotic dance as a butterfly. She becomes trapped in the web of a giant spider, but the creature seems to force her to fall from stage into the basement. Visiting friend Andre Dubois (Curt Bois) finds Lillian has failed to accept that her dance career is over until she discovers she can no longer accomplish the necessary movements.

Uncle Bill tells Andy he should be looking after Lillian. Teddy, realizing Lillian will never love him but only Andy, joins Bill in concocting a scheme to unite the stubborn lovers. Andy, told Lillian is suicidal, blames Teddy and shoots him in a struggle as Lillian arrives—but Teddy had put blanks in the gun. The farcical overtone of the ending is incompatible with the otherwise completely serious demeanor of the movie. Curiously, Wodehouse's original ending had the heroine (named Katie) informing Uncle Bill of her suicide plans after breaking her ankle during a rehearsal, and of her desire for Andy to never know the truth. Bill talks her into delaying, showing her suicide note to Andy, finally uniting the couple. Teddy and Dubois were absent entirely from the original.

The serious artistry of *Der Goldene Schmetterling* separates it from other Wodehouse adaptations. It succeeds as a product of very high cultural tone, far beyond the more populist, entertainment-directed aims of other adaptations and of Wodehouse's own writings. The new characters added a complexity that would otherwise have been lacking, endowing the story's development with romantic subplots appropriate to the casting of vampish Damita as the star. As a rendering of the story itself, *Der Goldene Schmetterling* would be regarded as a failure save for the fact that it entirely reinterprets the original for its own purpose, one that is memorable in its own right, more so than some attempts to simply imitate the source. The fact that the original included a suicide attempt already placed it outside of the conventional Wodehouse parameters; only his authorial voice could convert it into a source of light amusement. Save for the ending, many of the incidents in *Der Goldene Schmetterling* are taken from the story, yet their generic context is entirely shifted from farce to tragedy.

Of all the foreign plays Wodehouse adapted for the English-speaking stage, none has had as many screen incarnations as his version of Jacques Deval's *Dans sa candeur naïve*. Valerie Wyngate had adapted it into the stage play *Her Cardboard Lover* for producer-director Gilbert Miller. However, the try-out was unsatisfactory, and Miller asked Wodehouse to rewrite the show during February 1927. It opened on Broadway on March 21, 1927, running for 152 performances. Jeanne Eagels was the female lead, Simone, and Stanley Logan and newcomer Leslie Howard were philandering ex-husband Tony and cardboard lover Andre, respectively. Wodehouse was so confident in his rewriting that, prior to its opening, he bought out a one-third share for $10,000 and was soon making a $2,500-a-week profit.[20] The production lasted until Eagels's drinking prevented her from performing.[21] On October 31, 1927, Daniel Frohman sold the film rights to Paramount Famous Lasky, who in turn sold them to Metro-Goldwyn-Mayer on December 20, 1927 (the film rights purchase mentioned only Wyngate's name).

Marion Davies and Nils Asther in *The Cardboard Lover* (1925).

The play was first brought to the screen the next year, in 1928, in a film preserved at the Library of Congress. This 71-minute silent version, entitled *The Cardboard Lover*, credited the original Deval source. In the movie, as adapted by Carey Wilson, the gender base is switched: instead of two men fighting over a woman susceptible to the charms of each, it is two women dueling for a champion tennis player, Andre. (Probably this was the reason for the title modification from *Her* to *The*.)

Marion Davies stars as Sally, a flapper on tour in Monte Carlo, where she becomes determined to secure Andre's autograph. This leads her to follow him and learn of the flagrant infidelity of his amour, Simone, in this case with an aging opera singer whose ungentlemanly inscription in her autograph book Sally tears out. Continuing her pursuit, Sally calls "Bunko!" in the casino and finds herself $50,000 in debt. Andre saves her, but only after securing her promise to help keep him from Simone.

However, it is a pledge he wishes she would forget, for Simone has him firmly in her grip; even a vicious parody of her mannerisms, with Sally in a costume evoking Simone, fails to turn him. Simone need only announce she is on her way for Andre to once again become her slave, until she walks out when Sally appears in pajamas and brushing her teeth as if she had taken up a liberal residence with Andre. Not until Sally finally punches Andre, and he pushes her in response so that she falls, does he realize he loves her and only her. Surrounded by flowers and gifts, Sally takes her time about her recovery, knowing she has won all Andre's love.

Davies gives a riotous performance, justifying her reputation as a skilled comedienne. Nils Asther fits the role of Andre, as does Jetta Goudal that of Simone, and the movie steadily builds momentum as it captures the essential silliness and delight of the play under Robert Z. Leonard's direction.

The Cardboard Lover was almost issued by the time of the opening of the play in England on August 21, 1928, with Tallulah Bankhead taking the female lead opposite Tony Melford as Tony, and with Leslie Howard continuing as Andre. The first sound film production of Wodehouse was *Her Cardboard Lover*, released by British Photophone in England in April 1929. This five-minute short, directed by Clayton Hutton and shot in Berlin, doubtless took advantage of the superior recording studios there, and featured a scene of Bankhead as Simone undressing while talking on the telephone.

Surprisingly, for an author so dependent on dialogue and language, the silent era was the most prolific in the quantity of cinematic adaptations of Wodehouse. The "talkies," while taking Wodehouse himself to Hollywood, did not bring quite as many adaptations to the screen; not until the coming of television would Wodehouse again prove so popular a source.

The years of the silent cinema had also been the ones in which Wodehouse had reached the height of his popularity as a playwright and gained fame for his short stories and novels. He acquired a reputation for sophisticated, elegant, and witty humor with an English background in prose; but just as significant was his work for the theater, both in adaptations or musical comedies. Examples of all of these had been brought to the screen, as Wodehouse found success in prose, theater, and cinema. Film rights alone were bringing an amount equivalent to his payment for a books' magazine serialization. In addition, many of the plays, novels, and stories composed during this period, including *A Damsel in Distress*, *Piccadilly Jim*, and *Her Cardboard Lover*, would be remade in the following decade.

II

Screenwriter

Hollywood, with the coming of sound, was searching for script writers appropriate to the new medium, especially individuals with stage experience. During the summer of 1929, having traveled to New York to collaborate on a Flo Ziegfeld production experiencing endless delays, Wodehouse decided to make his first visit to the film capital in August. In chapter 17 of *Bring On the Girls*, he describes this somewhat fancifully as a summons to join Guy Bolton at Metro-Goldwyn-Mayer and write a script for W.C. Fields. The comedian tells them that, as appalling as conditions were before sound, with talkies they are now much worse, with everyone in the industry walking around in circles and clutching their heads. The supervisor on the production was to be a man named Palmer, whom Bolton and Wodehouse had first met as the wretched cook on board a poor excuse for a yacht owned by a chiseling theatrical impressario, Henry W. Savage.[1]

Although feeling that Hollywood should have little terror for two men who had survived life on Broadway, Wodehouse added that he felt like Alice, "after mixing with all those weird creatures in Wonderland." In the wake of the experience, Wodehouse described the role of the author in talkies and how writers become scenarists in a satirical piece entitled "Slaves of Hollywood," published in the December 7, 1929, issue of the *Saturday Evening Post*. It appeared in modified form as "The Hollywood Scandal" in the 1932 anthology *Louder and Funnier*, and was excerpted elsewhere in his reminiscences.

Ethel Wodehouse had been impressed with the money Guy Bolton was making in Hollywood, and thought his stage collaborator should make as much as well. While the Wodehouse income was comfortable, she had experienced major losses in the stock market.[2] The town's social scene seemed infinitely promising to her. Wodehouse didn't want to move to Hollywood until spring, when he would finish his new novel. As well, he wanted to arrange for at most a six-month stint, while other offers were for a full year. He was approached by Samuel Goldwyn, who had known Wodehouse since the first film of *A Gentleman of Leisure*, but wouldn't meet

An ad for *Sally* (1929).

his price. As Wodehouse commented, "The poor chump seemed to think he was doing me a favour offering about half what I get for a serial for doing a job which would be the most ghastly sweat."[3]

In November, while Wodehouse remained in London, Ethel negotiated a contract for her husband that fulfilled all his demands. He was proud of her efforts. He was to be a screenwriter at M-G-M and earn $2,000 a week. (His income tax of around 5 percent was deducted in advance before receiving his check each Saturday.)[4]

In the interval between signing the contract and arriving in Hollywood, new and changing media had indicated the fresh avenues opening to him. At the end of 1929, the first Wodehouse sound film in the United States was released, a remake of *Sally*, already filmed in 1925. This time, however, the screen version included Marilyn Miller reprising her stage role. For her, film seemed a fresh direction for her own career after *Rosalie* a year earlier. Her pay of $100,000 for ten weeks of work on the film was widely advertised, but when *Sally* was not finished on time, she walked away until she was paid the promised $16,800 a week to continue.[5] The movie's principal success lies in best capturing, of all her three movies, the charisma that made her so famous on Broadway.[6]

On the other hand, the 1929 film version of *Sally*, on which Wodehouse did not receive credit, is also an astonishingly dull film. (The "Sally" of the play is unrelated to the "Sally" of Wodehouse stories.) The movie was presented in the stilted manner that plagued many early musicals, although it is not as bad as some, and was critically praised and popular in its time.[7] Emblematic of the pacing is the fact that the first song, "Look for the Silver Lining," is not performed until 21 minutes into the movies. The plot is typical of the musical formula, with only a few novelties, such as an exiled nobleman working in a restaurant for his former chef. Joe E. Brown costars in this role (created on Broadway by Leon Errol) as a refugee from Czecho-Govina, and for once his acting is on target, lacking the tendency toward excess that was typical of his persona.

Wodehouse had also coauthored a 20-minute radio operetta heard over the BBC on March 27, 1930. Titled *Zara*, it was fifth in a sort of review titled *A Café in Vienna*. Wodehouse provided the lyrics to music by Tony Lowry, for a book by Leonora Wodehouse and C. Denis Freeman. Zara was the name of one of the characters, a Viennese singer; others included a waiter, an English diplomat, and two Austrians, a nobleman and a secret service agent. Taking place in the present, it also included a prewar flashback. Unfortunately the script of this modest effort does not survive. The contributors split a fee of £30 between them.[8] (At the time, Leonora seemed to be inclining toward a writing career of her own.)

Joe E. Brown and Marilyn Miller in *Sally* (1929).

Less than a month had passed after the radio broadcast before Wodehouse disembarked from the White Star liner *Majestic* on April 22, 1930. His arrival won press coverage: "Wodehouse Here to Write Movies," the *New York Times* headlined.[9] He was age 49 when he arrived in Hollywood on May 8, accompanied by Leonora; Ethel joined them in July.

They moved into a home at 724 Linden Drive in Beverly Hills, then owned by actress Elsie Janis; the property had previously been held by Norma Shearer, first lady of M-G-M, as lead actress and wife of studio head Irving Thalberg. Wodehouse's daily life was predictable, and he loved the climate and the simple pleasures it allowed, like breakfasting in his garden. "This sunny garden with the palms—it is what every Englishman dreams about on a muggy day at home."[10] He arranged with the studio to work at his residence, so he often would not leave home for four days on end. "My days follow each other in a regular procession. I get up, swim, breakfast, work till two, swim again, work till seven, swim for the third time, then dinner and the day is over. When I get a summons from the studio, I motor over there, stay there a couple of hours and come back."[11]

The Wodehouses seldom went out, but his wife often gave parties. Initially his dinner companions were other New York writers and theater friends. Many of the actors in Hollywood at the time were those he had known in the theater. He wrote,

> Ethel has been entertaining largely lately. She starts by asking two people to lunch, then "Who can we get to meet them?" This gets it up to four. Then come all the people who would be hurt at being left out, and eventually the thing becomes a Hollywood orgy. This afternoon we had fifty people to lunch! It's not as bad as it sounds, because in this lovely climate you feed out of doors. We had bridge tables spotted about the garden and patio and a large table with cold food in the dining room, so that people simply helped themselves. As usual, Ethel feels it was a frost, but it wasn't really. It went off splendidly.[12]

He noted how dinners began at 7:15, but participants were expected to wait and drink cocktails until 9:30, when the last guest had arrived and dinner was finally served. He enjoyed scandal as much as anyone, such as the story about the Henry Daniells. "Apparently they go down to Los Angeles and either (a) indulge in or (b) witness orgies—probably both.... And what I want to know is—where are these orgies. I feel I've been missing something."[13]

Under the leadership of C. Aubrey Smith, Wodehouse helped to found the Hollywood Cricket Club, of which he became a vice president, along with Ronald Colman, George Arliss, and Leon Errol. Wodehouse took the minutes at the inaugural meetings. He had played against Smith years before in England. The club attracted many in Hollywood's British colony and became its social center.

Wodehouse found the writing process in Hollywood very different from the collaborations and responsibility of authoring stage plays. As he wrote a few years later in his short story, "The Castaways,"

> Few who have not experienced it can realise the eerie solitude of a motion-picture studio. Human intercourse is virtually unknown. You are surrounded by writers, each in his or her little hutch, but if you attempt to establish communication with them you will find on every door a card with the words "Working do not disturb." And if you push open one of these doors you are greeted by a snarl so animal, so menacing, that you retire hastily lest nameless violence befall.... Ever and anon the stillness is broken by the shrill cry of some wheeling supervisor. But for the most part a forlorn silence prevails.

Wodehouse explained,

> The actual work is negligible. They set me on to dialogue for a picture for Jack Buchanan. I altered all the characters to Earls and butlers, with such success that, when I finished, they called a conference and changed the entire plot, starring the earl and the butler. So I am still working on it. So far, I have had eight collaborators. The system is that A. gets the original idea, B. comes in to work with him on it, C. makes a scenario, D. does preliminary dialogue, and then they send for me to insert Class and what-not. Then E. and F., scenario writers, alter the plot and off we go again.[14]

He failed to see that the Hollywood writing system offered any advantages. "I cannot see why just two people should not be sufficient to collaborate on a scenario—the author and a good continuity writer. Why must it be sixteen or more? How can an author's idea possibly materialise as he envisioned it when so many people take a hand in its preparation for the screen?"[15]

Wodehouse was also used to working much faster than he found to be typical of Hollywood. He had written his adaptation of Ferenc Molnar's *The Play's the Thing* for Gilbert Miller in three days in 1926. By contrast, Wodehouse needed even less time for the script to which he was assigned. "I could have done all my part of it in a morning, but they took it for granted I should need six weeks. The latest news is that they are going to start shooting quite soon. In fact, there are ugly rumors that I am to be set to work soon on something else."[16] However, the transition from writing to prose, and from stage to screen dialogue, was not one Wodehouse found easy; he complained of the difficulty of having to condense dialogue to a few lines rather than extend it for pages in a story.[17]

Wodehouse was initially set to rewriting *Those Three French Girls*, with a script to be ready by July 8. He was credited with the dialogue; the adaptation and continuity were by Sylvia Thalberg and Frank Butler, the story by Dale Van Every and Arthur Freed. As Wodehouse explained in a letter to Guy Bolton, "I really believe I must have had the softest job on record. A horde of scenarists have constructed the picture, even to the extent of writing the dialogue. All I have had to do is revise and adapt their dialogue. And they never expect me to go near the studio unless there is a conference."[18] A month later, Wodehouse wrote, "I fear I shall not be able to string out the dear old picture I've been tied up with ever since I arrived much longer, as they really do seem to be starting the shooting on Monday, and they may give me something tougher to do next time."[19] *Those Three French Girls* was shot in 30 days, and by mid-September was edited. It cost just over a quarter million dollars to produce, and upon release on October 11 was modestly profitable.[20]

Samuel Marx recalled an incident in the production of the film:

> Even with five scenarists, director Harry Beaumont was having trouble with an important scene. "It reads funny but it doesn't play," he complained.
>
> Thalberg ... told Beaumont to have the British humorist rewrite it. Wodehouse usually worked in the sunlit garden of his Beverly Hills mansion. I advised him that the director wanted him to do the revision at the studio for immediate shooting. A studio limousine was sent to fetch him but when it got there, Wodehouse wasn't home.
>
> Two hours later he showed up and announced he had walked the five-mile distance in record time. He assured the director he could easily fix the scene but wanted to do it outdoors. I found a sunny spot for him on a saloon porch on the Western street and provided him with desk, chair, and writing paraphernalia.
>
> Beaumont waited until late afternoon, with no word or words from Wodehouse. An assistant director was then dispatched to the back lot, but returned to say the saloon set was uninhabited. The equipment had also disappeared. It was

> subsequently learned that Wodehouse developed a ravenous appetite from his long walk, so he went to lunch. While he was gone a watchman saw the deserted desk and typewriter, thought it was mislaid by the prop department (not an uncommon occurrence) and returned it. When Wodehouse saw that it had been removed he took it as a hint his work wasn't needed after all. He went home the same way he came to the studio. He walked.[21]

As Leonora noted to family friend John H. Miller, Wodehouse once completed the six-mile walk from his home in Benedict Canyon to the studio in Culver City in 70 minutes— but of course the top brass of M-G-M never walked anywhere.[22]

Wodehouse learned his lesson:

> When you are engaged to work at Hollywood, you get a cable saying that it is absolutely vital that you be there by ten o'clock on the morning of June the first. Ten-five will be too late, and as for getting there on June the second, that means ruin to the industry. So you rush about and leap into aeroplanes, and at ten o'clock on June the first you are at the studio, being told that you cannot see your employer now, as he has gone to Palm Springs. Nothing happens after this till October the twentieth, when you are given an assignment and told that every moment is precious.[23]

Despite the fact that the script was a committee effort, Wodehouse clearly also had a certain degree of input into the plot and characters, and Thalberg hoped to distinguish the picture by the Wodehouse flavor.[24] *Those Three French Girls* starred Reginald Denny, an ideal choice in a very Wode-

Reginald Denny chivalrously tosses the Wodehousian flowerpot to protect *Those Three French Girls.*

Everyone matched when Cliff Edwards and Edward Brophy join Reginald Denny and *Those Three French Girls.*

housian role as Larry, a wealthy, chivalrous, but not terribly bright young Englishman. He is introduced with a "what-ho," and the dialogue for which Wodehouse received sole credit demonstrates his typical phraseology, highlighting his signature phrases to almost an excessive extent.

Fortunately, the Wodehouse dialogue is matched to a story that is very similar to his own in style, and verges on the musical comedy form, with several brief songs. *Those Three French Girls* opens in France with Larry driving up as three girls, Charmain (Fifi D'Orsay), Madelon (Sandra Ravel), and Diane (Yola D'Avril), are arguing with their landlord over their eviction. Larry stops to help them, escalating the war of words by throwing flowerpots on the landlord's head (an idea Wodehouse had used in his stories, most prominently in his 1924 novel *Leave It to Psmith*). The fracas lands Larry and the girls in jail, where they are joined by two rowdy and musically inclined Americans (played by Ed Brophy and Cliff "Ukelele Ike" Edwards, best remembered as the voice of Jiminy Cricket in Walt Disney's *Pinocchio*), veterans of the war who have returned to France.

While incarcerated, the men and women pair off, and eventually escape jail by fooling the police through behaving like monkeys. When their car is stranded in a storm, the six take refuge in a barn, where Larry declares his love to Charmain. Arriving at Larry's chateau the next morning, Parker, the butler, warns Larry's uncle, the Earl of Ippleton (George Grossmith, who had starred in the Wodehouse–Fred Thompson play, *The Golden Moth*), of his involvement with Charmain. Ippleton tries to buy her off, but picks the wrong girl, then tells Charmain that he always has to bail Larry out of misbegotten love affairs. Charmain, angry, ends the engagement to Larry, refusing to let him explain that the one who had to be saved from romantic entanglements was, in fact, Ippleton.

Ippleton buys the three girls a modiste's shop; Charmain is now engaged to him, and Larry is bitter. The two Americans try to help by going to the girl's apartment, but arrive during their morning shower and only succeed in alienating them further. Larry has a plan, however; he drives his mini-automobile into his uncle's home the morning of the wedding, to assist with the rehearsal. Finally, by exposing Ippleton as a confirmed bachelor who is far too old and cantankerous for Charmain, Larry wins her back.

Those Three French Girls, as directed by Harry Beaumont, is an amusing if uneven farce, belonging to the early days of sound cinema. Its style, together with the treatment of the women's motivations and costumes in a manner that was only allowed in this period before censorship, gives it an archaic feeling to modern audiences. Sadly, it is seldom seen today.

For Wodehouse aficionados, the movie has special resonance because his dialogue was applied in a thorough way to an appropriate narrative and characters. This was recognized at the time; *Empire Theatre News* proclaimed that this was the first screen effort of Wodehouse to be of interest as such.

In fact, the parts of the Earl of Ippleton and Parker, a butler in the mode of the famous "Jeeves," are essentially in the Wodehouse style. For instance, what could be more ludicrous than the dallying conversation between Denny and Grossmith:

> "You're an old blighter!" snaps Denny.
> "A blighter?" gasps Grossmith.
> "A bally blighter!"
> "Here — I have only two words to say to you — one is 'get' and the other is 'out!'"
> "And I only have two words to say to you — one is 'right' and the other is 'ho!'"[25]

Ironically, although he had just begun in Hollywood, *Those Three French Girls* was as close to a success as Wodehouse was to have at M-G-M, the only film from his first stint in Hollywood to thoroughly reflect his contribution. His only other credits were minimal, and the other projects he labored over were not produced.

The most frustrating assignment Wodehouse received was the musical film *Rosalie.* He had already been involved with the stage version, contributing lyrics with Ira Gershwin. Inspired by the recent American tour by Queen Marie of Romania, *Rosalie* had been a hit on the stage with Marilyn Miller in the title role, running for a year in New York. Work on the film version had begun in 1928, with the first script prepared by Frances Marion, dialogue changes by Salisbury Field, and a new script by Elliot Nugent and Harry Beaumont, all in 1929. In 1930, new treatments were prepared by Gene Markey, with another by Hans Kraly and Fred Niblo, Jr. *Rosalie* was sometimes also titled *Crown Prince Josephine* or *American Eagle Inc.* There had already been an aborted production starring Marion Davies.

Other than deciding it should be rewritten for the screen, there was little consensus about the project; Wodehouse recalled, "No one wanted me to hurry."[26] On August 16, 1930, a temporary complete screenplay was submitted, from a treatment by Hans Kraly, revised by Robert Z. Leonard (who was to direct), with dialogue by Wodehouse, Markey, and Fred Niblo, Jr.

In October, Wodehouse's contract was renewed for another six months, as work on *Rosalie* continued. By then, however, Wodehouse had come to dislike living in the region. "California scenery is the most loathsome on earth—a cross between Coney Island and the Riviera—but by sticking in one's garden all the time and shutting one's eyes when one goes out, it is possible to get by."[27] Taking up his option, he knew, did not mean the studio would find a more productive use for him. Over 20 years later, he would write, "There were authors who had been on salary for years in Hollywood without ever having a line of their work used. All they did was attend story conferences. There were other authors whom nobody had seen for years. It was like the Bastille. They just sat in some hutch away in a corner somewhere and grew white beards and languished. From time to time somebody would renew their contract, and then they were forgotten again."[28] Wodehouse came to regard his tenure as not so atypical.

After his renewal, Wodehouse attended a story conference in Santa Barbara, during which Thalberg outlined his own proposed adaptation of *Rosalie.* Wodehouse was commissioned to write it as a novelette. To Wodehouse, the task was onerous, and by then he was calling *Rosalie* "a perfectly rotten picture." He regarded the novelette as "exactly eight times as much sweat as doing an ordinary picture. What the idea was, I don't know, unless they thought that, writing it in that form, I would put in a lot of business which they could use. It ran to 45,000 words."[29] However, assigning a noted writer to such a version, although not common, was hardly an exceptional practice, allowing the publication of a literary tie-in with the film's planned release to gain extra publicity by the name of its author. Wodehouse turned in the completed work at the end of January 1931, and it remains unpublished.

Two West Point cadets, Runt O'Day and wealthy Bob Warwick, are vacationing in Romanza, a principality desperately in need of cash. Although Princess Rosalie is to marry for reasons of state, her mother Honoria, who rules the royal household, would be content for her to marry Warwick. He avoids the reception in his honor to instead visit the Liberty Festival. There he sees a girl in danger from mashers and rescues her, not realizing it is Rosalie. She is angry with him for avoiding her earlier. They meet for an idyllic day on an island and fall in love before a misunderstanding separates them. They next meet when Bob is assigned to escort the family on a tour at West Point, and the two resolve to marry, Rosalie deciding to give up her throne for love.

Hardly vintage Wodehouse, the novelette lacks the layered plot and character interaction typical of even his lesser stories. Despite the constraints involved in working from an outline, and the predictability of the story, the result has his typical charm. He takes advantage of the prose form to recast some of the story, for instance adding the day on an island to confirm their love, rather than having them simply meet briefly at a festival. Wodehouse also suggested that Rosalie be shown on parade in Romanza, rather than relying on the standard scenes of West Point that Thalberg preferred. There are few examples of his typical prose twists; one describing Bob provides the flavor: "He goes over to a foreign country and falls for a femme — falls good and hard — and then, just when everything's going nice and smooth, she pulls off her whiskers and says 'April Fool, you fool! I'm no lady, I'm a Princess!' A nice thing to happen to a poor guy on furlough. If that was what furloughs were coming to, it was about time they were stopped."[30] The story reads like a regular romance, without the sense of a need for breaks for songs or musical numbers.

Wodehouse considered trying to publish his novelette of *Rosalie*. He asked his agent, Paul Reynolds, to acquire story rights from the musical's co-librettists, William Anthony McGuire and Guy Bolton. Wodehouse was aware of the potential complications with M-G-M, and asked Reynolds not send telegrams on the matter to the studio. There, it was customary to open the telegram and telephone the recipient, reading him the contents.[31] Surely his contract dictated matters of ownership for writing produced for the studio.

Rosalie was cancelled by the studio as musicals seemed to be in decline, and when it was finally filmed in 1937, it deviated significantly from this outline. Rosalie became a dancer, and the plot began and ended in the

United States, with a section in Romanza in the middle. Only the ending placed at West Point had anything in common with the outline Wodehouse had known. Similarly, the play's original songs were replaced with new Cole Porter compositions.

In early 1931, Plum and Ethel spent a week at San Simeon, the estate of publishing tycoon William Randolph Hearst and his mistress, Marion Davies. She had first met Wodehouse in 1917 while appearing in his play, *Oh, Boy!*, had already appeared in the film *The Cardboard Lover*, and was the prospective star of the film of *Rosalie*.

Wodehouse would later mock Hearst's excesses in a number of bits in various stories and articles. He enjoyed telling how, at the dinner table, the first evening after your arrival you were seated next to the host, but with each passing day were placed farther and farther away. Similarly, with the zoo on the premises, a bear, elephant, or even Samuel Goldwyn might be encountered on the way to the house.[32]

Early in 1931, M-G-M credited Wodehouse, along with Sarah Y. Mason, as author of additional dialogue on a picture adapted by Mason, from the previous year's H.M. Harwood play, *The Man in Possession*. Wodehouse made clear his feelings about this credit in several of his short stories of the Mulliners in Hollywood. In "George and Alfred" the narrator remarks that "The lot of a writer of additional dialogue in a Hollywood studio is not an exalted one—he ranks, I believe, just above a script girl and just below the man who works the wind machine"; he later equates the position to that of "a Yes man." In "The Nodder," the title position, a man who nods after the Yes-men have indicated verbal agreement, is described as lying "socially somewhere between that of the man who works the wind-machine and that of a writer of additional dialogue." Noting the similarity between the humorous twist in both lines, it is clear Wodehouse did not think highly of such a credit. Reportedly, only three of Wodehouse's lines were used; certainly less than a half-dozen lines resemble his style, unlike the way his dialogue had pervaded *Those Three French Girls*.

The Man in Possession tells the story of a stern family of two brothers, one of whom, Raymond Dabney (Robert Montgomery), is recently out of jail for an apparently innocent financial error; the other, Claude (Reginald Owen) is seeking to marry Crystal (Irene Purcell), who he believes is an heiress. Montgomery refuses the family directive that he depart England for the colonies, and gets a job as a bailiff, whose first task is to take possession of Crystal's property. He assists her by pretending to be her butler, only to be astonished to discover that he is waiting on his own family when Claude brings his parents to meet Crystal. Eventually

Robert Montgomery serves his mother, played by Beryl Mercer, and his brothers, portrayed by C. Aubrey Smith and Reginald Owen, in the home of the latter's putative fiancée, costar Irene Purcell, in *The Man in Possession* (1931).

Raymond and Crystal discover their love when her poverty causes Claude to end the engagement.

Montgomery recreated his role for an August 12, 1935, *Lux Radio Theater* version. *The Man in Possession* would be brought to television in 1953 for *Theatre Guild* on CBS, starring Rex Harrison and Lilli Palmer. M-G-M would hastily remake *The Man in Possession* in 1937 under the title *Personal Property*, with Robert Taylor now in the lead opposite Jean Harlow, in one of her last roles. Reginald Owen and Forrester Harvey played the same roles in both versions, and while the 1931 film alternates between comedy and drama, the 1937 remake is in a comedic vein throughout, with the spiciness of the original toned down considerably.

While Wodehouse received no credit in 1937 (with the script attributed to Hugh Mills and Ernest Vajda), *Personal Property* highlights more clearly two aspects of the original that may have given Wodehouse ideas for his future writing, or may have been his contributions. One was a play on the words butler, and the act of "buttling"; he had written an article entitled "Butlers and the Buttled" for the British magazine *Piccadilly* in

A poster for *Personal Property*.

April 1929 that would be largely reproduced in the book of essays *Louder and Funnier*. More important was that the brothers' family is in the business of manufacturing ladies' undergarments, and the treatment of Owen's selfish character is linked to this background. This foreshadowed the fascist Roderick Spode's secret of Eulalie (a name brand for his designs in intimate women's apparel) in Wodehouse's 1938 novel *The Code of the Woosters*. In the original play, the family was in the underclothes business (gender not specified), regarded as a certain sign of financial success. Adding to the intertextuality was a Harwood line referring to a modern Wodehouse-type servant, excised in the screen adaptations.

The search for an appropriate project to be given as a task to Wodehouse veered steadily farther from the natural association with comedy. In October 1930, he had been asked to write dialogue for the adaptation of Vincent Lawrence's play *Among the Married*, eventually filmed the next year under the title *Men Call It Love*. The Hays office, after reading a January 1930 draft of the script, had already informed M-G-M that the movie "would violate the Code and would encounter major censorship difficulties." A report cited in the *American Film Institute Catalog of Feature Films*, noted that "None of the drinking or the dialogue and paraphernalia concerned with the drinking seems justified under it, and more importantly, the spirit of the Code lacks conformance in implied adultery between Helen and Jack and the intended adultery between Ethel and Bill."

The script had already been given its form first by Madeline Ruthven, then Edith Fitzgerald. Simultaneously, Wodehouse worked on an 82-page rough draft (a "temporary incomplete screenplay"), which had yet to be fully broken down into scenes, so that much of the dialogue was prepared without the full context of how it would be staged or visualized.

At the time of Wodehouse's association, his draft, and comments in the script, indicate that the tone had not been decided for this story of adultery among the New York social elite. The version from which Wodehouse worked had more emphasis on the philandering mores of an upper class social set, and the characters were fundamentally more sympathetic. Part of the reason for Wodehouse's assignment to this property may have been his humorous short stories about golf, for in *Among the Married* the rakish hero is a golf champion whose female partners, always married women, are also his lovers; his new girlfriend is a novice to the game. Wodehouse tried to interject comedy, to make the film belong to that amorphous combination genre, "Comedy-Drama," but his efforts were ill fated. From comments scattered throughout the script and initialed "P. G.W.," he seems to have found the source obscure, eliminated occasional lines, corrected some business, and awkwardly tried to insert new bits of business for the actors to be spread throughout a scene.

The project was next turned over to Doris Anderson, who completed the script in time for production to commence at the beginning of the year. Anderson won sole screenplay credit for "dialogue continuity," and the final film was entirely dramatic, without any attempt at humor. How-

Norman Foster and Leila Hyams play a couple whose marriage is nearly destroyed by Adolphe Menjou in *Men Call It Love.*

ever, many of the dialogue passages were the same as had been found in the version on which Wodehouse worked.

The love between Tony Minot (Adolphe Menjou) and Helen Robinson (Mary Duncan) is widely known; her bespeckled, dyspeptic husband can do nothing to control her roving eye. Yet the love between Tony and Helen has grown cold, now that he has turned to Connie Mills (Leila Hyams) and is teaching her to be "loose" in her golf game. However, Connie and her husband, Jack (Norman Foster), are much in love, despite the fact that Jack has concealed a brief affair with a Follies girl from her. Jack is jealous of Connie, and Tony's interest in her. She learns, inadvertently, through Tony, of Jack's Follies girl. Then she sees the result of Helen's determination to seduce Jack, when his interest in boxing makes her regard him as a possible replacement for Tony. Connie tells Jack they will have an open marriage and tries to accept Tony's offer of an affair. Tony, however, loves Connie too sincerely, and even wants to marry her. Ultimately the married couple is reconciled, while Tony is left as the odd man out, along with Helen's husband, who cannot cease loving her despite her infidelities.

Men Call It Love stiffly directed by Edgar Selwyn, demonstrates the weaknesses of early stage dramas in the talkies, with many early scenes resembling fragments awkwardly following one another. The key performances are also weak, other than Menjou in a very typical role for his persona. Today the film belongs to the category labeled "pre-code," when Hollywood could more frankly depict marital infidelity than would be the case only a very few years later.

The assignment of Wodehouse to *Men Call It Love* is less surprising given his next projects, covering many of the same themes. He wrote dialogue for *Just a Gigolo*, in which Lord Robert Brummel (William Haines) is involved with married women in Paris. As a result, Brummel is forced by his uncle, George Hampton (C. Aubrey Smith), to marry Roxana Hartley (Irene Purcell) or lose the allowance he has misspent on love affairs. Robert, believing all women unfaithful, wagers George he can prove that Roxana will deceive him, by impersonating a gigolo. He fails, and when she learns the deception, she pretends a flirtation, then slaps him, finally uniting the pair. *Just a Gigolo*, like other Wodehouse projects at M-G-M, was adapted from a play, this one entitled *Dancing Partner*. It had been produced a few months earlier by David Belasco, and based on a German piece adapted into English. Wodehouse did not receive screen credit, which went to Hans Kraly, Richard Schayer, and Claudine West; Jack Conway directed the 70 minute movie.

In August, 1930, *Candle-Light* opened at the Biltmore Theater in Los Angeles, with movie actors Alan Mowbray and Reginald Owen in the leads, and Owen in charge of the staging. Graham John's version of the Siegfried Geyer play had been performed successfully in London as *By Candlelight*, but producer Gilbert Miller thought it needed to be revised for a New York audience. Wodehouse had been given the task, with the title changed to *Candle-Light*. He watched the play enter rehearsals and oversaw the last minute changes before opening in 1929 at The Empire Theater with Gertrude Lawrence, Leslie Howard, and Owen. After the Los Angeles premiere, M-G-M bought the screen rights, and Wodehouse sold his share for £500, which he considered "gross overpayment for what I did on it."[33]

Candle-Light defies all the conventions associated with the author. It is very frankly continental in its outlook, concerning several attempts at seduction, most notably by the valet, Josef, who believes Marie is a titled, married woman, a type that has always held a secret appeal for him. Josef impersonates his employer, Prince Rudolf Haseldorf-Schlobitten, for Marie's benefit, and when Rudolf unexpectedly returns home early, he sympathetically tries to help Josef by pretending to be him. Marie secretly reveals to Rudolf that she is in fact only Mitzie, the maid of Baroness Von Rischenheim, who is also married and is secretly being courted by Rudolf. Marie, based on her believed social affinity with Rudolf, makes a play for his affections, which he is on the verge of accepting twice despite his assurances to Josef that he respects his servant's clear affection for her. The only aspect of *Candle-Light* typical of Wodehouse is the mixture of classes, with master and servant becoming involved in the affairs of the other. There is a moral at the end, with Rudolf saying, "Take it from me, Josef, if a woman is the right woman her rank doesn't matter a hang." However, this is the *only* moral in *Candle-Light*, whose title is reputedly from an old maxim, "Choose neither women nor linen by candle-light."

Wodehouse was assigned to prepare a screen version to star John Gilbert, but felt discouraged from the outset, as he later recalled. *Candle-Light* was to be one of four pictures the studio would produce with Gilbert, paying him $250,000, but the contract was signed before it became widely rumored that Gilbert's voice recorded as "squeaky" (which was, in fact, not true). Wodehouse recalled, "So they decide his next picture will be such a flop that he will make a settlement. And the disturbing thought that occurs to me is that when it is essential that a picture shall lay an egg, does the cry go around the studio 'Wodehouse is the man. Send for Wodehouse.'"[34]

A film of *Candle-Light*, even if toned down for the screen, would have been in the vein of the sophisticated comedies popularized in the American cinema by director Ernst Lubitsch. Indeed, Lubitsch's frequent collaborator Hans Kraly was brought in to work on the script immediately after Wodehouse's efforts, while F. Hugh Herbert was also working separately on the project both before and after Wodehouse turned in his treatment on March 18.

The bedroom theme, if such it can be labeled, is unquestionably most evident in Wodehouse's adaptations of works by continental playwrights; not only Geyer, but also Jacques Deval, Ferenc Molnar, Ladislaus Fodor, and Sacha Guitry. While extramarital affairs and infidelity are largely absent from Wodehouse stories, and even love is treated in an innocent, comic manner, the continental side of Wodehouse's writing can best be seen today in the film versions of those same plays. In his writing for the stage, Wodehouse felt pressured to write for certain audience demands, principally the relationships of men and women. He believed his only commercial successes were collaborations, either musicals or adaptations of European plays, which necessitated different themes from his prose.

The studio was apparently unwilling to film any of his novels. "Thalberg, the head man, told me that *Leave It to Psmith* was his favourite novel, but when I suggested that he should come across with money for the movie rights he merely smiled sheepishly and the matter dropped."[35] (The novel would be filmed in England in 1933.) When considering a film around the Wodehouse character Jeeves, Thalberg reportedly decided against buying film rights when he discovered that his chauffeur thought Jeeves was his wife's butcher.[36]

Wodehouse had his own explanation. "Naturally my reputation is for light humor, jolly nonsense. I was led to believe they felt there was a field for my work in pictures. But I was told my sort of stuff was 'too light.' They seem to have such a passion for sex stuff. I wonder if they really know the tastes of their audiences."[37] By March, still working on the script of *Candle-Light*, Wodehouse doubted his contract would be renewed. He adopted the role of a sycophant, noting that "My only hope is that I have made myself so pleasant to everyone here that by now I may count as a relative. The studio is full of relatives of the big bosses who do no work and draw enormous salaries."[38]

To M-G-M, Wodehouse's reputation in the theater, then considered the medium closest to "talkies," was of more significance than his stories and novels. While probably vaguely aware that adaptations of this work had been done at other studios, M-G-M's only previous Wodehouse movie had been *The Cardboard Lover*, and the projects handed to him demonstrate the recollection of its nature and subject matter. His assignment to *Rosalie* and *Candle-Light*, projects he had been involved with on stage, reflect this conception of what he had to offer. Even the one novel that was bought (but never produced) reveals this same tendency. The studio paid $25,000 for the rights to the new Wodehouse novel, *If I Were You* (serialized in *American Magazine* from April to July 1931, published in book form in September)—which he had written, from a play coauthored with Guy Bolton, during spare time on the M-G-M payroll.[39] The play *If I Were You* was published in book form but apparently never performed; Bolton and Wodehouse revised it under the title *Who's Who* in 1934 for a London staging, but it was a failure.

Wodehouse's contract ended on May 9, 1931, when M-G-M did not renew it. Wodehouse remarked in a letter, "The movies are getting hard up and the spirit of economy is rife. I was lucky to get mine while the going was good. It is rather like having tolerated some awful bounder for his good dinners to go to his house and find the menu cut down to nothing and no drinks."[40] He realized how he preferred writing his own work while supposedly composing scenarios by day: "It's odd how soon one comes to look on every minute as wasted that is given to earning one's salary."[41]

After his arrival, Wodehouse had found that he came up with an idea for a new short story every day for a week, and that southern California encouraged one to work. Sometimes he would remain unassigned to a picture while at home and could work on his prose, still on the M-G-M payroll. He summed it up by saying that he was required to do so little work that he had time to write a novel and nine short stories (including "The Story of Webster"), "besides brushing up my golf, getting an attractive sun-tan and perfecting my Australian crawl in the swimming pool."[42]

On June 7, 1931, he gave an interview with *Los Angeles Times* correspondent Alma Whitaker, at M-G-M's request. He could hardly feel mistreated by the studio, considering his generous salary and the purchase of *If I Were You*, not to mention permission to work at home; even Leonora (then in her late 20s) had been hired as an assistant at the studio.[43] Wodehouse could only complain that he was receiving too much pay for too little work.

> "I cannot see what they engaged me for," he said wonderingly, as we sat beneath the cocoanut palms beside his glistening swimming pool in Benedict Canyon. "The motion picture business dazes me. They were extremely nice to me—oh, extremely—but I feel as if I have cheated them. It's all so unreasonable....
>
> "You see, I understood I was engaged to write stories for the screen....
>
> "Yet apparently they had the greatest difficulty in finding anything for me to do. Twice during the year they brought completed scenarios of other people's stories to me and asked me to do some dialogue. Fifteen or sixteen people had tinkered with those stories. The dialogue was really quite adequate. All I did was touch it up here and there—very slight improvements.... That about sums up what I was called upon to do for my $104,000. Isn't it amazing? If it is only names they want, it seems such an expensive way to get them, doesn't it?"[44]

Of course it was a humble understatement of what he had done. Wodehouse would later describe interviewer Whitaker as charming on the outside, but beneath as hard-boiled and poisonous as a Gila monster.[45]

However, his words, gentle as the were, proved the most damning indictment of all. The first inkling Wodehouse had of the impact of his remarks came with a call from Reuter's early the next morning, asking if the *Los Angeles Times* interview was authentic, and if it could be cabled to London. When another call was received shortly afterward, Wodehouse finally went out to get the morning paper, and saw that the interview had merited a headline.[46]

The interview appeared in abridged form in the *New York Times* on June 9, but the next day the *New York Herald Tribune* used it as the basis for an editorial on practices in Hollywood. The interview merely confirmed years of anonymous reports, and that a figure of Wodehouse's literary stature would acknowledge the waste of his talents gave it added credence to shareholders and gossipmongers. "Mr. Wodehouse must be among the first to bring it out into the open, to mention names and firms, and thus assure us of the truth in the astounding legends. He confirms the picture that has been steadily growing — the picture of Hollywood the golden, where 'names' are bought to be scrapped, talents are retained to be left unused, hiring of distinguished authors is without rhyme and firing without reason."[47]

The ensuing controversy was picked up in the *Literary Digest* of June 27. *Variety* mentioned an English playwright and author making $2,500 a week "without contributing anything really worthwhile to the screen."[48] Wodehouse family friend Maureen O'Sullivan, to whom he would dedicate his 1932 book *Hot Water*, reported that there was resentment of him in Hollywood, and after his interview *Variety* even accused him of refusing to attend story conferences.[49]

Nor was the anger only felt from industry brass. In the interview, Wodehouse mentioned the story of a fellow screenwriter, Roland Pertwee, who was believed to have been told that he was fired by the policeman at the studio gate. Pertwee wrote a letter to the *New York Times*, published on July 30, saying he had been dismissed in a merger. He added, "Unlike my friend Wodehouse, I am in no sense appalled at the amount of salary I drew, nor am I troubled by any pangs of conscience about the amount of work I did."

When M-G-M's New York office complained about the wastefulness Wodehouse had exposed, they were simply told that writers were needed to make movies.[50] Whatever the actual outcome, the incident acquired a reputation for having caused "the bankers who control Hollywood to order drastic cuts in authors' wage scales."[51]

Ethel felt obliged to tell a local newspaper that her husband only meant to say he felt badly that he hadn't turned out a major hit. On June 14, he wrote a letter to the *Los Angeles Times*, printed on June 20, noting not only *Those Three French Girls*, but also *Men Call It Love*, *The Man in Possession*, and *Just a Gigolo*, crediting himself with much of the dialogue on the last three. He added, "I contributed various other bits of dialogue — a scene here and a few important lines there — to a number of other pictures," which, he indicated, the studio felt earned his salary. Indeed, much of this work had been overlooked, and *The Man in Possession* and *Just a Gigolo* were just going into release at the time of his departure. Still, upon the conclusion of his contract, he was no longer the same lionized figure in Hollywood, who had been deluged with speaking invitations, as many as nine in two days, during his first weeks. His early hope of preparing original screen stories had not been realized, whether his initial assignment to a Jack Buchanan comedy, or his wish to compose for Marion Davies (so perfect in *The Cardboard Lover*).[52]

Perhaps not until Wodehouse's naiveté led him to make the German broadcasts did his candor have more disastrous results. Wodehouse's remarks resulted in a firestorm, which he summarized best himself:

> That interview of mine seems to have had something of the effect of the late assassination at Sarajevo (which, if you remember, led to a nasty disturbance). I can't quite understand why, seeing that I only said what everybody has been saying for years, but apparently the fact that I gave figures and mentioned a definite studio in print has caused a sensation all over the world. One of the bosses at Paramount said I had done as much damage as if a hundred picture houses had been closed.
>
> The trouble is, you see, all these Jews out here have been having a gorgeous time for years, fooling about with the shareholders' money and giving all their relations fat jobs, and this gives the bankers an excuse for demanding a showdown. Well, if it results in Mr. Louis B. Mayer having to cut his salary (which at present is a snappy eight hundred thousand dollars a year), I shall feel I have done my bit.[53]

Ultimately, the Wodehouse interview was a storm in a teacup, a matter primarily for gossip, and for the most part rather quickly forgotten.

However, Wodehouse's own belittling of his efforts to Whitaker continued to echo through subsequent years. A 1934 article on Wodehouse's tax difficulties quoted his salary, commenting that "he was a high-paid scenario and dialogue writer, an occupation which he did not take seriously.... saying that he was ... paid ... without exacting any work from him."[54] It was, of course, false; he had done much to earn his salary, even when his writing was not filmed at M-G-M.

Wodehouse remained for several months before returning to England in November. Even Leonora simply said that Hollywood bored Plum.[55] However, his emotions ran far deeper. After 18 months in California, he was determined never to return, according to an August 7, 1932, interview given to the *New York Times* from the French Riviera:

> "By the time you see your brain children on the screen, they are not yours any longer," he says. This is not an original complaint, but that makes it none the less valid.
>
> "Every one takes a hand in helping along your product. I suppose even the office boys and the gatekeepers at the studio have their say. And what a manhandling it is!
>
> "I don't know if other writers feel as I do. But they should.
>
> "No, I won't ever again write for the movies, not even if they should offer me enough dollars to put England back on the gold standard.
>
> "The theatre, yes! But not the movies," the humorist concluded.[56]

He was to express the degree of his bitterness in a manner unique for him.

III

Satires

As a result of his experience, Wodehouse returned to prose and created a carefully drawn, parallel Hollywood universe, based on what he had seen. It required minimal exaggeration to achieve comedic effect. In a series of stories, Wodehouse methodically outlined various Hollywood jobs and types of people that had an obvious basis in the studio system.

This is well beyond what Wodehouse admitted to having written. He would claim that these stories were inherently unreal, with his fictional Hollywood no less imaginary than his fabled British estates or clubs for the idle rich.[1] However, the author typically belittled the serious undertones to be found in his work, whether the reflection of class stratification, inherited wealth, the mockery of authority figures from constables to clergy, or the pretensions of highbrow artists.

Despite the studied air of innocence he tried to convey in the Alma Whittaker interview, Wodehouse was about to demonstrate what he had learned as a studio employee. Already he had long been far more aware of filmmaking than he was prepared to admit. This sometimes only came through in brief glimpses, such as this passage from *The Luck of the Bodkins*: "All this sort of thing, he presumed, would have been the merest commonplace of everyday life in Hollywood, but to one who, like himself, was mixing for the first time in motion-picture circles it was rather breath-taking. He felt as if he had been plunged into the foaming maelstrom of a two-reel educational comic."[2] A similar reference appears in "The Ordeal of Osbert Mulliner," published in 1928. Two-reel comedies had long been a staple of film programs, and Educational Pictures was one of the most prolific of low-budget producers in the form, to the point that their product had become known as "Educationals" despite the apparent misnomer.

Wodehouse, like other authors, made veiled jests about overblown movies in his early writings from the 1910s forward. In his 1927 story "Came the Dawn," Wodehouse recounts how a young man has evidently just been rejected in love because he lacks the necessary income. His expressive face is spotted by the head of the Bigger, Better, and Brighter

Motion-Picture Company and placed under contract. By introducing Hollywood at the end, Wodehouse also satirized the need of movies to provide a last-minute "happy ending."

Wodehouse had actually begun creating his own self-contained movie world, with its own range of renowned titles. *Where Passion Lurks*, starring Loretta Byng, Oscar the Wonder-Poodle, and Professor Pond's Educated Sea-Lions, was mentioned in "The Passing of Ambrose" (1928) along with "The Rise of Minna Nordstrom." Gloria Gooch had starred in *A Girl Against the World* and *Tried in the Furnace*, while Pauline Petite was the star of *Bonds of Gold, Passion's Slaves, Purple Passion, Seduction,* and *Silken Fetters* in "Lord Emsworth Acts for the Best," published in 1926. *Fangs of the Past, Love or Mammon, A Modern Cinderella, Prairie Nell, A Society Mating,* and *Wed to a Satyr* were among those movies attended by Freddie Threepwood in *Leave It to Psmith*. There was even a cartoon, *The Adventures of Sidney the Sturgeon*, mentioned in the 1936 short story "Buried Treasure."

During Wodehouse's 1930–1931 year as a screenwriter at Metro-Goldwyn-Mayer, he had felt obligated not to write a satire of the studio, but, "Now that the pay envelope has ceased, maybe I shall be able to write some stuff knocking them good."[3] Shortly after leaving Hollywood, Wodehouse found himself committed to writing a number of stories about American characters, and set in the United States, at the request of the editor of *American Magazine*. Although he didn't regard Americans as inherently humorous, his recent experiences provided a solution to the problem.

From December 1932 through March 1933, Wodehouse's sharpest satire on Hollywood appeared in *American Magazine*, with the sequence of stories titled "Monkey Business" (originally entitled "A Cagey Gorilla"), "The Nodder" (originally entitled "Love Birds"), "The Juice of an Orange" (originally entitled "Love on a Diet"), and "The Rise of Minna Nordstrom" (originally entitled "A Star is Born"; the first of the films of this title was not released until 1937). They were printed simultaneously in England in *Strand Magazine*, and the series ended in June with "The Castaways." This story was not published serially in the United States, deliberately, since Wodehouse felt it "isn't quite up to the mark."[4] All five stories were eventually collected as "the Mulliners of Hollywood" in the 1935 short story volume, *Blandings Castle*.

Following the Mulliner short stories were two 1935 novels, *Laughing Gas*, set in Hollywood, and *The Luck of the Bodkins*, with movie personalities away from their Hollywood lair. The original *New York Times* reviewer of *Blandings Castle* in 1935 was initially a bit uncertain what to make of these stories, preferring the more typical Wodehouse tales set in

England.[5] The following year, the same reviewer, encountering *The Luck of the Bodkins*, again wrote of preferring "Wodehouse when he is not under the Hollywood influence."[6] J.B. Priestley, critiquing Wodehouse, commented that "he has shaken a fist at Hollywood" and seemed on his way to becoming an American humorist.[7]

Another reviewer of *The Luck of the Bodkins* for the *New York Times* was certain they detected something new.

> I don't know what P. G. Wodehouse did to Hollywood.... But whatever he did or did not do to Hollywood, it is fairly apparent, from a faintly querulous asperity ... that Hollywood has done something to sear Mr. Wodehouse's large and ample soul. Not that Mr. Wodehouse has been knocked off his pins; it would take more than Hollywood — yes, even more than the whole United States— to ruffle the surface aspects of the Wodehousian aplomb. Yet even Achilles had his heel, and the canker may feed at the fairest damask cheek. Apparently Hollywood has pinged Mr. Wodehouse in the heel. And his cheek is ever so slightly wan.... Not being able to beard the movie magnates in the Hollywood den, Mr. Wodehouse has lured one of the breed into the lair of P. G. Wodehouse, novelist. In his own lair Mr. Wodehouse is a tiger.[8]

For one of the few times in his writing, the Hollywood Mulliner stories, and the subsequent novel *Laughing Gas*, brought Wodehouse unusually close to pointed social satire.[9]

In future years, Wodehouse would not hesitate to indicate the actual names he most detested. Louis B. Mayer, who had come up in the infamous 1931 newspaper interview, was portrayed in a negative light. As star Mervyn Potter drunkenly relates to Cyril "Barmy" Fotheringay-Phipps in chapter 5 of the 1952 novel *Angel Cake* (titled *Barmy in Wonderland* in England),

> "You ever been cornered by a wounded studio executive, Phipps? No? It's an experience every young man ought to have. Broadens the mind and helps to form the character. How well I remember the day when I was wandering through the jungle on the Metro-Goldwyn lot and Louis B. Mayer suddenly sprang out at me from the undergrowth. He had somehow managed to escape from the office where they kept him, and I could see from his glaring eyes and slavering jaws that he had already tasted blood. Fortunately I had my elephant gun and my trusty native bearer with me."

Wodehouse wrote these words at the very time Mayer had been removed as boss of the studio, two decades after his experience with him. In 1954, in chapter 17 of *Bring on the Girls*, Wodehouse places an anecdote in the mouth of Bob Benchley: "He said I mustn't believe the stories I had heard about ill-treatment of inmates at the studios, for there was very little actual brutality. Most of the big executives, he said, were kindly men, and he had often seen Louis B. Mayer stop outside some nodder's hutch and push a piece of lettuce through the bars."

However, in the 1930s, Wodehouse still felt obligated to cloak his portraits of real people. In "The Rise of Minna Nordstrom," Wodehouse provides his own version of Marcus Loew's 1924 merger of Metro Picture Corporation, Goldwyn Picture Corporation, and Louis B. Mayer Pictures into Metro-Goldwyn-Mayer, under the ownership of Loew's, Inc., with Louis B. Mayer as vice president and general manager. In the Wodehouse version, Jacob Z. Schnellenhamer, like Mayer, rules a company including the name of a producer, Goldwyn, who has long since left the fold. Schnellenhamer's Perfecto-Zizzbaum Corporation is the result of a merger between his own company, the Colossal-Exquisite, with Isadore Fishbein's Perfecto-Fishbein and Ben Zizzbaum's Zizzbaum-Celluloid. In a town run by such figures as Carl Laemmle at Universal (best known for his many relatives on the payroll), Adolph Zukor of Paramount, Harry Cohn of Columbia, or the Warner brothers, Wodehouse's version does not seem so farfetched. Nor was the company name so imaginary; Wodehouse may have drawn its name from the company behind the 1918 adaptation of his novel *Uneasy Money*, produced by Essanay and Perfection Pictures as one of their "Ultra Features."

Schnellenhamer is modeled on Mayer, and is the leading mogul of the "Mulliners of Hollywood" series. Like Mayer, Schnellenhamer is portrayed as the most powerful magnate in Hollywood. Following the mold of his prototype, Schnellenhamer is unintellectual, tyrannical, and paternalistic, a man who rewards obedience and sees the company as one big family.

In "The Juice of an Orange," Wilmot Mulliner tells Schnellenhamer, "'Don't dream of cutting your salary... You're worth every cent of it. Besides, reflect. If you reduce your salary, it will cause alarm. People will go about saying that things must be in a bad way. It is your duty to the community to be a man and bite the bullet, and, no matter how much it may irk you, to stick to your eight hundred thousand dollars a year like glue.'" (And as it turns out, Schnellenhamer was only thinking of cutting Wilmot's salary, not his own.) The $800,000 figure, previously quoted by Wodehouse in a response to his 1931 interview as Mayer's salary, clearly identifies the model for Wodehouse's fictitious studio head.

In "The Nodder," Schnellenhamer is described physically. "Even at the best of times, the President of the Perfecto-Zizzbaum, considered as an object for the eye, was not everybody's money." In "The Rise of Minna Nordstrom," it is revealed that he contents himself with remembering "that morning he had put through a deal which would enable him to trim the stuffing out of two hundred and seventy-three exhibitors," but "Like all motion-picture magnates, he had about forty-seven guilty secrets, many of them recorded on paper."

Schnellenhamer is a man of negligible intellectual attainment; in "The Nodder" he is described as "modestly proud of knowing words of two syllables." However, he and other studio heads have a grasp of language typical of the legendary malapropisms of movie pioneers, which reaches its pinnacle in a dialogue between Schnellenhamer and an assistant, Isadore Levitsky, from "The Juice of an Orange":

> "Every time I said anything, it seemed to me he did something funny with the corner of his mouth. Drew it up in a twisted way that looked kind of ... what's that word beginning with an 's'?"
>
> "Cynical?"
>
> "No, a snickle is a thing you cut corn with. Ah, I've got it. Sardinic. Every time I spoke he looked sardinic."
>
> Mr. Levitsky was out of his depth.
>
> "Like a sardine, do you mean?"
>
> "No, not like a sardine. Sort of cold and sneering, like Glutz of the Medulla-Oblongata the other day on the golf-links when he asked me how many I'd taken in the rough and I said one."

In chapter 5 of *Angel Cake*, Mervyn Potter offers Barmy some advice. "I've just remembered something that may be useful to you. When a studio executive charges you, look to the left but leap to the right. This baffles the simple creature."

Wodehouse provides two memorable parodies of the Hollywood story conference. In "The Juice of an Orange," a scenario calls for a husband, after seeing his wife kissing another man and not realizing it is her brother, to leave for Africa to hunt big game. As he is about to be devoured by a lion, one executive proposes he have a vision of a cabaret sequence, while Schnellenhamer decides that what is needed is the arrival of the United States Marines.

In "The Nodder," with 11 writers in the room, along with yes-men and secretaries, Schnellenhamer continues the scripting of the picture, leaving off at the last scene. Here, "Cabot Delancy, a scion of an old Boston family, has gone to try to reach the North Pole in a submarine, and he's on an iceberg, and the scenes of his youth are passing before his eyes." One of the writers suggests that one of the scenes passing before his eyes is that of a polo-game. "'No good,' said Mr. Schnellenhamer. 'Who cares anything about polo? When you're working on a picture you've got to bear in mind the small-town population of the Middle West. Aren't I right?" And all agree. Minutes later, after the other authors have offered their suggestions, Schnellenhamer has the solution. "'He sits on this iceberg and he seems to see himself—he's always been an athlete, you understand—he seems to see himself scoring the winning goal in one of these polo-games. Everybody's interested in polo nowadays. Aren't I right?" And all agree.

A second vision for Delancy has "to be something that'll pull in the women." Schnellenhamer has his next brainstorm. "'This fellow's with this girl in this old-world garden where everything's burgeoning ... and when I say burgeoning I mean burgeoning. That burgeoning's got to be done *right*, or somebody'll get fired ... and they're locked in a close embrace. Hold as long as the Philadelphia censors'll let you, and then comes your nice comedy touch. Just as these two young folks are kissing each other without a thought of anything else in the world, suddenly a cuckoo close by goes "Cuckoo! Cuckoo!" Meaning how goofy they are. That's good for a laugh, isn't it?'"

In "The Castaways," Wodehouse compares writing dialogue for the talkies to being castaways on a desert island, explaining that few who write film dialogue are actually authors, and they are gathered in a manner reminiscent of the old press gangs. "The executives of the studios just haul in anyone they meet and make them sign contracts. Most of the mysterious disappearances you read about are due to this cause. Only the other day they found a plumber who had been missing for years. All the time he had been writing dialogue for the Mishkin Brothers. Once having reached Los Angeles, no one is safe."

Bulstrode Mulliner, trying to pick up his hat, which has been accidentally taken from a train by Schnellenhamer, is signed as a writer in this manner.

> "Miss Stern," he [Schnellenhamer] said, addressing his secretary, "what vacant offices have we on the lot?"
>
> "There is Room 40 in the Leper Colony."
>
> "I thought there was a song-writer there."
>
> "He passed away Tuesday."
>
> "Has the body been removed?"
>
> "Yes, sir...."
>
> The Leper Colony, to which Bulstrode had been assigned, proved to be a long, low building with small cells opening on a narrow corridor. It had been erected to take care of the overflow of the studio's writers, the majority of whom were located in what was known as the Ohio State Penitentiary.

Management has forbidden the writers in the Ohio State Penitentiary from associating with those in the Leper Colony.

Room 40 is assigned to Bulstrode, where he is one among a mere ten other writers working separately on the script of *Scented Sinners*. This is a "'powerful drama of life as it is lived by the jazz-crazed, gin-crazed Younger Generation whose hollow laughter is but the mask for an aching heart,' said Mr. Schnellenhamer. 'It ran for a week in New York and lost a hundred thousand dollars, so we bought it. It has the mucus of a good story. See what you can do with it.'"

However, writers have already been laboring over *Scented Sinners* for years. When all the writers laboring on it are summoned, they are a motley collection, shuffling listlessly. "There were young writers, old writers, middle-aged writers; writers with matted beards at which they plucked nervously, writers with horn-rimmed spectacles who muttered to themselves, writers with eyes that stared blankly or blinked in the unaccustomed light. On all of them *Scented Sinners* had set its unmistakable seal." Screams are heard from their building, with one of the writers working on the treatment shouting "No, no! It isn't possible!," but the secretary is confident that it is just the warm weather and the ordinary process of writers going cuckoo.

Scenarists discover they are chained to the lot by their contract, unable to quit, as Schnellenhamer explains.

> "Here are the contracts, duly signed by you, in which you engage to remain in the employment of the Perfecto-Zizzbaum Corporation until the completion of the picture entitled 'Scented Sinners.' Did you take a look at Para. 6, where it gives the penalties for breach of same? No, don't read them ... You wouldn't sleep nights. But you can take it from me they're some penalties. We've had this thing before of writers wanting to run out on us, so we took steps to protect ourselves...."
>
> "And anyway," he said, speaking now in almost a fatherly manner, "you wouldn't want to quit till the picture was finished.... It wouldn't be right. It wouldn't be fair. It wouldn't be cooperation. You know what 'Scented Sinners' means to this organization. It's the biggest proposition we have. Our whole programme is built around it. We are relying on it to be our big smash. It cost us a barrel of money to buy 'Scented Sinners,' and naturally we aim to get it back."
>
> He rose from his chair and tears came into his eyes. It was as if he had been some emotional American football coach addressing a faint-hearted team.
>
> "Stick to it!" he urged. "Stick to it, folks! You can do it if you like. Get back in there and fight. Think of the boys in the Front Office rooting for you, depending on you. You wouldn't let them down? No, no, not you. You wouldn't let me down? Of course you wouldn't. Get back in the game, then, and win — win — win ... for dear old Perfecto-Zizzbaum and me."

Wodehouse was recalling his own stint at M-G-M when he wrote, "There is a miasma in the atmosphere of the Perfecto-Zizzbaum lot which undoes all who come within its sphere of influence."

In authoring "The Castaways," Wodehouse remembered his long months of labor on the unused scripts of two plays, *Rosalie* and *Candle-Light*, especially the fact that *Candle-Light* was ultimately filmed at another studio. Only when Schnellenhamer's aid, Isadore Levitsky, reminds the chief that actually Medulla-Oblongata-Glutz had outbid them for *Scented Sinners*, and they don't own the property at all, are the writers freed from their contracts.

In "The Nodder," Wodehouse elucidates the corporate structure from top to bottom:

> It is not easy to explain to the lay mind the extremely intricate ramifications of the personnel of a Hollywood motion-picture organisation. Putting it as briefly as possible, a Nodder is something like a Yes-Man, only lower in the social scale. A Yes-Man's duty is to attend conferences and say "Yes." A Nodder's as the name implies, is to nod. The chief executive throws out some statement of opinion, and looks about him expectantly. This is the cue for the senior Yes-Man to say yes. He is followed, in order of precedence, by the second Yes-Man—or Vice-Yesser, as he is sometimes called—and the junior Yes-Man. Only when all the Yes-Men have yessed, do the Nodders begin to function. They nod.

In "Monkey Business," Montrose Mulliner is an assistant director at the Perfecto-Zizzbaum Motion Picture Corporation:

> It is one of the drawbacks to being an assistant director that virtually everything that happens to him is of a nature to create an inferiority complex—or, if one already exists, to deepen it. He is habitually addressed as "Hey, you" and alluded to in the third person as "that fathead." If anything goes wrong on the set, he gets the blame and is ticked off not only by the producer but also by the director and all the principals involved. Finally, he has to be obsequious to so many people that it is little wonder that he comes in time to resemble one of the more shrinking and respectful breeds of rabbit. Five years of assistant-directing had so sapped Montrose's morale that nowadays he frequently found himself starting up and apologizing in his sleep.

George Pybus, of the press department, suggests to Montrose that he and his fiancée, Rosalie Beamish, be married in the gorilla's cage as a publicity stunt. As Wodehouse advises, "The brains of members of the Press departments of motion-picture studios resemble soup at a cheap restaurant. It is wiser not to stir them." When Montrose refuses, Rosalie accuses him of cowardice. The gorilla's agent complains that all the publicity goes to the human stars, giving the publicist an idea. One afternoon the gorilla is let out of its cage to menace hundreds, although no one of consequence need worry. "The stars have all been notified and are off the lot. So are the directors. Also the executives, all except Mr. Schnellenhamer, who is cleaning up some work in his office. He will be quite safe there, of course. Nobody ever got into Mr. Schnellenhamer's office without waiting four hours in the ante-room." Montrose impresses Rosalie and wins a promotion when he discovers the studio's secret—the gorilla is actually a man in a suit. As the Balliol-educated actor tells him, "The initial expenditure comes high, of course ... you don't get a skin like this for nothing ... but there's virtually no overhead." And, of course, a gorilla star is as much in need of a good agent as a human-faced performer.

Wodehouse makes use of a typical stock figure in "The Juice of an Orange":

> One of the things which have caused the making of motion pictures to be listed among the Dangerous Trades is the fact that it has been found impossible to dis-

pense with the temperamental female star. There is a public demand for her, and the Public's word is law. The consequence is that in every studio you will find at least one gifted artiste, the mere mention of whose name causes the strongest to tremble like aspens. At the Perfecto-Zizzbaum this position was held by Hortensia Burwash, the Empress of Molten Passion....

A procedure, accordingly, had been adopted not unlike that in use during the raids in the War. At the first sign that the strain had become too much for Miss Burwash, a siren sounded, warning all workers on the lot to take cover. Later, a bugler, blowing the "All Clear," would inform those in the danger zone that the star had now kissed the director and resumed work on the set.

"The Nodder" deals with child stars, and whether they are actually played by midgets—a question "that has occupied the minds of thinking men ever since these little excrescences first became popular on the screen. Some argue that mere children could scarcely be so loathsome. Others maintain that a right-minded midget would hardly stoop to some of the things these child stars do." Yet, in "The Nodder," the star of *Baby Boy* is Little Johnny Bingley, "The Idol of American Motherhood" and "The Child with the Tear Behind the Smile"—actually a hard-boiled midget in his early forties.

Wilmot Mulliner, a nodder, is in love with Mabel Potter, Schnellenhamer's private secretary. She "has imitated the call of the cuckoo from the Palace, Portland, Oregon, to the Hippodrome, Sumquamset, Maine, and taken three bows after every performance," but she rejects Wilmot as a mere serf. Drowning his sorrows at the nearby speakeasy, Wilmot is astounded to meet Bingley. Learning of it the next morning, Schnellenhamer fears that Wilmot may have discovered that Bingley is a midget, although in fact Wilmot can remember little. At the next day's story conference, Wilmot has a hangover, but Schnellenhamer mistakenly interprets his new, less obsequious attitude as evidence that he must be quieted if he is not to reveal Bingley's secret to the press. Schnellenhamer grants Wilmot an executive position "with brevet rank as a brother-in-law."

In the sequel, "The Juice of an Orange," the reader learns how Mabel, like many a girl who "has fallen into a man's arms," has wriggled "out of them at a later date." Love so fills Wilmot with benevolence that he agrees to a pay cut, causing Mabel to end the engagement. Going on an eating binge to compensate for his loss, Wilmot is soon compelled to diet, to which, Wodehouse remarks, "may be attributed all the unhappiness which is afflicting the world to-day." This allows him to commiserate with fellow-dieter Hortensia Burwash, star of *Hearts Aflame*, becoming her agent and regaining respect in Mabel's eyes.

The gorilla star of *Black Africa* is a far more sympathetic kind of actor in "Monkey Business." This picture was described as

> a celluloid epic of the clashing of elemental passions in a land where might is right and the strong man comes into his own. [The gorilla's] capture in its native jungle was said to have cost the lives of seven half-dozen members of the expedition, and at the time when the story begins it was lodged in a stout cage on the Perfecto-Zizzbaum lot at a salary of seven hundred and fifty dollars a week, with billing guaranteed in letters not smaller than those of Edmund Wigham and Luella Benstead, the stars.

Again, the resemblance to reality during the time Wodehouse was in Hollywood was pronounced. For many years actor Charlie Gemora was known as the performer behind Hollywood's ape masks, although he was never given the privilege of star billing. M-G-M's *Trader Horn* had just returned from the most elaborate African location shooting up to that time, and *Tarzan of the Apes*, the first of the Johnny Weissmuller films costarring Maureen O'Sullivan, was beginning production as well. Simian madness was standard in filmmaking during these years, from the falsified documentary *Ingagi* to the menace of *Murders in the Rue Morgue* and the gigantic threat of *King Kong*.

"The Rise of Minna Nordstrom" begins in the milieu where every maid, butler, waitress, barber, secretary, watchman, and bootlegger hopes to be a star, and even a local policeman has "specially taken sex-appeal in the College of Eastern Iowa course of Motion Picture acting." All the moguls need liquor immediately, since Mrs. Zizzbaum is about to give a party for the vice president of Switzerland, Mrs. Fishbein for the ex-king of Ruritania, and Mrs. Schnellenhamer for "the Duke of Wigan, who, as so many British dukes do, was at this time passing slowly through Hollywood." Schnellenhamer's wife is a former silent star who had been known "as the Queen of Stormy Emotion, and she occasionally saw to it that her husband was reminded of this." But with their bootlegger playing an archbishop on the Outstanding Screen–Favorites lot, Schnellenhamer, Fishbein, and Zizzbaum finally decide to break into the liquor cellar of their rival, Sigismund Glutz of Medulla-Oblongata-Glutz (abbreviated M-O-G, another play on M-G-M, and with the first two words taken from the part of the brain that tapers into the spinal cord). At Glutz's home is Vera Prebble, the maid for Schnellenhamer, Fishbein, and Zizzbaum who had been fired by each when she tried to audition for them at home. Prebble has taken her revenge by reporting the liquor supply in the homes of Schnellenhamer, Fishbein, and Zizzbaum to the police. Alone with the three moguls in the only remaining home with liquor in Hollywood, Prebble demands and wins herself a starring contract (under the name of "Minna Nordstrom"), also compelling the merger of the three companies.

Three of the Mulliner Hollywood short stories were adapted into two episodes of the television series *Wodehouse Playhouse*. "The Rise of Minna

Nordstrom" (1975) was adapted from the story of the same name, while "The Nodder" and "Monkey Business" became the basis for the episode entitled "The Nodder" (1976). Like the made-for-television film of "The Old Reliable" over a dozen years later, these proved that Wodehouse's satires of Hollywood were ideal screen fare, although all three made significant variations on their source. They capture a mythical Hollywood past, in which the secrets of tyrannical moguls are discovered and used by underlings. However, in *Wodehouse Playhouse*, as opposed to "The Old Reliable," there is not only a wackier tone, but also a greater sense of specificity and a sharper perspective on Hollywood life.

The *Wodehouse Playhouse* version of "The Nodder" presents a broader view of the studio system than the more narrow focus of "The Rise of Minna Nordstrom." In "The Nodder," Wilmot finds the woman he loves, Mabel, Schnellenhamer's secretary, unimpressed with her prospective suitor's lowly position in the line of yes-men. "The Nodder" presents his hapless position at the typical story conference presided over by Schnellenhamer. Progress inches along on an absurd scenario with a battery of writers mined by the mogul for his own almost surreal notions of what constitutes a narrative. Meanwhile, Wilmot refuses a studio publicity plan to marry Mabel inside the cage of the company's resident gorilla. However, he accidentally discovers that the studio ape is, in fact, a man making a living wearing an ape suit — Schnellenhamer's secret. When Schnellenhamer's pet Nodder becomes suddenly assertive, although he is actually trying to impress Mabel, Schnellenhamer knows he must give the couple a promotion.

Both "The Rise of Minna Nordstrom" and "The Nodder" add elements to their source, "Nordstrom" with a presentation of her Al Jolson–style debut in talkies that merely serves to pad the running time. However, "The Nodder" ideally combines the two stories that serve as its sources, and both shows achieve an impressive comedic success, capturing a laugh-inducing satirical view of Hollywood's golden age, as Wodehouse presented in prose.

In Wodehouse's first novel about Hollywood, *Laughing Gas*, an Englishman and child star exchange bodies while under the ether. (He acknowledged that the idea was taken from an 1882 boys' classic, *Vice Versa*, by F. Anstey.[10]) It is in many ways one of Wodehouse's most unusual books, and his only novel to be an outright fantasy. Reggie Havershot, third Earl of Havershot, is sent to Hollywood because his cousin Egremont Mannering has escaped and is rumored to be engaged to a woman there — certainly no suitable wife for Egremont.

On the journey west, Havershot meets the absurdly-named actress

April June, and believes her to be his soulmate, "an angel in human shape."[11] She tells him, "It may seem odd to you, considering that I'm in pix, but I'm really at heart just a simple little home body. I am never happier than among my books and flowers. And I love cooking."[12] She adds, "Money and fame mean nothing.... My reward is the feeling that I am spreading happiness, that I am doing my little best to cheer up this tired world, that I am giving the toiling masses a glimpse of something bigger and better and more beautiful.... It's sort of a religion with me. I feel like a kind of priestess. I think of all those millions of drab lives, and I say to myself what does all the hard work and the distasteful publicity matter if I can bring a little sunshine."[13] Havershot finds Eggy at one of the parties that April says she dislikes but is expected to give, and learns that his fiancée is Ann Bannister, to whom Havershot had once been engaged himself.

The flare-up of a wisdom tooth sends Havershot to the dentist's chair at the same time as Joey Cooley, the leading child star and the idol of American motherhood. In the waiting room, Havershot hears that the kid Cooley misses his home in Chilicothe, Ohio, and eating his mother's fried chicken, but is bound by a five-year contract. However, when Havershot goes into the dentist's chair for the laughing gas, he awakes to see he is no longer age 27 but has long blonde hair in ringlets and is wearing knickerbockers and stockings. He realizes that, "owing presumably to some bad staffwork during the period when we were simultaneously sauntering about in the fourth dimension, or whatever they call it, there had been an unforeseen switch."[14] Havershot is in Cooley's body, with the voice of a child but the thoughts and words of an adult, while the mischievous Joey is quite content now that he is free to take a "poke in the snoot" at his enemies using Havershot's adult body.

Laughing Gas is told in the first person by Havershot, and during most of the story he is trapped in Cooley's juvenile body. He is taken from the dentist back to the home of the head of the Brinkwater-Magnifico Motion Picture Corporation, where he is under strict supervision and forced to subsist on a spartan diet of dried prunes to control his weight. Havershot learns that Ann is Cooley's governess, and Eggy his elocution teacher. "Since the talkies came in, you can't heave a brick in Hollywood without beaning an English elocution teacher. The place is full of Britons on the make, and if they can't get jobs on the screen, they work the elocution-teaching racket. References and qualifications are not asked for. So long as you're English, you are welcomed into the home."[15]

Havershot even learns that while under the ether June had burst into the dentist's office, shrieking "I want my little pal" for the benefit of photographers. When Havershot visits her, with the thoughts of Havershot but in Cooley's body, he finds that she loathes the scene-stealing child star and kicks him in the pants, proving as well in other ways that she is hardly the divinely selfless girl she had given Havershot to believe. Cooley is kidnapped by some would-be screenwriters, angry that "the Hitlers and Mussolinis of the picture world ... ship these assortments of New York playwrights and English novelists out here and leave it all to them."[16] After Cooley has got hold of their gun, he learns the abduction is a publicity stunt, to end in his rescue by June. Instead, Cooley and Havershot are knocked unconscious by a bicycle and return to their proper bodies. Havershot realizes he loves Ann, while she and Eggy ended their engagement when Havershot, in Cooley's body, told Eggy who he really was. This had convinced Eggy to end his drinking and follow the advice of a woman proselytizing for Sister Lora Luella Stott's temperance crusade at the Temple of the New Dawn (a reference to Aimee Semple McPherson).

Unlike the short stories of the Mulliners of Hollywood, which were set largely in and around the studios and adopted a parallel of their organizational structure for their cast of characters, *Laughing Gas* is a more traditional Wodehouse novel, set in homes and with the staff as supporting characters. However, it remains unique in providing a behind-the-scenes perspective of one branch of Hollywood as seen through the eyes of an adult forced to live as a boy. As the novel unfolds, Havershot's thoughts and actions become increasingly childlike, in a metaphor for his takeover by Hollywood. The characters generally think, and talk, in movie clichés, and the narrative structure of the novel is clearly meant as a parody of the unlikely coincidences and happy endings that are the elements of many Hollywood plots. At the same time, the more acidic parody of the Mulliners of Hollywood is absent from *Laughing Gas*.

When Havershot finds unguarded liquor and cigarettes, he forgets he is in Cooley's body; he quickly becomes drunk and is photographed by a columnist, ruining Cooley's career in an instant. Yet Cooley is hardly resentful of Havershot's error: both main characters in *Laughing Gas* yearn for home and find nothing appealing in Hollywood.

Discontent is everywhere: T.P. Brinkwater bemoans, "Look at me now. President of the organization, worth every cent of twenty million dollars... Got to stand up there in spats, with everybody staring at me... You get on just the least little bit in this world, and first thing you know they're putting up statues to you.... I ought to have stuck to the cloak and suit business."[17] Brinkwater is a far more likeable mogul than Schnellenhamer. He joins forces with Cooley to forestall having to dress in a stiff collar and spats to unveil the studio founder's statue with the kid handing him a nosegay saying, "Pity f'owers for 'oo, Mithter B'inkwater."[18]

Even the English butler is infected with Hollywood malaise, although Havershot as Cooley suggests he save it for the winter evenings. In the butler's words,

> There's the yearning to be away from it all. There's the dull despair of living the shallow, glittering life of this tinsel town where tragedy lies hid behind a thousand false smiles.... Ah, Hollywood, Hollywood... Bright city of sorrows, where fame deceives and temptation lurks, where souls are shrivelled in the furnace of desire, where streets are bathed with the shamed tears of betrayed maidens.... Hollywood! Home of mean glories and spangled wretchedness, where the deathless fire burns for the outspread wings of the guileless moth and beauty is broken on sin's cruel wheel. If you have finished with the tray, sir, I will take it.[19]

Afterward, the butler convinces Havershot as Cooley to give him the tooth saved for him by the dentist, having him sign a certificate of authenticity so that the holy relic can be sold to a fan magazine for several thousand dollars. The butler then pockets the profits and leaves town.

The domestic staff is made up of would-be actors, and even Brinkwater's gardener is only made up to look Japanese, hoping to land a small part in a forthcoming production. A neighboring child actor, Orlando Flower, with red hair and spots, is jealous of Cooley's climb to stardom, calling him "Little Lord Fauntleroy." Tommy Murphy, labeled another local junior excrescence, was replaced by Cooley in the screen affections of American mothers and now, like a thug, is only waiting to catch Cooley alone.

The basic theme of *Laughing Gas* is that Hollywood is a place to escape from, a Dartmoor rather than a Mecca. However, it lacks the comparative sophistication of the Mulliner stories' complex creation of a parallel Hollywood universe. Although certainly a Hollywood satire, *Laughing Gas* was gentle compared to much that had already been written—and had even appeared—on screen.

Hollywood was not the setting, but a subsidiary element, of another Wodehouse book of this period, *The Luck of the Bodkins*. Combining "English merriment with Hollywood hilarity," this shipboard romance has a plot enhanced by the work Wodehouse was doing simultaneously on the play that became *Anything Goes*. The first draft was a Hollywood satire, which the prospective producer rejected, compelling major rewrites of the piece.[20] *The Luck of the Bodkins* itself was first published in England, and then it was rejected by the *Saturday Evening Post*. Wodehouse, realizing it was too long, rewrote and condensed it into a much more tightly-structured form for publication a few months later by *Redbook* in the United States.

In *The Luck of the Bodkins*, Ivor Llewellyn, the president of the Superba-Llewellyn Motion Picture Corporation, is given orders by his wife, Grayce. She was one of leading panther-women of the silent screen, famous for the role of Mimi, the female Apache in *When Paris Sleeps*. He must obey, even though she wants him to smuggle a pearl necklace through customs on his return from France.

Mabel, Grayce's sister, proposes putting Monty Bodkin on the payroll as an advisor for the English sequences, mistakenly believing Bodkin to be an undercover customs agent who could be bribed in this fashion. Mabel also believes there is room on the payroll for British expertise, considering a past blunder of Llewellyn:

> Until this moment the emotion which any reference to that fox-hunting in July thing always caused him had held him dumb. It was a sore subject with him. One of the features of his super-film, *Glorious Devon*, it had been the occasion of much indignation in the English Press and of such a choking and spluttering and outraged what-whatting among purple-faced Masters of Hounds in the Shires as had threatened to produce an epidemic of apoplexy. This Mr. Llewellyn could have borne with fortitude. But it had also resulted in the complete failure of the picture throughout the island kingdom, and that had cut him to the quick.[21]

To Llewellyn's continual vexation, much of his family is on the payroll, even his wife's cousin Egbert's sister Genevieve, a reader at $350 a week. He shakes at the mere suggestion of having to put more such individuals on the payroll. "Often as he had been through discussions of this kind, he was never able to remain quite calm when they came up. When an opportunity of doing something at Llewellyn City for a relative or a friend of a relative or a relative by marriage or a friend of a relative by marriage was offered to him, it always made him feel as if his interior organs were being stirred up with a pole."[22]

Llewellyn succeeded Schnellenhamer as Wodehouse's principal fictional creation of a studio executive. While he has been compared to Samuel Goldwyn, Llewellyn seems to be an amalgam of a number of figures, probably most of whom Wodehouse did not actually work with, most particularly Harry Cohn.[23] Llewellyn is an obese man with three chins, who hums extracts from the musical scores of old Superba-Llewellyn features. It is impossible to appeal to his heart, or wring his neck, because he has neither. He only has use for those from whom he needs favors, and his word is notoriously unreliable. "Why, if Ikey had an only child and he promised her a doll on her birthday, the first thing she would do, if she was a sensible kid, would be to go to her lawyer and have a contract drawn up and signed, with penalty clauses."[24]

He is unpredictable and temperamental. "No motion-picture magnate is ever troubled by the *volte-face*."[25] He tends to avoid flattering those he seeks to employ, preferring to create an inferiority complex.

Like Schnellenhamer, Ivor Llewellyn's cultural awareness is minimal. Hearing that Tennyson is a famous poet, Llewellyn hires the first English author of that name he meets, unaware that the Tennyson of note has been dead for decades. He would just as easily have signed a man named Dante to a contract if he had heard the name before. When he learns that both writers are dead, he is partly confused, "but one thing was clear to him, that his brother-in-law George, not content with drawing from the coffers of the firm a thousand dollars more than he was worth, had been trying to fill up the Superba-Llewellyn lot with corpses; and for a moment all he felt was a very justifiable resentment against George." Yet Llewellyn also felt "that corpses would probably be just as good at treatment and dialogue as most of the living authors already employed by him."[26]

Monty's romance with Gertrude Butterwick is upset by the interference of actress Lotus Blossom, since she believes he can affect whether Llewellyn gives her boyfriend a contract. No less underhanded than Llewellyn, Blossom's actions are more whimsical than purely selfish. Star of such pictures as *Bozo the Ape Man* and *Shadows on the Wall*, Blossom is physically inspired by the red-haired Clara Bow.

> It was her hair that did it, principally. That and the fact that on the screen she seemed a wistful, pathetic little thing, while off it dynamic was more the word. In private life, Lottie Blossom tended to substitute for wistfulness and pathos a sort of "Passed-For-Adults-Only" joviality, which expressed itself outwardly in a brilliant and challenging smile, and inwardly and spiritually in her practice of keeping alligators in wickerwork baskets and asking unsuspecting strangers to lift the lid.
>
> But principally, as we say, it was her hair that caused the eye of the beholder to swivel in its socket and his breath to come in irregular pants. Seeming on the screen to have merely a decent pallor, it revealed itself when she made a personal appearance a vivid and soul-shattering red. She looked as if she had been dipping her head in a sunset: and this, taken in conjunction with her large, shining eyes and the impression she gave, like so many of her sisters of the motion-picture art, of being supremely confident of herself, usually hit the stranger pretty hard.[27]

When Lottie Blossom, actually a native of Hoboken and of Irish descent, hears that someone liked one of her pictures, she started like a war-horse at the sound of the bugle.

> "What picture was that?"
>
> "*Lovers in Brooklyn.*"
>
> "You should have caught me in *Storm over Flatbush.*"[28]

Lottie admits that success in the movies is "mostly a case of having a map that photographs well and getting a good cameraman and director."[29]

Blossom says everyone likes Hollywood. "There's something going on there all the time. Malibu. Catalina. Agua Caliente. And if you aren't getting divorced yourself, there's always one of your friends who is, and that gives you something to chat about in the long evenings. And it isn't half such a crazy place as they make out. I know two-three people in Hollywood that are part sane."[30] However, writers come in for her criticism. "The trouble with writers is, they're all loopy. I remember the fellow who did the dialogue for *Shadows on the Wall* stopping rehearsal once to tell me that when I said 'Oh!' on finding the corpse in the cabin-trunk I must let the word come slowly out in the shape of a pear. Well, I ask you!"[31] Indeed, in *The Luck of the Bodkins*, Hollywood is congested with people trying to break in, especially authors, who are starving in the thousands.

Studio life, the contract system, corporate management and mergers, the story conference, multiple writers composing scripts of a single property, the position of assistant directors, publicists, and stars, and the greed and stupidity of movie moguls—all the prominent features of Wodehouse's Hollywood were memorably covered in the Mulliner series. They were present, less pointedly, in *Laughing Gas* and *The Luck of the Bodkins*. None of his subsequent writing with a filmmaking background or Hollywood characters was so biting in its tone as that first response to his M-G-M experience.

IV

British and Hollywood Adaptations

Regardless of any general residual antipathy in Hollywood as a result of the Alma Whittaker interview or an awareness of the satires Wodehouse was writing, a spate of films from his writing were produced in the next few years. Within months of his leaving Metro-Goldwyn-Mayer, production began on another version of *Her Cardboard Lover*. Nils Asther was originally to appear in it, having been a costar of the silent version, and Robert Montgomery was also cast. Then, in early September 1931, M-G-M announced that it would shelve the picture, but only days later reactivated it with Buster Keaton announced as the lead.

Released in 1932, the new film was retitled (with a separate French version, *Le Plombier Amourreux*, also produced), with Irene Purcell, the feminine lead of *The Man in Possession* and *Just a Gigolo*, appearing as Patricia Jardine. Keaton and Jimmy Durante starred, in the first of the three pictures in which they were paired. *The Passionate Plumber* was filmed in a mere 19 days, and placing Keaton in this property was considered a measurement of his importance to the studio; he was still a box-office draw, but was well aware that he was miscast.[1]

Initially, Keaton and Durante seem imposed on the structure of the play, with it taking secondary importance to their antics. However, the casting becomes less intrusive as the movie's plot develops in Laurence E. Johnson's adaptation. As Elmer, played by Keaton, falls in love with Patricia, taking on the play's role of her "cardboard lover," he eventually wins her heart and saves her from a liaison with caddish Tony Lagorce (Gilbert Roland).

One of the projects Wodehouse had worked on at M-G-M, *Candle-Light*, from his own theatrical adaptation, was instead filmed at Universal in 1933 as *By Candlelight*. This was one of the last years the work could have been transferred to the screen; the lack of sexual morality underlying much of its plot would have been discouraged or banned outright by the new Production Code. The project arrived at Universal in a manner that must have inspired Wodehouse in his short story "The Castaways": Universal traded M-G-M their rights to H. Rider Haggard's *She* for *Candle-Light*, then discovered they didn't own *She* after all, and had to pay cash for *Candle-Light*. Ultimately nearly $15,000 was paid, along with the M-G-M scripts to date. Robert Wyler, the director who had convinced the studio to make *Candle-Light*, was replaced after a week of shooting by James Whale, who proceeded to complete the picture in a month.

By Candlelight is initially amusing, as the audience sees the well-practiced interplay between prince and butler to ensure the success of a lady's seduction, with the butler Josef hoping to one day be like his master, imitating all his lines and moves in a mirror. The prince, as played by Nils Asther (who had already appeared in two Wodehouse pictures, *Der Goldene Schmetterling* and *The Cardboard Lover*), is much harsher and less sympathetic than in the play. Paul Lukas, as Josef, although far from optimally cast, proves better in the role than his persona would lead one to expect. Elissa Landi, in the female lead as Marie, the servant imitating nobility, fails to realize the role's potential.

The movie, by concentrating simply on the central gag of the valet imitating the prince, loses its focus. The play's sophistication lay in examining the results and ramifications of the exchanges of identity on all of the characters and the parallel couples. It was this complexity that had sustained the length of the play, and with its loss, *By Candlelight* gradually resembles more of a Cinderella story than an Ernst Lubitsch–style farce. The play had sought to erase class differences by demonstrating the characters' interchangeability through their similar behavior and instincts at all levels. In the movie, this playfulness is absent, and what works for the prince is not for the butler; the importance of class difference is reinforced and justified. A year after the release of the film, the play was also adapted on a *Lux Radio Theater* broadcast of June 9, 1935, with Robert Montgomery, Irene Purcell, and Alfred Shirley in the roles of the valet, the lady, and the prince.

In 1934, a small independent company, Liberty Pictures, bought the rights to Wodehouse's 1910 short story "The Watch Dog," which it transformed into the musical film *Dizzy Dames*, released the next year. Liberty was a short-lived company, part of whose program was to use the names of prominent authors with properties that could be obtained with minimal expense. As the *Hollywood Reporter* review noted, *Dizzy Dames* proved it was impossible to stage an impressive musical on a nickel and dime shoestring budget.[2] The banal plot concerns a boarding house for theatrical players; it is run by a retired actress, who has tried to keep her talented daughter from going on stage. Nonetheless, the lure proves too strong, especially when

Buster Keaton in *The Passionate Plumber.*

the girl falls in love with one of the players who helps train her for a successful singing career. The predictability, combined with music and songs that highlight the production's low budget, resulted in a dissatisfying movie that only looks worse with age. There is no resemblance to the purported Wodehouse source; perhaps the story was simply one whose rights were available cheaply enough to allow putting the Wodehouse name on the film.

Paul Lukas, Elissa Landi, Dorothy Revier, and Nils Asther in *By Candlelight* (1933).

On the British screen, two Wodehouse stories appeared in quick succession, both produced by British International Pictures and starring Gene Gerrard, Molly Lamont, and Tonie Bruce. First was *Brother Alfred* in 1932, filmed at the Elstree studio. The adaptation (from "Rallying Round Old George") and scenario by Henry Edwards and Claude Gurney did not conceal the thinness of the source, a play by Wodehouse and Herbert Westbrook that had failed on the stage, and was derived from a 1913 short story of the same title. With a tale that would have better suited the running time of a three-reeler, instead the story is stretched out to 77 minutes. Nor is there any novelty to the narrative's development, with every event telegraphed far ahead under Henry Edwards's direction.

When young George Lattaker (Gerrard) celebrates his engagement by kissing the nearest person to him, the servant of his fiancée Stella (Lamont), Stella assumes this is evidence of impending inconstancy. Drowning his sorrows with a new acquaintance, they create a disturbance at a nightclub. When the police arrive the next morning with the evidence of George's hat to prove his participation, he adopts the artifice of pretending to be his own fictitious twin brother Alfred. Having convinced every-

Trade paper advertisement for *Dizzy Dames*.

one, complications ensue when it turns out his drinking companion was Prince Sachsberg (Clifford Heatherley), who wants to reward George for his companionship. George appears to have outwitted himself until the truth is unintentionally given away. Only one gag is amusing, as George and the royal first meet, the obese prince pulling out a huge hip flask in proportion to his noble status; more typical is the punctuation of various scenes with shots of the yacht's anchor dropping. The lack of character development or major subplots leaves a stagnant feeling; only a parallel romance with two of the servants was deleted from the Wodehouse original. The problems were especially evident with the low caliber acting and the production cheaply made and stage-bound, confined for its setting largely to a single ship. The only intriguing bit of design is a shot of an apparent shelf of Wodehouse books in dust jackets with *Very Good, Jeeves* plainly readable on the end.

Similar themes were treated with vastly more skill in *Leave It to Me*, the film of another play Wodehouse had written, an adaptation of his novel *Leave It to Psmith*. Between 1929 and 1930, Wodehouse had teamed with Ian Hay (the pseudonym of John Hay Beith) in England to convert two of his novels and one of Hay's short stories for the stage: *A Damsel in Distress*, *Leave It to Psmith*, and *Baa, Baa, Black Sheep*, respectively. *A Damsel in Distress* was completed in record time, and the collaboration was enjoyable because it was like those with Guy Bolton. Hay "liked doing all the stuff himself. I was just to contribute the book. We talked it all over and got our scenario and the characters and everything and then he wrote it."[3] There was thought of a theater company to perform Wodehouse plays, but the idea was dropped when he left for Hollywood.

The stage version of *Leave It to Psmith* makes such alterations as changing Clarence's name to the Earl of Middlewick and eliminating all the plot strands tying the novel in to earlier stories of Psmith and Mike Jackson. Its comic dialogue also surpasses the very gentle, subtle humor of the novel. The film does revert to the use of the Emsworth name, and novel, play, and film each make their own set of variations and details on the story, straying steadily further from the source.

While less faithful to these sources than *Brother Alfred*, the scenario of *Leave It to Me*, by Gerrard, Frank Miller, and Cecil Lewis, follows the play's dialogue. It is filled with enough amusing lines and gestures, coming in rapid pace under Monty Banks's direction, to fulfill the basic purpose of a Wodehouse movie, although frequently veering too much toward slapstick. Nearly all the performances are appropriate, and the interplay of the large number of characters is effective, although naturally some must be slighted for a film of 76 minutes. Gerrard, as "Sebastian Help" in place of Psmith, is a lively figure, keeping up a continuous patter that represents almost a turn toward the manic Marx Brothers mode, emphasized by a harp recital — unlike Gerrard's comparatively subdued performance as George in *Brother Alfred*.

Help heads a large, frenetic, but unsuccessful office, Help, Ltd. Finally winning a promise of employment from a mysterious figure meeting him at a club, on the way he manages to ensnare a flowerpot with his cane, echoed later when Help drops one on Rupert Baxter (Gus McNaughton). He meets and falls in love with Miss Eve Halliday (Lamont), who will arrive later at Blandings, and the two share the first of two singing duets. Help is hired to keep an eye on the jewels of Lady Constance (Bruce). He finds the perfect cover when the poet Siegfried Veleur (Peter Godfrey; the character's name changed from Ralston MacTodd in the play and novel), scheduled to read his poetry at Blandings, asks Help to impersonate him. On the train Help meets his friend Freddie Threepwood (Melville Cooper), Lord Emsworth's son. A mix-up in suitcases with the criminal Ed Coots (George Gee) when the train arrives makes butler Beach (Syd Crossley) suspicious, for Help's bag is filled with tools of the burglary trade, and he informs Baxter, who realizes Help is an imposter. Ed is linked with Lida (changed from Alison Peavey, and played by Olive Borden), another undercover guest at Blandings who is after the jewels.

Help must continue the pretense of being the poet Veleur and recite his work in an amusing scene that maintains the satire of poets found throughout Wodehouse generally but that is not crystallized fully in any particular scene in the original play or novel of *Leave It to Psmith*. Halliday places Constance's necklace in the flowerpot, observed by Ed; she is suspicious of Help. Baxter and Beach behave like police in the subsequent investigation, Baxter firing his pistol at Help but hitting only flowerpots as Help escapes into the rain. In an entirely new climax having no basis in either source, Help trails Lida and Ed, enabling Halliday and Freddie to follow as the necklace is saved just as the crooks are about to leave on a vessel going abroad—until Help tosses the necklace to Freddie, who drops it into the sea.

Despite its use of many of the incidents from the stage and novel versions of *Leave It to Psmith*, this ultimate departure from its narrative places *Leave It to Me* as a lesser, if still worthy, member of the canon of Wodehousian screen adaptations. On the other hand, unlike the elemental sets of *Brother Alfred*, the production of *Leave It to Me* is far more lavish, with elaborate settings and elegant costumes and appropriate makeup. (Another British film, similarly entitled *Leave It to Me*, a 1930 George King production released by Fox within days of the play's premiere, also may have been inspired by it and the novel.)

The same year that *Leave It to Me* was released, 1933, another Blandings novel, *Summer Lightning*, was produced by British and Dominions Film Corporation at the Elstree studio. This 78-minute movie, a reasonably close approximation of the book, was described as "slow" by the *Film*

An advertisement for *Summer Lightning* feature the porcine Empress of Blandings.

Pictorial review of October 21, 1933. Maclean Rogers directed Ralph Lynn as Hugo Carmody, Winifred Shotter as Millicent Keable (sic), Dorothy Bouchier as Sue Brown, Miles Malleson (who also wrote the adaptation) as Beach, Helen Ferrers as Lady Emsworth, Esme Percy as Baxter, Gordon James as Pilbream (sic), and Horace Hodges as Lord Emsworth. In 1935, Lynn would commission Wodehouse to write a stage version of the novel *Hot Water*, to be retitled *The Inside Stand*. Wodehouse even persuaded his son-in-law to invest, but *The Inside Stand* closed disappointingly after 50 performances in London.[4]

Summer Lightning (titled *Fish Preferred* in the United States) was again filmed later in the decade as *Blixt och Dunder* (*Thunder and Lightning*) in Sweden in 1938 with many of the nation's top screen performers. As adapted by Hasse Ekman with Anders Henrikson directing, the names were altered, Emsworth becoming Hagerskiold. Characters were also shifted, the figures of Clarence and Constance becoming a couple rather

The "24 sheet" roadside poster for *Summer Lightning* highlighted the Empress as well as the human stars.

than brother and sister, with Ronnie Fish changed into their son. The porcine Empress is renamed "Helen of Troy" and dressed in pink. Three songs were also included. The movie earned varying estimations for lack of fidelity to the Wodehouse spirit, for instance opening with Galahad parachuting into his brother's pear tree.

At the beginning of 1936, Paramount released *Anything Goes*, although the credits did not mention Wodehouse; Howard Lindsay and Russel Crouse had revised the Guy Bolton–Wodehouse book when the two became unavailable. The play opened on Broadway in 1934 and ran for 420 performances, with Wodehouse receiving 2 percent of the gross.[5] However, the movie added new songs to those by Cole Porter (Wodehouse's lyrics were performed only in England). There are no adaptation credits on the screen. On behalf of Wodehouse, Bolton had sold the rights along with those of another version, *Hard to Get*, while reserving television and broadcast rights—a prudent decision, considering the play was adapted several times to the small screen in the 1950s. The 1936 movie of *Anything Goes* was subsequently reissued for television in a shortened version under the title *Tops Is the Limit*, eliminating the title song.

In this version of *Anything Goes*, a seagoing vessel is the setting for the antics of a man (Bing Crosby) who 1) accidentally remains aboard while seeing his boss off on a trip, necessitating disguise; 2) falls in love with a woman who seemed to be in danger (Ida Lupino); 3) is helped in his romance by another woman (Ethel Merman) who loves him; and 4) becomes involved with a gangster disguised as a minister (Charlie Rug-

An ad for *Anything Goes* (1935).

gles). While the diverse plot strands and the songs merge surprisingly well, neither Lewis Milestone's direction nor the cast muster the necessary panache or style required for a memorable example of the musical comedy genre. The picture moves from scene to scene with little logical motivation, and only Merman is ideal, repeating her Broadway role. Lupino is merely decorative, while Ruggles is unbelievable as anything more than a bumbler. Arthur Treacher plays Lupino's protector, a stiff Englishman eager to learn American slang, in a foreshadowing of the Jeeves role he would undertake shortly at Fox. *Anything Goes* was only modestly profitable at the box office.

On October 16, 1935, Twentieth Century Fox bought the film rights to *Thank You, Jeeves*, along with a one-year option on the other stories and the right to make additional films centered around Jeeves. The contract, negotiated with Société Anonyme Siva, Wodehouse's Swiss company set up for tax purposes, authorized payments to go to the American Play Company. Wodehouse sold the rights to the initial Jeeves novel for $15,000. Until January 1, 1937, Twentieth Century Fox had the option to continue to purchase one story annually for $5,000 from the 39 Jeeves short stories already published at that date, or $15,000 for the novel *Right Ho, Jeeves* (titled *Brinkley Manor* in England). Also mentioned was the unpublished and unproduced, nonmusical play titled simply *Jeeves*. The contract could be extended for 20 years, but the exclusive rights given to the studio would expire two years after the last story was purchased.[6]

Looking for potentially prolific — and profitable — properties, Twentieth Century Fox was interested in any character who seemed to have the ability to lure filmgoers to film after film, no less than in modern television series. Earlier in the year, Fox's merger with Twentieth Century had enhanced the studio's status. A "B" unit was organized under Sol Wurtzel, who had a $6,000,000 annual budget for 24 B films per year. These pictures averaged between $150,000 to $200,000 apiece in cost, involved two to three months of preparations and three weeks of shooting, and had access to the top equipment, sound stages and technical personnel used by the studio's biggest budget films.[7] Although B's were typically intended for screening on the bottom half of double bills, many of the series B's focused on a character, had especially high production standards, and were reliable attractions for moviegoers. Fox had a notable success with its Charlie Chan series, bringing to the screen the late Earl Derr Biggers's detective, and Chan was the studio's most popular "star" after Shirley Temple.

Jeeves had been brought to the notice of the American reading public in the *Saturday Evening Post*, as had Chan. The Jeeves series seems to

Ethel Merman, Arthur Treacher, and Charlie Ruggles in *Anything Goes* (1935).

have been launched on what was perceived as a sure bet, casting Arthur Treacher, known for such roles, as the famous literary butler. However, while the Chan series was cast and presented in a manner consonant with Biggers's literary creation, the Jeeves films revealed no understanding of the situations and character patterns that had made Jeeves successful in stories and books.

Nearly a year after purchasing the rights, the studio released the first movie, *Thank You, Jeeves.* There was scarcely a mistake that was not made in its 56 minutes. Dispensing with the plot of the novel, or that of any other Jeeves story, screenwriters Joseph Hoffman and Stephen Gross substituted a bizarre combination of incidents interspersed in an incredibly unlikely account of Bertie and Jeeves becoming involved with espionage. (The novel *Thank You, Jeeves* would be adapted again with greater fidelity in two 1991 episodes, "Jeeves in the Country" and "Kidnapped!," of the television series *Jeeves and Wooster.*) As Wodehouse noted later, "They didn't use a word of my story, substituting another written by some studio hack."[8] The attempts at humor were either forced or, in the case of a few lines that might have been amusing, presented in such a way as to conceal any comedic potential. Even worse was the lackluster, unimaginative direction of Arthur Greville Collins, who was seemingly wholly unaware of the demands of a comedic presentation. *Thank You, Jeeves* so utterly fails in

Herald for *Thank You, Jeeves.*

its essential purpose that it is easy to watch the whole picture without so much as cracking a smile.

Only the opening, as Bertie loudly plays the drums to the accompaniment of music on the radio, recalled the milieu of the Wodehouse stories. Subsequently, a mystery woman who is followed by agents, Marjorie Lowman (Virginia Field), knocks at the door. Bertie, proud of his chivalrous ancestors and hoping to emulate them, offers her shelter, but she disappears in the night. Jeeves, after threatening to give notice, persuades the bored Bertie that he should take a vacation in the country, and he knows just the place—Mooring Manor Inn. By the logic of Hollywood, this hotel is, of course, the headquarters of the spies, and just the place Marjorie will turn up next. When the spies introduce themselves to Bertie as men from Scotland Yard, he accepts them at face value, surrendering Marjorie (an actual crime-fighter). In the final scene of fisticuffs in the hotel basement, Bertie wields the medieval artifacts lying about while Jeeves reveals himself to be a former amateur boxing champion. Making amends for his earlier errors, Bertie finally has become worthy of Marjorie's love, although Jeeves must accept that Bertie's new bride has other plans for a gentleman's gentleman.

The most lamentable addition to *Thank You, Jeeves* is the black comedian Willie Best as the saxophone-playing "Drowzy," a wandering min-

At right, Virginia Field and David Niven encounter spies in *Thank You, Jeeves.*

strel performer. Best was sometimes billed as "Sleep 'n' Eat," and his role was strongly reminiscent of Stepin Fetchit, who was under contract at Fox and a popular comedian at the time. Today these scenes recall the worst type of Hollywood racial humor during the 1930s. In one dreadful scene, Jeeves tries to teach Best a British march, which Best turns into swing. The mutual pounding of their feet breaks through a trap door into the basement where Bertie and Field are held prisoner.

Treacher's Jeeves is intended as a model of social grace who is appalled by any breach of etiquette or improper behavior, according to publicity suggestions in the American pressbook. It urges the exhibitor to arrange with a local newspaper for a series of drawings in which Treacher as Jeeves appears, horrified at the commission of some *faux pas.* "Jeeves can be shown serving at table which would afford an opportunity of showing guests using wrong forks, putting napkins under chin, tipping soup plate, drinking coffee with spoon in cup, 'dunking' toast or doughnut, etc. etc. Wrong clothes for certain occasions, improper introductions, etc., can be illustrated. In drawings Jeeves should appear as the essence of correctness and stiffness, immaculately attired as a gentleman's gentleman who is being constantly unnerved by the series of social errors."

Instead, on screen he is excessively irritable and petulant, lacking the adaptability of the Wodehouse creation. "Treacher's Jeeves fusses, complains, shouts, bays like a beagle," complained one Wodehousian critic.[9] Wodehouse himself said that Treacher "'pulled faces all the time. Awful.'"[10] He added, "That supercilious manner of his is all wrong for Jeeves."[11] More important, there is none of Jeeves's trademark Machiavellian cleverness in the Treacher characterization, simply an annoyingly starched and stuffy, standard-issue English servant.

David Niven made an acceptable Bertie, effectively capturing his comic perplexity.[12] Niven later wrote of how, at the time, "he was getting together a 'whole repertory of looks that passed for acting from boggling my eyes to furrowing my brow.'"[13] Although Niven was only given third billing, after both Treacher and Field, *Thank You, Jeeves* was one of several pictures at the time that helped to raise Niven toward star status. He was then under contract to Samuel Goldwyn, who typically loaned Niven out only for a single picture. Hence, obtaining Niven for a return engagement as Bertie would have been a problematic and expensive proposition. In marrying Bertie, *Thank You, Jeeves* not only makes it possible not to hire Niven for subsequent movies in the series, but also seemed to be part of a strategy to eliminate half of the Wodehouse team in adapting the stories to the screen, judging Bertie to be a dispensable character.

Thank You, Jeeves, a 1936 release, was followed the next year by *Step Lively, Jeeves*, which this time is not even ostensibly based on any Wodehouse work, but admits to being an original creation. While critics were unaccountably kind to *Thank You, Jeeves*, they were too harsh on the sequel. The first picture in the series had been so bad that the second was an improvement; there was nowhere to go but up. Although *Step Lively, Jeeves* is a screwball comedy far from the Wodehouse tone, it at least is predominantly humorous, unlike the espionage situations that had marred *Thank You, Jeeves*.

There is no consistency in characterization between the two pictures. *Step Lively, Jeeves* reflects a new concept of the whole idea of a Jeeves series, rather than a logical follow-up to *Thank You, Jeeves*. Perhaps the studio recognized what a misstep the first film had been. Bertie is not mentioned in *Step Lively, Jeeves*, and indeed the butler's former employer is mentioned as Lord Fenton. Overall, *Step Lively, Jeeves* is much more intriguingly scripted (and nearly a quarter-hour longer) and better realized under director Eugene Forde. The result is a pleasant if thoroughly undistinguished movie that does contain a few mild, brief laughs—modest achievements, but significant improvements over *Thank You, Jeeves*. However, *Step Lively, Jeeves* was still far from having the necessary quality to sustain a series.

Whereas Treacher's Jeeves in *Thank You, Jeeves* had been a fussy, schoolmarmish figure, in *Step Lively, Jeeves*, he is naive, with the brain of Bertie Wooster. Indeed, the "Rupert Hedgewick" (not Wodehouse's "Reginald") Jeeves of *Step Lively, Jeeves* is almost the result of a merger of the separate Wodehousian characters of Bertie and Jeeves. The Jeeves name and figure remain, but he has the Wooster brain, perpetually befuddled and confused.

While *Thank You, Jeeves* was ostensibly based on one of the Wodehouse stories, and *Step Lively, Jeeves* was not, there are nearly as many incidents from the source in the latter as the former. In *Step Lively, Jeeves*, Jeeves scolds another butler for his poor choice of clothes for his master, making far wiser suggestions for color and design coordination. After joining a celebration, going on a bender, and traveling by bicycle, Jeeves awakes with a hangover. He is given a pick-me-up: a scene perfectly brings to life the before, during, and after of the drink, vividly showing its effect—except that its larger purpose is gone. Whereas the pick-me-up was, in Wodehouse's world, a demonstration of its inventor's knowledge, as Jeeves administered it to Bertie, in *Step Lively, Jeeves* the concoction is the brainchild of a minor character, needed by Jeeves.

Jeeves has far less time on screen than he had in *Thank You, Jeeves*, and the idea for *Step Lively, Jeeves* seems to have been conceived less as a Jeeves vehicle than a comedy in which any one of many characters could have portrayed the central dupe. The original story by Frances Hyland, as scripted by Frank Fenton and Lynn Root, concerns two con artists who develop a scheme to promote a supposed direct descendant of Sir Francis Drake—an actual racket practiced in America for years, according to the trade journal *Variety*. Indeed, it resembles the plot described in chapter 17 of Wodehouse and Guy Bolton's *Bring on the Girls*: the last in a long line of pawnbrokers discovers his ancestor loaned the money to Queen Isabella to finance Columbus, and now owns 10 percent of America.

Even Bertie Wooster would have trouble falling for this obvious, transparent line, but the Jeeves of *Step Lively, Jeeves* proves easily persuaded that Drake was his ancestor, qualifying him for the title Earl of Braddock and to inherit millions accumulated over the centuries in interest. The con men, in turn, intrigue a gang headed by a woman in their scheme, without either realizing they are also dealing with lawbreakers. While the narratives of both *Thank You, Jeeves* and *Step Lively, Jeeves* combine crime and humor, *Step Lively, Jeeves* is far more consistent, constructing its gangsters and con men as amusing characters, unlike the conventional criminals of *Thank You, Jeeves.*

In *Step Lively, Jeeves*, the compulsory love subplot is provided by a

Patricia Ellis and Robert Kent portray the new couple who hire Arthur Treacher's Jeeves at the end of *Step Lively, Jeeves.*

ne'er-do-well and one of the ubiquitous female reporters of 1930s cinema, who combine forces to expose the shenanigans of con men and gangsters alike during a costume party. They convince the gangsters not to take out their disappointment in a shower of bullets, since their primary aim had been merely to use the "Earl" to crash society. Jeeves is only mildly disillusioned, and he is poised to begin life anew in the service of the couple (Patricia Ellis and Robert Kent).

Given the proper material, a long-running Niven-Treacher pairing could have succeeded. Nor is the fact that both Jeeves films abandoned their original sources surprising. While contractual reasons compelled an early Niven exit from the series, another appropriate actor should have been obtained; it is difficult to imagine producers believing Treacher had the star power to carry a series on his own.

It is more probable that American audiences were regarded as unlikely to accept a series positing a truly sagacious English butler, instead seeing such a figure purely as a source of comedy, meaning that the rights to the Wodehouse stories were bought for the name only, not the narratives. This same reasoning seems to explain the inspiration for *Step Lively, Jeeves*—using the character to create comedy by utilizing national types, the English elite versus the nouveau-riche American, both keenly aware of class

Pressbook advertisement for *Thank You, Jeeves.*

difference.[14] In that film, gangsters epitomized the opposition of Englishman and American; the notion of the butler and the gangsters together seems to have been regarded as appealing. One ad pictured Jeeves as a chimp: "Gentle Jeeves Goes Berserk!! ... and no wonder! He didn't mind being bamboozled ... he could abide a bit of buffeting ... but gunsters, or no gunsters, they mustn't use bad manners!" Even the British advertisements echoed this thinking: "The world's favourite gentleman's gentleman teaches gangsters to mind their manners." Perhaps the most pungent expression was "Gangland's in a deuce of a dither!" It was far from the Wodehouse conception, as was clear from another slogan: "He's so sad-eyed, so gentle, so utterly, utterly proper ... till a gangster's social error makes him a fightin' terror!"

The Jeeves series became one of the worst executed ideas under Sol Wurtzel's Fox "B" unit, an effort that fully justified the aphorism about Fox B's, "from bad to Wurtzel." The short-lived Jeeves film series was canceled at Twentieth Century Fox over the summer of 1937, just as Wodehouse himself was in Hollywood scripting *A Damsel in Distress* at RKO.

In a radio broadcast that same year, Hedda Hopper interviewed Wodehouse and spoke as if the pictures had never been made.

> Hopper: You know, Mr. Wodehouse, I don't believe Jeeves would be very popular in Hollywood. He's much too bright. Why heavens, he might even know what's wrong with pictures. And that would never do.
>
> Wodehouse: Well, Hedda, perhaps we had best leave Jeeves back in London with Bertie.
>
> Hopper: You're right, Plumey.[15]

Only in the 1960s, and later again in the 1990s, would the memory of the Treacher series be erased when the Jeeves stories (*with* Bertie) were successfully transferred to the new medium of television.

Nonetheless, the plot idea of the film adaptation of *Thank You, Jeeves* was perhaps remembered by Wodehouse. Twenty years later, contemplating a play to be titled *Betting on Bertie*, he used the picture's device of a true romance that would finally end in a Wooster wedding and the departure of Jeeves. Similarly, the idea of a solo Jeeves story without Bertie's participation, as portrayed in *Step Lively, Jeeves*, would reappear in the early 1950s. Wodehouse and Guy Bolton coauthored *Come On, Jeeves*, the only Jeeves play that Wodehouse was to see produced, although only in outlying English provinces. It was rewritten in novel form as *The Return of Jeeves*, and retitled *Ring for Jeeves* in England. However, while Jeeves is surrounded by characters with different names, they are simply variations on Bertie and his friends, and the intellectual integrity of Jeeves remains. In the notion of Jeeves persuading his temporary master to become a bookie, and serving him in that capacity (all of which is presented in the past tense rather than directly portrayed), is there a distant echo of the plot of *Step Lively, Jeeves*. Dissimilar though the Fox Jeeves films were from the tone of Wodehouse works at the time, they did provide the first examples of experiments with the Wooster-Jeeves formula that Wodehouse himself would later attempt.

V

Screenwriter Once More

In June 1934 Paramount approached Wodehouse, living in France, about placing him under contract at $1,500 a week. He was simultaneously having trouble with the Internal Revenue Service (at the time, the same income was taxed in both England and America), who believed he was eager to take a screenwriting contract. "But they don't know that I don't want to go to Hollywood," Wodehouse explained to a friend.[1] "I had to refuse because I am public enemy number one in America, and can't go there. But it's rather gratifying after Hollywood took a solemn vow three years ago never to mention my name again."[2]

Two months later, in August, Metro-Goldwyn-Mayer was offering $5,000 for the screen rights to the 1917 novel *Piccadilly Jim*, which Wodehouse's agent Paul Reynolds recommended he accept but also would be held up in the same tax dispute. Wodehouse replied to Reynolds that in fact the screen rights to *Piccadilly Jim* were held by Guy Bolton; to resolve their dispute 18 months earlier out of court, Wodehouse had signed over motion picture rights to certain plays. On June 8, 1933, the rights to *Piccadilly Jim* had gone to Bolton, while Wodehouse retained *Leave It to Psmith*. This of course had already been staged successfully in 1930 and filmed only months before signing the agreement, so it seemed at the time the more valuable property. Within just over a dozen years, the film rights to *Leave It to Psmith*, bought by the filmmakers, would revert to Wodehouse.[3] Bolton had done the dramatization of *Piccadilly Jim* in 1918, a difficult adaptation for him, and had participated in the rights to the 1919 screen version of the 1917 novel.[4] Wodehouse had told Bolton that *Leave It to Psmith* incorporated "a good bit of your stuff from the dramatization of *Piccadilly Jim*. There was a scene in an employment agency where I drew very largely on the Bolton genius."[5] Hence the exchange seemed reasonable to them.

Bolton sold all motion picture rights for *Piccadilly Jim* to Loew's on November 5, 1934, for $5,000.[6] The remake of *Piccadilly Jim* was initially to be produced by then M-G-M producer David O. Selznick in early 1935, with songs provided by Harold Adamson and Burton Lane. Rowland Lee

Newspaper advertisement for *Piccadilly Jim* (1936).

was assigned by Selznick to complete work on the screenplay, which was initially written by Robert Benchley. J. Walter Ruben was set to direct, and Chester Hale had prepared dances.

After two years of scripting by at least nine writers, the new version of *Piccadilly Jim* became overlong, finally clocking at 100 minutes. One-time screenwriter Benchley joined the cast. Rather than being a musical, *Piccadilly Jim* turned into a vehicle for Robert Montgomery, who had previously appeared six years earlier in *The Man in Possession.* Montgomery as the title character James Crocker was aptly cast, one of the few Hollywood comedians who could play an Englishman who simultaneously combined intelligent and "silly ass" traits. Equally appropriate were Eric Blore as his valet, Frank Morgan as his father (the elder Jim Crocker, an unemployed ham actor), and many of the supporting players. However, leading lady Madge Evans brought no sense of comedy to her role.

As adapted for film, the story concerned the father and son both falling in love, not

Billie Burke, Grant Mitchell, Frank Morgan, Robert Montgomery, Tommy Bupp, and Cora Witherspoon in *Piccadilly Jim* (1936).

with the same woman, but with related women, although neither knows this, and Jim initially does not yet even know Ann's last name. When Jim's father is rejected as a suitor by the arrogant in-laws, the son conceives of a comic strip, "From Rags to Riches," centered around the dictatorial mother, the henpecked husband, and their obnoxious son Ogden. (Unlike the novel, in the movie Jim's nickname derives from his skill as a caricaturist, more than his reputation for late London nights.) When the strip becomes a hit, it makes further romantic progress impossible, but contractually Jim must continue drawing it. The family can't remain in England because they are so widely recognized, so the Crockers pursue their beloveds to America, father in disguise, and son by concealing his true identity. Jim gradually changes the characterizations in the comic strip to make the family proud of the association, until only Ann, the niece, resists him.

Little of this is from the book; the main thread in common is the Pett family, with its meek father and rambunctious child, the title character's newspaper experience, and a few brief chapters that become the middle third of the movie, in which Jim follows Ann on board a transatlantic ship, using the name of his butler and pretending he is his father. Many of the movie's elements that had appeared in the novel and were standard Wodehouse devices, such as the eccentric butler, the henpecked husband, and the use of disguise and masquerade, compounded by mistaken identity, were also typical conventions of 1930s romantic comedy. Genuinely amusing passages scattered throughout the film are finally overwhelmed by too many dull stretches. Although *Piccadilly Jim* had potential, under the direction of Robert Z. Leonard (who had previously directed the estimable *The Cardboard Lover*) it fails to achieve the standard of many other more memorable comedies of the period.

By 1936, Wodehouse's tax problems were resolved, and he was free once again to visit the United States. At the beginning of August 1936, the *New York Times* noted that Wodehouse had engaged his Hollywood agent, Bill Stevens, to arrange his return to the ranks of screenwriters.[7] This did not seem likely, with three of volumes of Hollywood satire in bookstores: "the Mulliners of Hollywood" in *Blandings Castle*, *Laughing Gas*, and *The Luck of the Bodkins*. Nevertheless, to Wodehouse's own surprise, by September he was sailing to America and returned to Hollywood on October 10, 1936. He and Ethel took a home in the Hollywood hills at 1315 Angelo Drive. He had a new contract at M-G-M, this time for $2,500 a week for six months, with an option for six more.

Adding to his eerie sense of *deja vu*, he was assigned to *Rosalie*, the still unproduced film he had originally worked on during his 1930 stint. Almost simultaneously, one of Wodehouse's songs, "March of the Musketeers," was used in the studio's musical extravaganza of 1936, *The Great Ziegfeld*. At the beginning of 1937, the new movie of H. M. Harwood's *The Man in Possession*, called *Personal Property*, went before the cameras.

This time Plum and Ethel lived quietly. Leonora was no longer part of the household; she had married in 1932 and now had a daughter of her own. Wodehouse confided to a friend that he hated the people he had to meet and was bored by them, especially at big parties, and would prefer the life of a hermit.[8]

Wodehouse liked his boss, Sam Katz, and worked amicably with a former cast member of a Bolton-Wodehouse-Kern show, McGowan, "who seems to be fighting the heads of the studio all the time."[9] William Anthony McGuire was the producer and Wodehouse was told to write *Rosalie* under his supervision.

However, the experience soon soured. Wodehouse learned that his brother Armine had died a month earlier but was told he could not leave Hollywood to join the widow because of the urgency of the production, so Ethel went to England alone. McGuire proved to be taking all the credit for his collaborator's work. As Wodehouse told Bolton, "By degrees I found that I was being quietly frozen out. Everything I turned in he rewrote, keeping the substance of my stuff but changing it enough so that he could tell the men higher up that it was his work. Eventually it got so that I couldn't make any progress, and now the thing has poofed out and Bill is writing it by himself."[10] The studio told Wodehouse they had wanted McGuire to write it all along. "I have had another frost with them.... There seems to be a curse over M-G-M, as far as I am concerned."[11] Wodehouse's option was not renewed, and he finished at the studio in early April 1937. *Rosalie* was finally released at the end of the year, becoming one of the 20 top box-office films of 1937.

While under contract, Wodehouse was asked along with other authors Rupert Hughes and Jim Tully to attend the premiere of *The Good Earth*, one of M-G-M's most prestigious pictures of the year. The purpose was to write an impromptu review to be sent by wire around the nation. Wodehouse's byline credited him as "Noted Author and Playwright" rather than studio employee. His review appeared in the *Los Angeles Times* on February 21, 1937, with typical Wodehouse style, for example praising "Albert Lewin, associate producer, for his masterly associate producing."

On the advice of George Gershwin, RKO producer Pandro Berman decided to purchase *A Damsel in Distress*. Pathé transferred their interest in the 1919 version to Ernest De Journo. On January 19, 1937, RKO bought the rights, including radio and television rights, to both the novel and the Wodehouse–Ian Hay play by successive contracts with Wodehouse, with Wodehouse and Hay, and with Wodehouse's company, Siva. Gershwin had collaborated in the theater with Wodehouse before he wrote the novel, and believed that the book's character George Bevan, a music writer, was based on him (both character and Gershwin had been born in Brooklyn). RKO was interested in filming *A Damsel in Distress* because the novel's romantic lead was a musical comedy composer, allowing a singer and dancer to be cast in the role—and RKO needed a Fred Astaire vehicle.

After the option on Wodehouse's contract was not taken up at M-G-M, a strike at the studios closed down the industry in May. He wrote Leonora, "I wouldn't take another salaried job like the last one for anything."[12]

However, offers came in, including one from David O. Selznick (which instead went to Ben Hecht) and one from Walter Wanger. Wanger wanted Wodehouse to script a Hollywood satire, Clarence Buddington Kelland's *Stand-In*. Kelland was a writer Wodehouse did not admire, and his decision to avoid the project turned out to be a wise one. The film of *Stand-In* that Wanger brought to the screen that year was heavy-handed and different from the type of spoof that was Wodehouse's specialty. Wodehouse explained, "I got myself in bad enough last time by criticising Hollywood, and I didn't want to do a picture which would have been an indictment of the studios."[13] However, contrary to what Wodehouse believed, parodies like *Stand-In*, and his own "Mulliners of Hollywood" series, *Laughing Gas*, and *The Luck of the Bodkins*, had hardly lessened potential Hollywood interest in him or his works.

At Warner Bros., Wodehouse was proposed as a dialogue writer to inject humor and a period sense for the planned production of *Adventures of Robin Hood*, eventually filmed a year later.[14] Wodehouse knew the problem. "The fact is, I'm not worth the money my agent insists on asking for me. After all, my record here is eighteen months at a huge salary, with only small parts of pictures to show for it."[15]

In May 1937, Wodehouse was asked to adapt *A Damsel in Distress* for the screen at RKO. The 1919 film, at the time of its original publication, had been faithful to the novel. In 1928 Wodehouse had collaborated on the stage version with Ian Hay, preparing the book with him while Hay did the actual writing. Instead of turning it over to producers, Hay, Wodehouse, and two partners each contributed £500 and put it on themselves, and it was a great success. The play had condensed and rearranged some scenes for stage limitations (such as placing the cab scene in a theater instead), while retaining the highlights of the book. Like *Leave It to Me*, based both on the play and book *Leave It to Psmith*, the film *A Damsel in Distress* would also be based on both theatrical and novel versions, except that this time Wodehouse himself adapted the previous work for the screen. (Other prose versions appeared in the December 1937 issues of *Movie Story Magazine* and *Screen Romances*.)

Initially Wodehouse's assignment was to be a brief polishing job for four weeks. As he wrote to Leonora, "I must say it is altogether different working at RKO on a picture based on my own novel from being on salary at M-G-M and sweating away on *Rosalie*! I like my boss, Pandro Berman, very much. He is the first really intelligent man I have come across here — bar Thalberg, whom he rather resembles."[16] He explained, "When they bought it, they gave it to an ex-drugstore clerk to adapt, and he turned out a frightful script all about crooks— no resemblance to the novel. [Perhaps an echo of the film of *Thank You, Jeeves*?] Then it struck them that it might be a good thing to stick to the story of the novel, so they chucked away the other script and called me in. I think it is going to make a good picture."[17]

He also wrote to Leonora,

> Everything is made very pleasant for me, and I like the man I am working with—a chap named Pagano. The way we work is, we map out a sequence together, then I go home and write the dialogue, merely indicating business, and he takes what I have done and puts it into screen play shape. Thus relieving me of all that "truck shot" "wipe dissolve" stuff!
>
> It is also pleasant to be working on something that you know is a real live production and not something that might be produced or may be put away in a drawer for years! As far as I can gather, we are going to start shooting this picture in about a week. We have actually completed about sixty pages out of probably a hundred and fifty, but this isn't as bad as it sounds, because we can write twenty pages while they are shooting two. There is a whole sequence laid in London which will take them at least ten days to shoot, I imagine, and they can be getting on with that while we are finishing the script.[18]

Indeed, the London sequence used many of the ideas of the book, as Alyce takes refuge in stranger Jerry's cab, pursued by Keggs the butler, who provokes an altercation with the police. In the movie, Jerry escapes only through participating in a street show and singing a song long enough to climb aboard the first passing bus.

Wodehouse finished work on August 14, three weeks after shooting began, having made $14,500 (by comparison, the original magazine sale to the *Saturday Evening Post* in 1920 had earned him $10,000). However, work on the script continued until September 25, with shooting taking place from July 22 to October 16; the final screenplay credits Wodehouse, Ernest Pagano, and S.K. Lauren. "I have really come across with some good stuff, so that my name is big in the picture world. Wodehouse, the man who gets paid $1500 a week for mere charm of manner has been supplanted by Wodehouse, the fellow who delivers the goods."[19]

Whereas *Piccadilly Jim* had retained most of the characters of his novel, but largely dispensed with the plot, the film of *A Damsel in Distress* retained the basic plot outline and many of the highlights—as had the Ian Hay stage version—but unlike it, deleted and merged a number of the characters, and added others, becoming a second, separate Wodehouse variation on the novel. Names are changed; George Bevan becomes Jerry Halliday, and Maud becomes Alyce (although retaining her identity, not becoming the Alice Faraday of the novel).

The female lead was chosen in a manner similar to Ida Lupino's placement in *Anything Goes* as Bing Crosby's nonsinging romantic partner. For *A Damsel in Distress*, Joan Fontaine was cast opposite Astaire. She was only then emerging from low-budget films, having just been placed under contract to RKO, and had yet to become a star. (Earlier choices for the role included Ruby Keeler and Jessie Matthews.) Although appropriately aristocratic, Fontaine was chosen to be as unlike Astaire's usual partner, Ginger Rogers, as possible. Fontaine and Astaire have only one brief number

Lobby card from *A Damsel in Distress* (1937) with Fred Astaire and Joan Fontaine.

together, acknowledging that she was unable to dance adequately opposite Astaire. Fontaine believed that the movie actually set her career back; her first successful role would be in 1940 in *Rebecca.*

To compensate for the risk associated with casting a relative unknown as the love interest, and to add box-office insurance, George Burns and Gracie Allen were brought in from Paramount (at $10,000 a week) to partner Astaire in gags and dance routines. Burns and Allen play Jerry's press agent and his secretary, using their own names as they did in most of their movies. While their participation was definitely outside the original, and the humor different from the Wodehouse style, Burns and Allen provide the picture with needed additional amusement. Burns recalled, "As we signed our contracts, all I could think about was how good this was going to be for our careers. Dancing with Astaire to music by the Gershwins, directed by George Stevens in a story by Wodehouse, playing real characters rather than doing four-minute segments as Burns and Allen. Not bad for two vaudeville comics. Gracie thought it was unbelievable too—the worst dancer in her family starring in a Fred Astaire movie." Wodehouse later remarked in a radio interview with Hedda Hopper, "I'm sorry I didn't meet Gracie Allen until after I had written *Damsel in Distress*. I would have

A title card for *A Damsel in Distress.*

tried much harder had I known at the time that Gracie was going to be in it. She's one of the funniest women I have ever met."[20]

Reginald Gardiner had played the role of Percy, the antagonist in the romances, in the Hay version on the London stage; he had also portrayed Freddie Bosham in the original theatrical production of the Hay-Wodehouse *Leave It to Psmith.* In the movie, by contrast, Percy is eliminated, and Gardiner is cast as Keggs the butler, whose part is rewritten to take over much of the role played by both Reggie and Percy in the novel and the play. As a result, Keggs becomes a much more sprightly and unlikely character. For instance, rather than Percy, it is Keggs who follows Alyce to London, and ends up imprisoned when he believes Jerry is her secret boyfriend and has a scuffle with him. Keggs is also turned into an opera addict whose instinct is suppressed by Lady Caroline, Alyce's aunt, but who is compelled to sing and must finally reveal his true (dubbed) voice in the garden. Gardiner was an ideal choice, an English comedian with range but also in the same tradition as Wodehouse; it is unfortunate he had not been cast as Jeeves in the Twentieth Century Fox series, instead of Arthur Treacher.

Reggie's much reduced character, of the rival for the girl, is played by bandleader Ray Noble, with his only distinguishing trait being an addiction to swing, to which Caroline also objects. Reggie has a brief romance with Gracie before she decides to instead marry George Burns (in the movie). The secondary romances in the novel and the play, of Alice Faraday and Reggie, and Lord Marshmoreton and Billie Dore, are eliminated in the movie, along with both of these female characters. (The script retains the novel's name as Marshmoreton, although subsequent publicity and writing on the film changed the spelling to Marshmorton.)

Alyce's father remains the curmudgeonly Marshmoreton (ideally portrayed by Montagu Love), whose joy is his garden; he delivers Jerry's message to his daughter, supporting the romance. Constance Collier ferociously portrays Caroline, who only agrees to the wedding of Jerry and Alyce to avoid a scandal. Unlike the stage play, in which the novel's Albert the page becomes Albertina, Albert in the movie remains his original impish self. As portrayed by Harry Watson, Albert hopes to preserve his stake in the drawing against Keggs's continual machinations.

Instead of opening, as did the novel and play, with the meeting of the future romantic couple, the movie begins by establishing the conflict between the family's determination to sequester Alyce in the castle and her desire for love. In the servant's hall, a lottery offers the names of Alyce's prospective suitors, introducing the interplay between Keggs and Albert to see who will win the prize. As in the novel, Albert's support helps foster the romance, but in the movie it is the crucial motivating factor. The page writes a spurious note from Alyce that spurs Jerry's interest, rather than, as in the book, the hero finding love at first sight when she enters his taxicab. Instead of Bevan beginning as a man who has avoided women as a consequence of his life in the theater, as in the novel and play, in the movie Jerry yearns for a real woman, after his publicist, George Burns, has concocted fictional romances for the gossip columns that have given him legions of giddy feminine followers.

Jerry first visits "Totleigh Castle" (already renamed thus in the play from the novel's "Belpher Castle") with Burns and Allen, who join Keggs's public tour of the grounds. Gracie uses her typical combination of ignorance and malapropisms to befuddle her guide. He shows the visitors the site of Leonard's Leap, a dangerous escape from a castle balcony, used in the middle ages to preserve a lady's honor. Jerry, refused entrance by Keggs, gets in through a ruse of Albert's. Twice during the film, in a move resembling Wodehouse's use of a minstrel group to help Bertie Wooster in his 1934 novel *Thank You, Jeeves*, Jerry enters the house pretending to be associated with musicians.

Jerry meets Alyce upstairs, and when she seems unwilling to discuss love, convinces her to talk about it in the third person, consequently failing to realize she loves someone else. However, Jerry must make a quick exit onto the balcony, where Albert drops him a sheet with which to climb to safety, convincing Alyce that Jerry must have escaped by heroically repeating the legendary Leonard's Leap. (Later he will actually perform the feat, breaking his fall by using tree branches, and impressing Alyce.) As he leaves the grounds, Jerry gives a note for Alyce to Marshmoreton, assuming he is the gardener. Jerry moves into "Leonard's Manor" instead of the novel's cottage "down by Platt's," and the visiting Marshmoreton soon clarifies his identity. He even serves to confirm his daughter's love for Jerry, believing he is the American ski instructor she truly loves.

In these sequences, ideas from the novel are used but are combined with fresh material, as the movie increasingly strays from the source. Some of the incidents most directly inspired by the novel seem awkward on the screen, such as the cab fracas, and Keggs and Albert overhearing key events, trading drawing tickets.

Reggie is supposed to propose to Alyce at a local fair, but when Jerry arrives ahead of him and kisses Alyce, he receives a slap in the face. (The movie's subsequent funhouse sequence is the musical and choreographic highlight.) Afterward, Alyce tells her father she now loves Jerry, and Marshmoreton explains why Jerry believed she loved him. (The film dispenses completely with the climactic meeting with her previous lover, now grown fat and obnoxious, that in the novel and play made her realize her true love; as a result, in the movie Alyce seems to be fickle.) Meanwhile, Jerry is thoroughly confused when Alyce goes to the manor to say she loves him, and urge him to come to the evening ball at the castle. The now advancing romance is abruptly halted when Burns places a newspaper item citing Alyce as heartbreaker Jerry's twenty-eighth victim. This time it is Keggs who helps Jerry into Totleigh, now that he has taken his ticket from Albert.

The recurring gag of everyone infectiously saying "Right-ho" to one another, to Marshmorton's frustration until he is saying it too, is a nod to Wodehouse's presence on the film. Similarly, the song "Stiff Upper Lip" is the most colloquial in its wording, and its lyrics are reminiscent of Wodehouse's prose.

A major screen credit seemed to open up the possibility of a new career, though Wodehouse claimed he would not come over to Hollywood for more than three months at a time.[21] Berman told Wodehouse's agent he wanted him for the next Astaire picture at RKO.

Wodehouse appeared in an interview on one of Hedda Hopper's weekly radio talks about Hollywood, writing it out in advance in comic form, "full of good lines (which I gave mostly to her — nothing small about me) and it was a great success— in spite of the fact that she killed my gags by laughing in front of each one and putting 'Well' at the head of each line."[22] Nonetheless, Wodehouse and Hopper remained friends.

Edmund Goulding hired Wodehouse to collaborate on a scenario at Warner Brothers, but Wodehouse noted, "I am not finding it very pleasant, because he has his own ideas about the thing and rewrites all my stuff, thus inducing a what's-the-use feeling and making it hard not to shove down just anything."[23] After receiving $10,000 for six weeks of work, he was to be paid $2,000 a week thereafter (a third of which went for taxes), but by October Wodehouse had decided to leave, canceling plans to stay until the following spring.[24]

Even during the optimistic period at RKO, Wodehouse had noted, "I don't like doing pictures. *A Damsel in Distress* was fun, because I was working with the best director here — George Stevens— and on my own story, but as a rule pictures are a bore."[25] On November 4, 1937, Wodehouse returned to his home at Le Touquet, France. The following day, a one-hour radio version of *A Damsel in Distress* was presented over CBS on the weekly series *Hollywood Hotel* starring Astaire, Fontaine, and Burns and Allen. As late as November 16, Wodehouse was still considering a return to Hollywood.[26]

A Damsel in Distress was released on November 19, but proved to be the first Astaire picture to lose money at the box office. This was probably inevitable; after seven vehicles together, audiences expected to see Astaire paired with Ginger Rogers. Moreover, their previous two pictures had not done as well as expected. (One of those films, *Swing Time*, had also been directed by Stevens.) Reviewers inevitably compared Fontaine unfavorably with Rogers. Both Astaire and Rogers were pressing RKO to make separate pictures, which she had already done during their collaboration. However, the failure of *A Damsel in Distress* would compel Astaire to agree to two more movies with Rogers, although their reunion in *Carefree* (1938) also met with a lukewarm box office reception. Hence, the reaction to *A Damsel in Distress* was hardly unique for Astaire at this point in his career.

Previous Astaire films had also emphasized a partnership, and the grace of a romantic duet with Rogers, while *A Damsel in Distress* placed Astaire front and center, emphasizing the solitary aspect of his performance, and it was not to audience taste. Only the presence of Burns and Allen keep the entire picture from pivoting entirely on Astaire. The expectations of a romantic musical comedy usually call for a couple at the center, but *A Damsel in Distress* opts for a solitary lead, or a trio (when Burns and Allen are also on screen)— an inherent imbalance in the genre.

The disappointing box office results stung Wodehouse as well. This was not only because of his involvement in its creation, but because his name had become a more prominent part of advertising and promotion than on any of his previous films, and far more than on any of the other pictures he had worked on in Hollywood. Adapting his own original work to the screen was an opportunity he would never have again. Near the end of his life, in a new preface to a 1975 paperback edition of the novel, Wodehouse looked back on *A Damsel in Distress* and wrote:

> It was handed over to the hired assassins who at that time were such a feature of Dottyville-on-the-Pacific. The result was a Mess which for some reason is still shown occasionally on American television and causes sets to be switched off from the rockbound coasts of Maine to the Everglades of Florida.... The first thing they did was to eliminate the story and substitute for it one more suitable to retarded adults and children with water on the brain. Then there was the hero. There was not much they could do here, but they did their best by engaging Fred Astaire and giving him nobody to dance with, so that he had nine solo numbers.

Wodehouse should have realized that *A Damsel in Distress* was sold to the public primarily as an Astaire vehicle (and to a lesser degree as one for Burns and Allen), not a Wodehouse adaptation; its commercial failure had to be accounted for as a passing disenchantment audiences had with the star, not the writer.

Wodehouse may also have been glad to leave Hollywood when he became involved in a lawsuit over the publication of a letter from fellow screenwriter Philip Dunne. Dunne, an acknowledged leftist, was a chief organizer of the new writer's union, the Screen Writers Guild. To combat it, the producers immediately recognized a competing union, the Screen Playwrights, of which Wodehouse was a member. Dunne, who had read Wodehouse's Jeeves stories, and had met him once in England, wrote what he admitted was an "intemperate" and "indiscreet" letter. Dunne wrote, "In effect, I asked Wodehouse if he realized that he was consorting with scabs and scalawags in an organization whose sole purpose was to break our virtuous Guild." Dunne claimed that Wodehouse showed the letter to the officers of the Screen Playwrights, who published it in *Variety*, announcing they were suing Dunne and the Guild for libel, along with the Guild's parent organization, the Authors League of America. However, the suit was quickly dismissed by a democratic judge as being the result of a political letter rather than a libelous one. Nonetheless, the matter caused Dunne to accuse Wodehouse of "right-wing leanings" and, later, anti-Semitism, based on the German broadcasts.[27] It could not have helped Wodehouse's future in Hollywood to have such a vitriolic and prominent critic.

A Damsel in Distress had an unusual follow-up. George and Ira Gershwin were both hired to write the score, but they arrived in Hollywood before the script had been written. Consequently, their libretto was based on their conception of the book and play. A number of the songs were

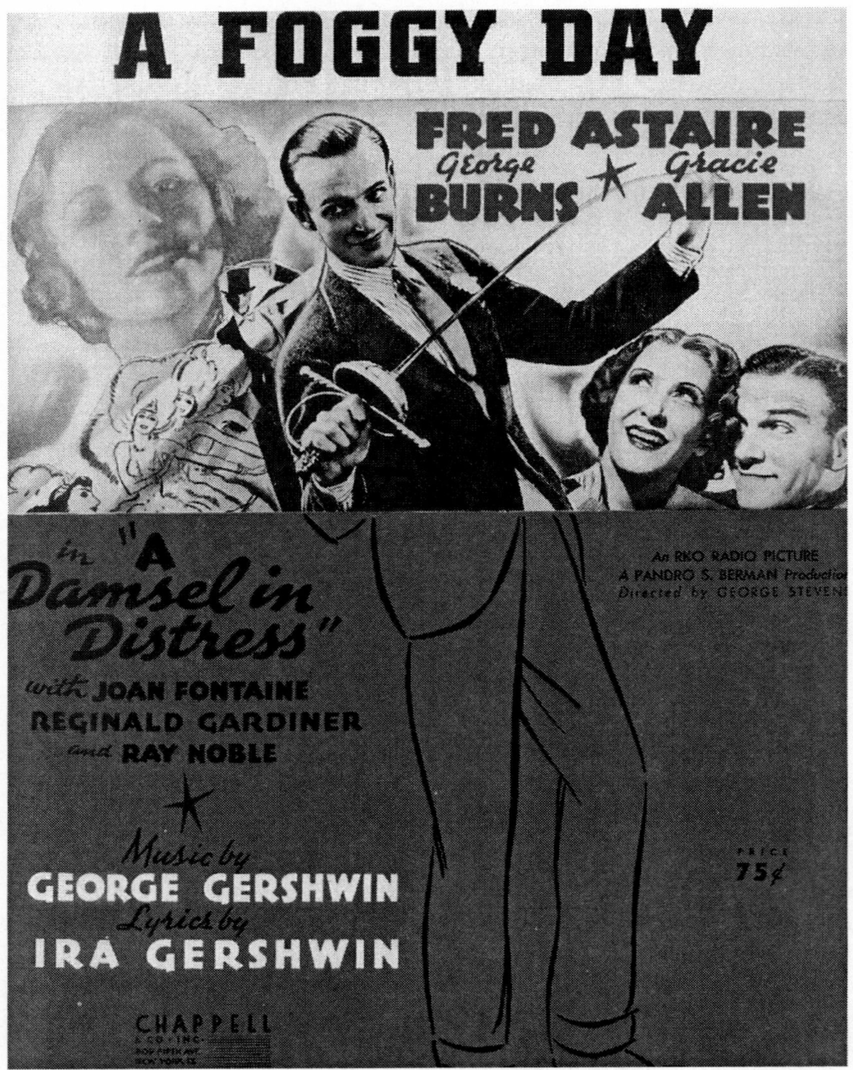

Sheet music for the song "A Foggy Day," which later gave the title to a theatrical version of *A Damsel in Distress* (1937).

dropped as the final script departed from the source, and George Gershwin died during production, from a brain tumor. In 1987, their adaptation was first staged as *Reaching for the Moon*, before having a more successful run in 1998, entitled *A Foggy Day* after one of the songs. The score, along with several songs Gershwin had written (a total of 16, with the film using nine), were included in a new stage musical of the Wodehouse novel. This time the play followed Gershwin's original conception of a songwriter looking for a damsel in distress to sweep off her feet.

To Wodehouse, there must have seemed a hex over Hollywood. While his return was more productive, it again ended in such a way as to leave him bitter. Moreover, there was no legacy of inspiration such as the first screenwriting stint provided. The studio life Wodehouse saw was perfectly normal, with quiet, unemotional directors, and no temperamental stars like those of his stories. In 1938, he wrote that he would like to author a Hollywood novel, but "I'm afraid, though, that I've used up everything I can write about Hollywood in *Laughing Gas* and the short stories."[28] In 1939, Wodehouse learned that his agent had become a producer at RKO without telling him, and there was little chance of going to Hollywood, where "they are now using the horny-handed $300 a week men to do the stuff."[29] There would be no return. Instead, the next dozen years placed Wodehouse in contact with filmmakers on the continent.

VI
War and Aftermath

On August 12, 1940, CBS broadcast on its *Forecast* series a pilot episode for a possible radio series, to be titled *Leave It to Jeeves*. After the disastrous reconception in the Twentieth Century Fox movies, this adaptation, by Stuart Palmer, wisely returned to the Wodehouse format while still constructing a narrative that was original in its details. In New York, Bingo Little (Donald Morrison) requests Bertie's assistance in ending his awkward engagement to Gloria LaTour (Ellen Wood), while Bertie is also assigned to pick up his Aunt Agatha's ring. Bertie takes Gloria out to convince her that Bingo is a poor prospect, but he somehow ends up engaged to her himself, with the ring so handy. Fortunately, when Gloria and her mother (Myra March) call for lunch the next day, Jeeves convinces them Bertie is slightly deranged. A grateful Bertie allows Jeeves to dispose of the yellow spats that he has found so irritating. Alan Mowbray is an ideal Jeeves, while a "Sonny Boy"–singing Edward Everett Horton is satisfactory but not quite on key in his characterization as Bertie, relying too much on malapropisms. Kenneth Niles was the director of the highly amusing 25-minute production.

In 1941, Tallulah Bankhead reprised her lead role in an American summer stock revival of *Her Cardboard Lover*, and a year later Metro-Goldwyn-Mayer remade the film, the last Wodehouse movie made in Hollywood. A decade had passed since the last remake as *The Passionate Plumber*. A musical version had already been considered only two years after that production, to star Maurice Chevalier and Grace Moore. Now George Cukor, who had previously directed the play on stage, was at the helm of the new production, the only one he did in both mediums. The leading female role was offered to Joan Crawford and Hedy Lamarr, who both turned it down, and it was taken by Norma Shearer, becoming her last role.

Considering that *Her Cardboard Lover* had already been treated satirically in *The Passionate Plumber*, Cukor concluded that "the plot was already too dated to engage a wartime audience."[1] The movie is amusing in its first hour, as songwriter Terry Trindale (Robert Taylor, in his sec-

Robert Taylor and Norma Shearer accidentally fall in love in *Her Cardboard Lover* (1942).

ond Wodehouse-related film, after *Personal Property* in 1937) impulsively puts himself in monetary debt to radiant socialite Consuelo Croyden (Norma Shearer) to announce his love. To pay off his debt, she hires him as her secretary and asks him to pose as her fiancé, because she finds roguish suitor Tony Barling (George Sanders) irresistible despite knowing he is a cad. Since Consuelo is drawn toward both Terry and Tony, the plot is not amenable to a ready resolution in a series of farcical boudoir situations. The script places Taylor in awkward positions, such as the pajama scene, that in the hands of Marion Davies in the 1927 version had been so delightful. Veering in new plot directions, the delicate balance necessary to the comedy collapses in the last half-hour of *Her Cardboard Lover*. As a result, it leaves a sense of disappointment in the viewer that has given the movie a much worse critical reputation than it deserves overall; reaction was particularly harsh at the time. A final adaptation of *Her Cardboard Lover* was heard on radio on May 6, 1953, starring Madeleine Carroll for the *Philip Morris Playhouse on Broadway*.

In 1939, Wodehouse and his wife, living in France, were reassured by the British officers stationed nearby that there was no immediate danger from German aggression. As a result, they and their neighbors did not try to leave until it was too late, with their automobile breaking down twice. Soon the male foreigners under 60 were interned, in conditions that caused Wodehouse to lose 42 pounds. A reporter accidentally encountered Wodehouse at one of the prisons, and friends began petitioning for his release. The Germans finally realized who the man was whose name had been taken down as "Widhorse."

Shortly before he turned 60, Wodehouse was released, but was required to live at a hotel in Berlin that was also the official German Foreign Office hotel. There he was delighted to meet an old friend from Hollywood and elsewhere, Baron Raven von Barnikow, who had once been engaged to Warner Bros. star Kay Francis. The Foreign Office employed Werner Plack, a minor actor Wodehouse had known in Hollywood, to look after the author. Wodehouse agreed to a proposal by the Foreign Office to make a series of five broadcasts to the United States, then still neutral. The topic was to be his experiences in the camps, presented uncensored, by one who had not received preferential treatment and was not a collaborator. It was to be in the spirit of his July 19, 1941, satirical article for the *Saturday Evening Post* (reprinted in the London *Daily Mail*) and another for the October 1941 issue of *Cosmopolitan* on camp life; similar talks to his fellow internees had been well received.

Wodehouse believed the radio broadcasts were a way to respond to the hundreds of letters he had received during internment from concerned Americans, to which he could not respond (only letters to relatives, and concerning business matters, were customarily allowed). He had made a lifelong habit of answering all his fan mail himself. Wodehouse could not see how material of this sort, written without German interference, could be used by them. He also believed he was demonstrating how the British kept up their spirits no matter the adverse circumstances. Even his American agent saw no moral quandary, believing the broadcasts might enhance sales.[2]

Wodehouse's release was extensively covered by the media. Even before the broadcasts, Wodehouse agreed to a scripted interview (as had been the 1937 one he had prepared for use with Hedda Hopper) written by Harry Flannery and performed over CBS. It expressed uncertainty over a British victory, and sandwiched between news of the war, was followed by the words of Elmer Davis, noting that Wodehouse was lucky not to have been in a concentration camp. Wodehouse was surprised at what he regarded as Davis's "nasty" tone.[3] (Davis became head of the Office of War Information when the United States entered the war.)

The subsequent five German broadcasts written by Wodehouse created a furor in the United States, and in England as well, even before they had been heard there. However, against the wishes of the Foreign Office, the Propaganda Ministry subsequently also turned the broadcasts toward England. They were then intended and received as word from the enemy, causing many to regard Wodehouse as a traitor. The Foreign Office had realized that once Wodehouse was perceived in this light, and not as neutral, his words would be of no value to them in the effort at the time to keep America out of the war.

In fact, Wodehouse had been using satire, and increasingly "dark comedy," against fascism since 1936. In the short story "Buried Treasure," a character noted of Hitler's moustache, "He can't go on sitting on the fence like this. Either a man has a moustache or he has not. There can be no middle course." In chapter 3 of *The Code of the Woosters* (1938), Bertie is disgusted to learn that the followers of a would-be dictator, Roderick Spode, wear black shorts, since there were no shirts left by the time their association was formed. In chapter 7, the language is more direct; even mild-mannered Bertie is driven to put the fascists in their place. "Just because you have succeeded in inducing a handful of half-wits to disfigure the London scene by going about in black shorts, you think you're someone. You hear them shouting, 'Heil, Spode!' and you imagine it is the Voice of the People. That is where you make your bloomer. What the Voice of the People is saying is, 'Look at that frightful ass Spode swanking about in footer bags! Did you ever in your puff see such a perfect perisher?'" Spode was modeled on England's actual home-grown, would-be British fascist leader, Oswald Mosley. Such satire had appeared on American screens as well, when Charlie Chaplin mocked fascism in *The Great Dictator*, and as late as 1942 the Jewish German expatriate director Ernst Lubitsch sought to ridicule Nazi Germany with comedy in *To Be or Not to Be*, although the latter was controversial.

After the broadcasts, Ethel, who had been staying with friends, was finally able to join her husband in Berlin. She had heard of the reaction in England. Wodehouse was not allowed by the Germans to return home and attempt to clear his name. He resumed writing, but he and Ethel maintained themselves by collecting foreign royalties from neutral countries, borrowing, and selling her jewelry.

Perhaps because their finances were so uncertain, by March 1942 Wodehouse was involved in negotiations to sell exclusive film rights to his novels for a year to a German company and to adapt one of them, probably to star Theo Lindgen.[4] Agenting the arrangements was Charlotte Serda, daughter of a well-known Berlin stage figure.[5] Eventually Wodehouse was paid 40,000 marks, about £3,200, for adapting *Heavy Weather*;

this was the same amount as the other highest source of income they had, from Ethel's sale of a bracelet.[6]

The purchaser was the Berlin Film GmbH, a company that existed between 1942 and 1945, and was founded as one of the four state-owned film production units of the Propaganda Ministry's UFA Film GmbH. Berlin Film produced 22 movies, and handled the lower-budget productions. Wodehouse insisted on a clause stipulating that production would only take place after the war, and was told that there were already plans for a considerable number of movies to precede it.[7] The contract also specified that such a film was to contain no propaganda content — a clause, of course, that would have been impossible to enforce. Wodehouse's own experience of Hollywood, and in the wake of the radio broadcasts, must have told him not to be so trusting. Indeed, mocking or undercutting English pretensions was a prominent theme in German propaganda. However, Wodehouse felt safe because he was told that the setting for the film of *Heavy Weather* would change from Shropshire to Pomerania and all the characters would be German.[8] Having gone to theaters, the Wodehouses were doubtless aware that most German films were devoid of overt party propaganda, which did not attract a mass audience.[9] Instead, German features offered subtle patriotism, attempting to present a continuity with the traditional popular entertainment, to conceal the impact of war and fascism.

After the war Wodehouse feared that the *Heavy Weather* contract, and his sale of *Money in the Bank* to Tauchnitz, might come under the law banning trading with the enemy. (Tauchnitz was a Leipzig firm which had been publishing English-language paperbacks on the continent for a century.) Nor were these arrangements all; Ethel had also met with a representative of Tobias Film Company about rights to make German productions.[10] As Wodehouse explained to the British authorities, "I am hoping that they will take a lenient view, realising that I acted in perfect innocence, on the assumption that only commercial undertakings came within the scope of the law relating to trading with the enemy, and that there would be no objection to a transaction of a purely artistic nature." It was disingenuous reasoning at best, especially since in the same letter to British authorities he noted that, despite the popularity of his writings in Germany, he refused offers to write in that country, composing only with the plan of postwar sale. He had declined offers to do a humorous film for Jenny Jugo, and to compose a comic opera with Edward Kunneke.[11] His distinction drawn between refusing to create an original, but selling an adaptation, seems a fine one to say the least.

Wodehouse pictures were considered for production elsewhere in

Europe during World War II, but the only one to actually come to the screen was another production in Sweden, a country that was neutral. *Gomorron Bill!*, released in 1945, was based on the play *Good Morning, Bill.* This was, in turn, Wodehouse's 1927 adaptation of a Ladislaus Fodor Hungarian original, which had starred Ernest Truex on the London stage. The screen version was adapted by Torsten Lundqvist and Lars Tessing. Lauritz Falk and Peter Winner directed, with Falk in the lead role of Bill.

Although released, Wodehouse was informed that he could be prosecuted for his wartime conduct, should he ever attempt to return to England. The situation would not change before his age precluded such a trip, despite the case having long since been closed. So Wodehouse decided to return to the United States in 1947, where he would eventually become a citizen in 1955. In this country, he hoped to find that his name was not inevitably linked with the controversy over the Berlin broadcasts, and such proved to be the case. A cordial media reception awaited him when he disembarked in April of 1947, including an appearance on the syndicated radio show *Luncheon at Sardi's.*

Edward Everett Horton asked Wodehouse to transform his 1948 novel *Spring Fever*, which included American characters from Hollywood but located in England, into a play, with an American setting. Wodehouse obliged, placing the story in Hollywood and recreating the butler role for Horton's persona. When Horton backed out, Wodehouse reworked the material a number of times, with Joe E. Brown at one point to star. Finally Wodehouse turned the project into his 1951 novel, *The Old Reliable*—which in its turn was made into a play by Guy Bolton that failed to sell. Despite the fact that its 1952 French translation was retitled *Hollywood Follies*, *The Old Reliable* does not take advantage either of the alternate world created in "the Mulliners of Hollywood" short stories, or of the surrealism of *Laughing Gas.* Its Hollywood content, while significant, is not pervasive or determinant; indeed, the only acidic comments are reserved for literary agents, portrayed as an indolent lot who do almost nothing for their 10 percent. More than a decade after Wodehouse's own Hollywood experiences, his portrayals of filmmakers were becoming more sympathetic.

"The Rise of Minna Nordstrom" is echoed, with a retired but still intimidating star of the silent era, Adela Shannon, as the lead in such pictures as *Gilded Sinners.* Once known as "the Empress of Stormy Emotion," she is now widowed several times and wealthy. Again, as in the previous story, two local policemen that Adela labels "Keystone Kops" imagine themselves as potential stars. Jacob (changed from Sigismund in "The Rise of Minna Nordstrom") Glutz is still head of the Medulla-Oblongata-Glutz, and is described as looking like a lobster.

Adela has hired her sister, Wilhemina ("Bill"), the reliable of the title, to ghost her autobiography. Wodehouse includes excerpts, using Hollywood hyperbole:

> "Who could have dreamed that in a few short years the name of Adela Shannon would have been known to the whole wide world from China to Peru? Who would have supposed that before I made my third picture, I would have become loved, worshipped, idolized by the prince in his palace, the peasant in his cot, the explorer in the jungle and the Eskimo in his frozen igloo? So true it is—so true.—Ha!" said Bill. "So true it is that one touch of nature makes the whole world kin and that courage, patience and perseverance will always find a way. I will now describe my first meeting with Nick Schenk."[12]

However, time had passed and the studio system Wodehouse knew was fast dissolving, and he acknowledged the contemporary decline of Hollywood. Yet, like his Hollywood stories of 15 years earlier, *The Old Reliable* still functions in a town ruled by ferocious studio executives, gossip columnists, and contract talent. As in his stories of upper class English life, time essentially stands still for Wodehouse, and here he portrays no fundamental change from the industry he knew firsthand.

Perhaps partly because of the novel's gestation, Wodehouse created in *The Old Reliable* a work reflecting his motifs and plot tropes. *The Old Reliable* is constructed around three elements typical of many Wodehouse stories: the attempt to steal a secret diary that could be used for blackmail; an underhanded butler; and the satisfactory conclusion of two love stories between contrasting couples. Bill discovers that her old flame, Smedley Cork, the brother of the man who left Adela a wealthy widow, lives with his sister-in-law, who is obliged to support him according to the terms of the will. ("Bill," named for the Wodehouse song in *Show Boat*, whispers the lyrics to another of the show's tunes, this one not written by Wodehouse, to express her emotion at seeing Smedley again: "Fish gotta swim, birds gotta fly, I gotta love one man till I die. Can't help lovin' that man of mine.") Smedley is hoping to make his fortune by finding the diary of the fiery Mexican star Carmen Flores, who died in a plane crash a year earlier. She was the previous owner of the property where he and Adela now live. Smedley is unaware that the butler, Phipps, has the same goal, but only Adela recognizes Phipps as a "reformed" safecracker; she was on the jury that convicted him.

Bill has just been fired by the Superba-Llewellyn, as has another pulp writer turned scenarist, young Joe Davenport, who is in love with Adela's daughter, Kay. Although Kay has rejected Joe's proposals of marriage, Bill has the sympathy for him born of having been shipped with Joe out to Hollywood together to the studio in a crate of 12.

Through a stroke of luck, Smedley finds the Flores diary—which is in Spanish—and already has an offer of $50,000 for it from the Colossal-Exquisite, before he has even contacted Medulla-Oblongata-Glutz. Adela takes the diary and places it in her safe, from which Phipps takes it, blackmailed by Bill into taking up his former profession. Wodehouse was aware of the melodrama; as Joe thinks at one point, "He was conscious of an unpleasant sensation of having been plunged into the middle of a B. picture of the more violent type and this was making him gulp a good deal."[13]

Wodehouse was mocking movie conventions, including a type becoming increasingly frequent in the postwar years. Before being fired by Superba-Llewellyn, Bill had come up with

> "an idea for the finest B. picture ever screened, and Superba-Llewellyn could have had it if they had not madly dispensed with my services. I shall write it up for *Horror Stories*. It's about a sinister scientist who gets hold of a girl and starts trying to turn her into a lobster."
>
> "A lobster?"
>
> "You know. Those things that look like studio executives. He collected a covey of lobsters and mashed them up and extracted the juice, and he was just going to inject the brew into the gal's spinal column with a hypodermic syringe when her betrothed rushed in and stopped him.
>
> "Why did he do that?"
>
> "He didn't want the girl he loved to be turned into something that looked like a studio executive. Isn't that good psychology?"
>
> "I mean why did the sinister scientist act that way?"
>
> "Oh, just a whim. You know what these sinister scientists are."
>
> "Well, it sounds fine. Full of meat."[14]

Phipps is described as the "Butler Supreme," and Wodehouse goes on to playfully connect him with the actor who had enacted his own best-known valet on the screen earlier, in the Jeeves movies. "He out-Arthurs Treacher. He lends lustre to the whole establishment. That harsh, grating sound you hear from time to time is the envious gnashing of the teeth of all the other Beverly Hills employers who haven't got him."[15] (Indeed, Wodehouse believed Treacher "would play Phipps better than Horton."[16]) Phipps ultimately takes the Flores diary for himself, setting a new pattern of butlers who serve themselves as much as their employer. He has also won an offer to play butlers on celluloid; such are the reasons why "It is a very impoverished butler in Beverly Hills who does not own his natty little roadster."[17]

The Old Reliable became the only one of Wodehouse's Hollywood novels adapted for the screen, when it was filmed for television in 1988 as a one-hour production for the American Public Broadcasting miniseries, *Tales from the Hollywood Hills*. "The Old Reliable" concentrated on the familiar Wodehouse device of the tell-all autobiography, of which there is only one copy, with prospective publishers and individuals named in the account jostling one another to steal it (situations best remembered from the Blandings Castle saga). In the adaptation, the fading "queen of stormy emotions" (Rosemary Harris) has Bill (Lynn Redgrave) ghost her life story to extort money from her five ex-husbands.

None of Wodehouse's lines or scenes actually make it to the script; instead his outline is the basis for an otherwise largely original work by Robert Mundy. The adaptation condenses some preceding episodes into the on-screen narrative of a single day, emphasizing the Hollywood elements of the novel throughout, particularly by adding the luncheon and the addition of Adela's ex-husbands as studio moguls (who disparage writers). Wodehouse had been content, in the book, to leave them off-stage, and the idea of the blackmail of the executives was minimized with a milder treatment of the diary and autobiography. Adela's mediocrity as a performer is emphasized, as a tour guide says she slept her way to the middle, but she is now broke, hanging on only to a pearl necklace which tempts Phipps (Paxton Whitehead). The adaptation makes Joe reluctant to abandon his little book of starlet's telephone numbers, instead of gladly leaving it behind for Kay (Lori Laughlin).

Bill switches sides over both profit and concern that her magnum opus may never see the light of day. As in the novel, she knows Phipps as a reformed safecracker, and sees to it that Adela's daughter is united with her love, while she happily resolves her own longstanding romance with a fading "stage-door Johnny" (Joseph Maher). All of it is handled under Michael Blakemore's direction with a lightness, frenetic pace, dialogue, and sense of character appropriate to Wodehouse adaptation, producing a quietly amusing hour. With its setting shifted to 1937, "The Old Reliable" captures the sense of a mythical Hollywood, a place of tyrannical moguls, egotistical stars, and a few relatively sane people trying to survive amidst them.

Wodehouse's earlier Hollywood stories had been distinct variations on his formulas, intruding on and shifting his narrative construction to take the setting into account, but subsequent works followed the precedent of *The Old Reliable* to become more distantly related to his own disillusioning experience. Hollywood became simply a background and inspiration that could be adjusted for a possible Wodehouse character type in one of his typical narratives. Filmmakers are used as characters, but living outside Hollywood and the studio system. For instance, egotistical actors, like Joey Cooley of *Laughing Gas*, appear in *The Mating Season* (1949) and *Angel Cake*.

In *The Mating Season*, vicar's daughter Cora Pirbright has returned from two years before the camera in Hollywood under the name of Cora Starr; she calls her dog Sam Goldwyn. Known as Corky to childhood chum Bertie Wooster, she has a role in a typical tangled web of sundered hearts in which he and Jeeves become involved. In 1950, Paramount bought the rights for $500 to use the title only of *The Mating Season*.[18]

Some 80 theatrical characters are scattered throughout Wodehouse's stories, with the 1921 novel *The Little Warrior* (entitled *Jill the Reckless* in England) the most important to use the stage milieu as its setting. After briefly keeping up with a traveling company trying out one of his plays, Wodehouse wrote another novel of the stage. This time a movie star was the leading performer, one who, like the comic lead in the recent play, was a lush. In *Angel Cake*, Mervyn Potter, the irresponsible idol of millions, involves young Cyril "Barmy" Fotheringay (pronounced Fungy)-Phipps in his escapades.

Potter "was one of those fortunate persons who seem to thrive on a shortage of sleep. If there was any criticism that could have been made of his appearance, it was that though the day was well advanced, it being now nearly lunch-time, he was still wearing the white tie and tails more conventionally allotted to the dinner hour. And the bizarre note was further stressed by the circumstance that some loving hand had written the words 'Oh, baby!' across his shirt front in lipstick."[19] Thanks to Potter, Barmy loses his job, but as the heir to a modest inheritance of $22,000, Barmy follows Potter's advice to go to New York and invest in his newest play. When the play premieres, Potter is too drunk to perform, and the audience reaction is poor. Full of satire of the theatrical world, its types and its methods, *Angel Cake* does for Broadway what "the Mulliners of Hollywood" did for filmdom.

VII

Television

From the birth of the small screen, television quickly emerged as the ideal visual medium for Wodehouse adaptations. The playlet format of 30 to 60 minutes allowed an emphasis on dialogue and incident from the source. By 1957, Wodehouse realized that he had at least a hundred short stories that would make good television material.[1] Producers also recognized the reservoir provided by Wodehouse's plays and prose. In particular, the half-hour length provided sufficient but not excessive running time for the fast-paced dramatization of a single short story. This was shown through such series as *The World of Wooster*, *The World of Wodehouse*, and *Wodehouse Playhouse*.

Two of his stage productions previously filmed in the 1930s were brought to the screen anew on several occasions in the early 1950s. In 1949, the first British television show from Wodehouse was *By Candlelight*, adapted by Harry Graham and produced by Harold Clayton in a 105-minute BBC version starring Robert Flemying, Clive Morton, Luise Rainer, and Anthony Shaw. *Candle-Light* was brought three more times to television in the United States. Two of these productions appeared in 1953, for the syndicated *Broadway Television Theatre* and *Kraft Television Theater* on ABC, with the third in 1955, for the ABC series *Pond's Theatre*.

During the same years, there were nearly as many new versions of *Anything Goes*, and also a new movie adaptation. Initially, an hour-long presentation was made for television in 1950 as the premiere episode of the NBC series *Musical Comedy Time*, with Martha Raye in the part Ethel Merman originated.

Another of a similar length, again on NBC, was broadcast in 1954 for the *Colgate Comedy Hour— The Ethel Merman Show*. An aging Merman played opposite a miscast Frank Sinatra in the gangster role. The program survives in kinescope form and provides a lesson in the inherent drawbacks of paring back a musical to a mere three-quarters of an hour, emphasizing only the songs. The dialogue is minimized, leaving the surviving characterization and humor sillier than it would otherwise seem. However, a few moments of verve sporadically triumph over the compressed, quick staging. At the same time, unlike the movie versions, this more closely resembles the original stage play.

The title credited it as "Cole Porter's musical comedy, by Howard Lindsay and Russell [sic] Crouse," with the concluding credits noting "Book by Guy Bolton and P. G. Wodehouse." The 1950 version of *Anything Goes* had cost $30,000 to produce, while in 1954 NBC and the sponsor spent $175,000 for the single performance—$65,000 more than the original budget of the show for its Broadway run.[2]

Finally, in 1956 a new movie version of *Anything Goes* was made, exactly 20 years after the 1936 original. It even had the same star, Bing Crosby, finishing the Paramount contract he had begun just two years before the first *Anything Goes*. This 1956 adaptation was the least faithful of all to the play. On the one hand, unlike the 1936 movie, this time Wodehouse was credited, and five instead of four of the Cole Porter songs were retained. However, and more important, the comedic content was diminished by replacing the original plot with a trite story of two show-business stars, teamed for the first time, who search for an appropriate female lead for their new production. Naturally, each makes a different selection. Sharing the lead with Crosby was Donald O'Connor as a television impresario, with Mitzi Gaynor and Jeanmarie as the two women competing against each other. Perhaps the closest reflection of Wodehouse was Phil Harris cast as Gaynor's father, an expatriate due to the income tax.

The first American Wodehouse television broadcast had been in 1950, a one-hour *Philco Television Playhouse* broadcast on NBC of *Uncle Dynamite*, a novel that had appeared two years earlier. The publisher, Didier, pocketed Wodehouse's share of the proceeds.[3] It seems almost inevitable that the star of "Uncle Dynamite" was Arthur Treacher, in his fourth Wodehouse screen appearance. Treacher's former partner as the 1930s movie Bertie Wooster, David Niven, also made further contributions to Wodehouse on the screen when he proved an ideal Uncle Fred in two television versions of "Uncle Fred Flits By." The first was in 1953, for *Hollywood Opening Night*, and the second in 1955, for *Four Star Playhouse*.

The latter survives, and is one of the most successful transpositions of Wodehouse, which Niven produced with Roy Kellino directing. The incidents of the short story provide a perfect amount of plot for a half-hour small-screen presentation, and each member of the little-known supporting cast was ideal. The segment fully captured the zaniness of the original while maintaining fidelity to the source, with the teleplay by Oscar Millard using much of the Wodehouse dialogue.

Wodehouse returned to the British television screen in 1956 with a presentation titled *Lord Emsworth and the Little Friend*, produced by Rex

Tucker. The 28-minute dramatization by C.E. Webber of the short story "Lord Emsworth and the Girl Friend," while rearranging the narrative for length and dialogue, remains entirely true to its spirit, and demonstrates what a brief television adaptation of one of the stories could achieve. Emsworth tries to avoid confronting the authoritarian personalities of Beach, MacAllister, and Lady Constance, while they try to determine his clothing, his garden, and the responsibilities of his position. As played by John Miller, Clarence emerges as a meek, tentative, somewhat absent-minded figure, with an amiability that retains sympathy while not losing the eccentricity that gives the characterization its delight. As in *Leave It to Me*, where Emsworth was slightly but not excessively daffy, showing off his chrysanthemums, in *Lord Emsworth and the Little Friend* he is possessed of a gentleness that contrasts with those around him. This is especially true of MacAllister's control of the garden and refusal to allow picking of its flowers. As a result Clarence is situated as the admirable figure, and his alliance with little Gladys (Margaret McCourt) is a model of effectiveness but also innocence and probity.

From the start of television, Wodehouse had followed when broadcasts of his stories were made. He had noted as early as 1948 that "money from your dead past keeps coming in. You open your mail one morning and find a check for $196.33 for radio or television performances of something you wrote in 1928."[4] Nonetheless, despite the flurry of adaptations that the new medium brought about, Wodehouse initially failed to see any future in the small screen. In 1952, he wrote, "We have a set and I enjoy the fights, but everything else on it is too awful for words."[5] Four years later, he said "It's odd about TV. One starts ... by loathing and despising it and gradually becomes tolerant." He watched the 1930s movies, remarking they "were a damned sight better than those of today."[6] By the early 1960s, he had become a devotee of the daily soap-opera, *Love of Life*, later adding *Edge of Night* and *Secret Storm* to his viewing routine. Other programs he enjoyed included *The Dick Van Dyke Show*.[7]

One of Wodehouse's plays, *Arthur*, not yet staged, instead appeared on television, as a 1960 segment of the hour-long anthology series *Ford Startime*. Retitled "Dear Arthur," it was based on Wodehouse's 1952 adaptation of a Ferenc Molnar play. (Around the same time, Wodehouse also adapted Molnar's *Game of Hearts*, and like *Arthur*, it remained unstaged.) The television version starred Rex Harrison, one of the few actors the easy-going Wodehouse openly detested. Harrison's persona was the opposite of the types Wodehouse had created in his own musical comedies. "Who ever started the idea that he has charm? I had always considered Professor Higgins the most loathsome of all stage characters, but I never realised how loathsome he could be till I saw Sexy Rexy playing him. Why everyone raves about the thing I can't imagine."[8] Yet, while Wodehouse's reaction is understandable given the much gentler characters typical of his own musical comedies, he could have asked for no better actor in the role for *Arthur*.

"Dear Arthur," as adapted for a one-hour television format by Gore Vidal, is a surprising story of a father and daughter, both of whom are blackguards. Sarah Marshall plays the golddigger, the widow of a husband who left her an income from a tin mine. Her father, as played by Harrison, is a smooth ex-convict who passes himself off as her attorney. With their true relationship a secret, the two are widely suspected of a romantic involvement. Harrison concocts a plan for the ultimate marriage of convenience of his daughter, to Arthur, an explorer perpetually away from home—a nonexistent man whose history he invents. Soon, others come forward as former acquaintances of Arthur, including a woman who says her daughter is his illegitimate offspring. Jealousy over Arthur adds to a wealthy young American's ardent wooing of the supposed neglected wife, and helps to bring them together.

Although the play reaches a natural conclusion at this point, there is a fourth act in which complications ensue after an apparent lover's rift. The plot expands from simple romantic comedy elements to include a political dimension, and Arthur is reported to have broadcast a speech denouncing Prince Rainier and urging democracy for Monaco (in the play, it was radio speeches denounced by both left and right). This was perhaps Wodehouse's jibe at his own German World War II broadcasts. Ultimately Harrison must succeed in killing off his own imaginary creation to enable the union of the couple; as in *Brother Alfred*, an imaginary person has changed from a convenience to become troublesome. Supplementing in "Dear Arthur" as a type of Greek chorus is wealthy socialite Angela Baddeley, who ends as the perfect next victim of Harrison's latest scam. The program is amusing and delightful, with many lines reminiscent of Wodehouse, including his adage that a husband has no use for brains—they just unsettle him (coming from Harrison as advice to his daughter).

For two decades, England and Hollywood had turned their back on movies derived from Wodehouse's short stories and novels, instead exploring their adaptability to television. Then a book was turned into a movie by John Bryan for Knightsbridge in England for 1961 release, *The Girl on the Boat*. It is a madcap romantic comedy, in black and white, made on a budget; it could just have easily been a product of the studio era in style and content. Occasionally, under Henry Kaplan's direction, the movie becomes laugh-out-loud amusing. However, more often it is, in the spirit

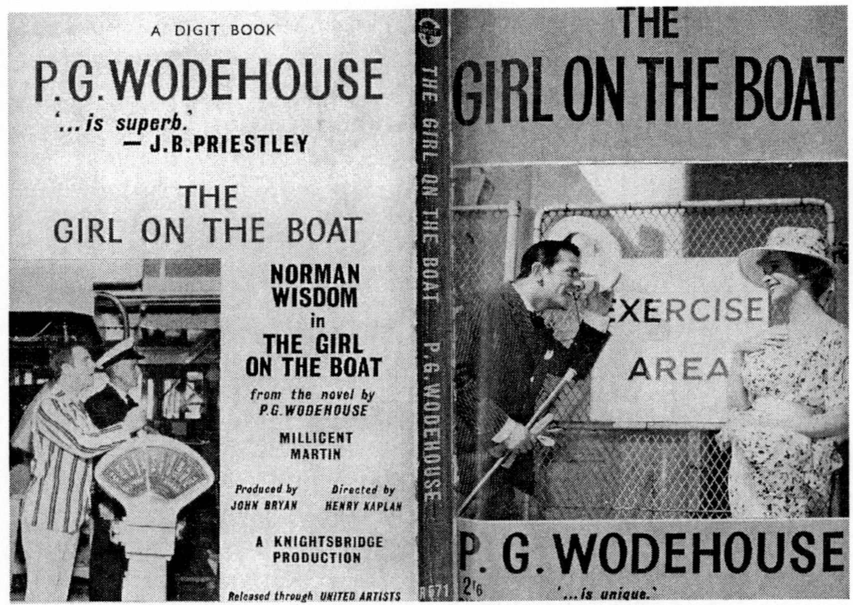

Cover art for the Digit tie-in for *The Girl on the Boat.*

of the book, light and diverting, although at times also bordering on silliness.

The Wodehouse source first appeared in 1921 as *Three Men and a Maid*; only the book publication in England took the title *The Girl on the Boat*. Reuben Ship's screenplay follows the story, with necessary adjustments and minor additions, but retains the original cast of characters even as they are adjusted slightly in importance. Many of the original gags from the book are retained, most notably Peter Cribbins as a legal secretary who is mistaken for a revolver-wielding maniac. Despite the modest budget, and the ready possibility of updating it, *The Girl on the Boat* wisely retains the 1920s setting and its mannerisms, costume, and behavior.

The high point of the film are the characters, created largely from the ideal casting. The performers perfectly bring to life the Wodehouse eccentrics, especially Richard Briers as a young man dominated by his mother, Athene Seyler. She prevents his initial wedding by taking his trousers, but later he finds his true perfect mate in Sheila Hancock, as a female big-game hunter looking for a man to protect. She brings off the unlikely feat of making such a part not excessively masculine, showing an attractive, feminine side despite her readiness with a gun. By contrast, the maid of the original title, Millicent Martin, engaged to three different men in the course of the story, is a redhead who reads Tennyson and is looking for her Sir Galahad. She is a typical Wodehouse female, sappy, but also hard-nosed when she suspects her prospective fiancés are less than they seem. Other supporting players were nearly as praiseworthy.

Only with the casting of Norman Wisdom as the romantic lead could one quibble; he was a major British comedian, on whose appeal the film based its advertising. However, his popularity never crossed the Atlantic, and *The Girl on the Boat* was conceived to expand his working-class roles, created for domestic consumption, into parts that would appeal to international moviegoers. Nonetheless, the film's only major stumbles are when it attempts to rework the book's plot for the star. *The Girl on the Boat* is a success, but too modest in its intentions and likely audience to suggest further Wodehouse adaptations on the large screen.

Hollywood's pathetic 1930s attempt to turn the Jeeves stories into a film series probably caused the author to look askance at such efforts. Yet, as early as 1953, a two-year option was taken on a Jeeves television series.[9] Success was again achieved with the stories in turning them into dramatic radio format. In 1964, two half-hour episodes, *Jeeves Takes Charge* and *Indian Summer of an Uncle*, closely followed the original texts, capturing the Wodehouse style. Only miscasting of the leads marred these versions. Roger Livesey was, or at least sounded, too aged for the role of Jeeves. By contrast, Terry-Thomas, while not quite surmounting his persona, manages to turn his mannerisms to proper effect. (He had bought an option on *Pigs Have Wings* in 1953, hoping to play Galahad.[10]) Only irritating musical segues that sound like a bad science fiction score mar this effort.

The success of this faithful approach may have been noted by the BBC. They had long considered Wodehouse's stories for television, but the idea had been regarded as unworkable. In their autobiographies, star Ian Carmichael and executive producer Frank Muir indicate that the problem was surmounted when narrative passages were shifted to dialogue, as impressions that Bertie tells Jeeves. The radio version had used this approach, as Terry-Thomas gave his first-person observations as well as the dialogue, a facility that remained unique to audio adaptations.

Each comedian who has played Bertram Wilberforce Wooster can be said to have endowed him with his own comic persona. That was certainly true of Hugh Laurie in the 1990s Granada *Jeeves and Wooster* television series, opposite longtime comedic partner Stephen Fry. David Niven's Bertie was based on his own light comedy typical of his very early career, in the single role in the movie of *Thank You, Jeeves*. So too was the 1960s interpretation by Ian Carmichael in the BBC's *World of Wooster*. Initially reluctant to take on the role of Bertie, Carmichael uses the nervous mannerisms of the affable, bewildered, overwhelmed innocent that he had brought to such Boulting brothers comedies as *Lucky Jim, Private's Progress*, and *I'm All Right, Jack*. He also adds a stammer that seems out of place for Bertie; while Carmichael's monocle is equally noncanonical, it seems less jarring. (His elocution is completely different from his other best-remembered role, as Lord Peter Wimsey, although these later Carmichael performances would have resonances as a detective who used a Wooster-type personality.) Carmichael was also, at age 44, plainly on the old side to play the "young master" so fond of late, carefree nights. Wodehouse recognized this, having regarded Bertie and his friends as "young scamps ... still in their early 20s."[11] Wodehouse, initially confident that Carmichael would be fine as Bertie, later believed he overacted terribly.[12] Despite these drawbacks, Wodehouse asked Carmichael to star as either Bertie or Jeeves in the musical comedy he was writing with Guy Bolton. However, Carmichael declined, feeling that his age precluded the one role and public perception barred him from switching to the other part. In subsequent years, Carmichael would return to Wodehouse with a number of audio book recordings, including such titles as *How Right You Are, Jeeves*, and the Blandings Castle novel *Summer Lightning*.

By contrast, Dennis Price's Jeeves is an older, stiff, dignified figure, regarding himself as superior to the proceedings around him, rather than participating in them or resolving them. Nonetheless, Wodehouse considered him "the best Jeeves he had ever seen."[13]

The first episode of *The World of Wooster* was "Jeeves and the Dog Mackintosh"; Richard Waring and Michael Mills shared the writing credit. "The Delayed Exit of Claude and Eustace" is the only surviving episode of the 20, shot in three separate series from 1965 to 1967, adapted by Waring and produced by Mills. Despite the title, it is based not only on that particular short story, but also on "Introducing Claude and Eustace" and "Sir Roderick Comes to Lunch," combining them all into a single entity centering on the deeds of Claude and Eustace, but also including portions of the Glossop story (Glossop was played by Paul Whitsun-Jones), while changing names. Using much of the Wodehouse material, some additional dialogue and situations are added by the screenwriter, giving the characters a sharper edge and heightening the tension between Jeeves and Aunt Agatha (Fabia Drake).

The series is filmed in a very minimal style, with economy-minded sets and an emphasis on medium shots and closeups to conceal the low production values. (Bertie's apartment is of modern design, with a central staircase and an intricate screen door.) The first six episodes in the series were shot over as many weeks.

Ian Carmichael and Dennis Price as Bertie and Jeeves on the cover of a Penguin tie-in to *The World of Wooster*.

Ralph Richardson as the Earl of Emsworth and Jack Radcliffe as McAllister, with the porcine Empress of Blandings, in the *Blandings Castle* series of *The World of Wodehouse*, as shown on the cover of a Penguin book tie-in.

Wodehouse only saw the first two episodes of the series, especially screened for him at his home by Muir, but expressed approval. *The World of Wooster* was widely popular and critically acclaimed, sparking a 1920s fashion in England among teens, and was distributed worldwide. Wodehouse was amazed at the amount of publicity *The World of Wooster* provided him.[14]

The series won awards for best script and comedy in 1965 from the Guild of Television Producers and Directors. However, by the end, Carmichael and others felt that they had used all the stories suitable for television adaptation, and after considering an adaptation of *The Code of the Woosters*, decided against it rather than change from the anthology to a serial format.

The breakthrough success of *The World of Wooster* quickly spawned two other series, filmed as *The World of Wodehouse* (1967). First was a six-part series of half-hour episodes from the Blandings Castle short stories, scripted by John Chapman. Ralph Richardson starred as Lord Emsworth, his wife Meriel Forbes as Lady Constance, Stanley Holloway as Beach the butler (who Wodehouse believed was miscast), and Jack Radcliffe as McAllister the gardener, browbeating his master.[15] The series was produced by Michael Mills and Frank Muir, the same team behind *The World of Wooster* Muir also provided the sounds of Emsworth's prize pig, the Empress of Blandings.

Muir considered the Blandings stories "the most autobiographical of Plum's works. Certainly Plum put much of himself in the character of Lord Emsworth: the agony of having to dress up and waste time being social; the disinclination to argue ... the dislike of facing the human race, singly or in bulk, at any time. And the sublime unworldliness, mind absent on higher matters...."[16] The Blandings series was described as having more charm than laughs, with the many exteriors shot in Penshurst Place, Kent. The opening episode was a remake of "Lord Emsworth and the Girl Friend." There was talk of a Blandings musical play, but series star Ralph Richardson was not interested, and the program itself did not repeat the popular success of *The World of Wooster*.[17]

The other *World of Wodehouse* series featured seven tales of Stanley Featherstonehaugh Ukridge starring Anton Rodgers, with Julian Holloway as Corky. Regrettably, like most of *The World of Wooster*, *The World of Wodehouse* is completely lost today, one of many British television series of the time deliberately destroyed as lacking further commercial value. Fortunately, enough does survive of this first decade and a half of Wodehouse television to reveal the perfect merging of author and visual medium.

VIII
Last Words

In their last decades, Wodehouse and Guy Bolton planned a variety of revivals of stage successes. There seemed to be encouragement when a 1958 off-Broadway return of *Leave It to Jane* drew unexpectedly large audiences, but nonetheless the plays did not enjoy the kind of renewed stature to make transpositions to film likely. It was not a new idea; in 1946 Wodehouse was enthusiastic over buying the film rights to *Oh, Boy!* in conjunction with Guy Bolton.[1] In 1968, Paramount did buy the rights to Wodehouse's two English language adaptations of the *The Play's the Thing*, originally commissioned by Gilbert Miller from Ferenc Molnar's Hungarian play. *The Play's the Thing* had opened in 1926 and run a year on Broadway and two years on the road. It had its London premiere in 1928, and was successfully revived on Broadway in 1948. However, both remained unproduced as a film, although *The Play's the Thing* is still one of Wodehouse's most popular pieces in stage revivals.

He also found himself the subject of a growing number of radio and television examinations of his own life and work, even as he began to turn out volumes of autobiography in the 1950s: *Bring On the Girls!*, *Author! Author!* (entitled *Performing Flea* in England, a compilation of his letters to William Townend, coedited by Townend), and *America, I Like You* (published in longer form in England as *Over Seventy*). He and Guy Bolton amplified on their written memoir, *Bring On the Girls*, in *Stagestruck: Fifty Years of Musical Comedy*, and were joined by William Gaxton, Vivienne Segal, and Fred Astaire on the hour-long October 30, 1953, special hosted by Mike Wallace. This was only one of a number of radio and television appearances that promoted the book. Now that he was a resident of the United States, living near New York, Wodehouse was interviewed for a myriad of other programs on subjects ranging from Jerome Kern (on *Today*, January 28, 1963) to living in the city, on *Comment* (June 20, 1971). Wodehouse appeared as a panelist on *Vim Electric — Quick on the Draw* (January 14, 1950, and November 16, 1950), and was the subject of a half-hour segment of *The Creative Person* aired over WNDT in New York on May 11, 1965.

Wodehouse recalled his dismay at all of this in a chapter entitled "Television" in *Over Seventy.*

> Every time I have a new book come out, it comes again ... the Finger. The telephone rings, and it is my publishers' publicity man informing me briskly that I am to appear on television next week—Monday 8:30, Sonny Booch's "Strictly for Morons" half-hour; Tuesday, 9:15, Alonzo Todd's "Park Your Brains in the Cloakroom"; and Thursday, 7:35, Genevieve Goole Pobsleigh's "Life Among the Halfwits." ...
>
> If they wanted to interview me on the radio, that would be different. I have an attractive voice, rich, mellow, with certain deep organ tones in it calculated to make quite a number of the cash customers dig up the $3.50. But it is fatal to let them see me.... On totters a spavined septuagenarian, his bald head coated with pancake flour to keep it from shining and his palsied limbs twitching feebly like those of a galvanized frog.... I wouldn't risk twopence on anyone who looks like I do on the television screen.

By 1958, despite residing in America, Wodehouse was being interviewed for such British shows as *Monitor.* In England, however, a continued focus remained on Wodehouse's World War II radio broadcasts from Germany, and whether they constituted collaboration or treason. He was pronounced guiltless of the latter on the occasion of an eightieth-birthday salute by Evelyn Waugh broadcast over the BBC on July 15, 1961, concluding with a tribute to his writing. He was again interviewed by such BBC figures as Robert Robinson, Alistair Cooke in 1963, and Malcolm Muggeridge in 1965. *Preview: The Chap with a Good Tale to Tell,* broadcast on October 15, 1971, examined a day at home with Wodehouse. Rehashing of the wartime questions was no longer central to the celebration of the legendary author on the occasions of his ninetieth birthday, with the ensuing media celebration.[2] The 1974 Argo LP record *Speaking Personally* offered Wodehouse reading from *Over Seventy* and other pieces. An interview with Bob Cromie was broadcast on January 17, 1974.

With the television renaissance of Wodehouse's work, Hollywood characters returned to Wodehouse's writing, and he resumed two earlier sagas. Wodehouse capped the "Mulliners of Hollywood" series with one more short story, "George and Alfred," published in 1967. "George and Alfred" was a softer reflection of its predecessors, set in an era when the Hollywood moguls have shifted their base to Europe for the production of super-spectacles.

Studio boss Ivor Llewellyn from *The Luck of the Bodkins* had also returned in Wodehouse novels. In *Cocktail Time* (1958) and *Biffen's Millions* (titled *Frozen Assets* in England; 1964), Llewellyn is an off-stage character, referred to but never actually appearing. In *Cocktail Time,* Llewellyn hears that the new book of that title would excite filmgoers if he can get it past the censors, and bids against Medulla-Oblongata-Glutz for the film rights.

In *Biffen's Millions*, Edmund Biffen Christopher hopes Llewellyn will give him a job in "pix," while Lord Tilbury must feign illness to provide an excuse for a missed luncheon with the powerful mogul, one of his principal advertisers. Biff uses knowledge of this to blackmail Tilbury into giving up his claim on his fortune. Tilbury's secretary finally wins his hand in matrimony after Llewellyn tells her that she is photogenic and should go to Hollywood.

Llewellyn once more became a principal character in two of Wodehouse's very last books, *The Plot That Thickened* (titled *Pearls, Girls, and Monty Bodkin* in England; 1972), and *Bachelors Anonymous* (1973). Both novels pick up where *The Luck of the Bodkins* had left off nearly 40 years earlier, and the tone toward Hollywood is much gentler, perhaps also a result of the success of *The World of Wooster* and *The World of Wodehouse*. By comparison with the other studio bosses of Wodehouse's imagining, Ivor Llewellyn is now a benevolent dictator, much changed from the character etched in *The Luck of the Bodkins*.

Most obviously, Llewellyn has changed religion. In *The Luck of the Bodkins* Llewellyn was, like most other studio heads, apparently Jewish, and was regularly called "Ikey" by intimates, a diminutive form of Isaac usually given to children. By the 1970s, Wodehouse has transformed Llewellyn into a gentile, a native of Wales. This removed any possible hint of anti-Semitism that might be mistakenly derived from Wodehouse's earlier Hollywood stories, especially in light of the charges of collaboration resulting from the wartime broadcasts.

In *The Plot That Thickened* and *Bachelors Anonymous*, Llewellyn left home after falling in love with a schoolteacher who wanted him to learn English literature. He recalled how he "came to America and got a job with Joe Fishbein, who was the big noise in pictures at that time, and one day discovered where he had buried the body, and of course after that I never looked back. I was like a son to him. So that sequence ended happily...."[3] Usually at the Superba-Llewellyn, one had to be a nephew or at least a brother-in-law — or at least the illegitimate son of one of the principal shareholders— to achieve a position of any importance.

At the studio, in *The Plot That Thickened*, Llewellyn is such a forbidding figure that he reminds Monty Bodkin "'of one of those unpleasant creatures in the Book of Revelations.'"[4] Despite having worked at the studio for a year, Bodkin remarks that "'whenever we meet my bones still turn to water and Dow-Jones registers another sharp drop in my morale. I shuffle my feet. I twiddle my fingers. My pores open and I break into a cold sweat, if you will pardon the expression.'"[5] However, Llewellyn becomes sympathetic; he is dominated at home, and placed on a strict diet. This wife is like the others; he has been wed and divorced several times already. He has only one excuse. "'That's Hollywood. You sort of drift into it. There's nothing much to do after office hours, so you go out and get married.'"[6]

All his wives ultimately cast him off like a soiled glove.[7] Llewellyn's fifth wife, Grayce, who is divorcing him by the end of the novel, continues to hearken back to her Oscar-winning role in *Passion in Paris*. During the course of its shooting, "she used up three directors, two assistant directors, and a script girl. They were never themselves again."[8]

Wodehouse begins *The Plot That Thickened* in Hollywood:

> As always when the weather was not unusual the Californian sun shone brightly down on the Superba-Llewellyn motion-picture studio at Llewellyn City. Silence had gripped the great building except for the footsteps of some supervisor hurrying back to resume his supervising or the occasional howl from the writer's ghetto as some author with a headache sought in vain to make sense of the story which had been handed to him for treatment.[9]

The novel commences as Monty Bodkin has completed a year as a production advisor at Llewellyn City, fulfilling the edict of his prospective father-in-law that he prove he can hold down a job.

When, in the second chapter, Bodkin returns to England to claim his bride, he is told that since he secured the job by blackmailing Llewellyn, his year's work is voided and he must begin again. Monty's former secretary obtains him another job with Llewellyn, who is visiting England to write his memoirs. Llewellyn is happy to hire his former employee in order to borrow from him, since he cannot access the joint bank account shared with his wife. The remainder of the narrative revolves around standard Wodehouse themes: uniting the right couple, a stolen necklace, and some amusing criminals.

In *Bachelors Anonymous*, Llewellyn, newly divorced from Grayce, leaves Los Angeles for a sojourn with the London production office. Despite his determination to avoid another marriage, he quickly meets temperamental stage star Vera Dalrymple. His lawyer, Ephraim Trout, is a member of a local group called Bachelors Anonymous, which uses the principles of Alcoholics Anonymous to persuade their members of the perilous fate that may result from so little as taking a woman to dinner. Trout is concerned over the potential danger in which Llewellyn may find himself; he typically proposes marriage only because he has no idea what more to say after talking to a woman for ten minutes.

Dalrymple's demands for changes in the script of Joe Pickering's play,

Cousin Angela, cause it to close in a week. Looking for a job, Joe takes a position with Llewellyn to try to keep Vera at bay and serve as a one-man local branch of Bachelors Anonymous. Because of Vera, Llewellyn had seen *Cousin Angela* three times, and told him, "With a little fixing, it might make a good picture. I don't say great, I don't even say colossal, I just say good. It flopped, yes, but the practiced eye like mine can see possibilities in the worst stage flop."[10]

Joe's romance with a journalist, Sally Fitch, is nearly upset by the distinctively-named wastrel, Sir Jaklyn Warner, Baronet — or, as he is known to those whose money he seeks, Jak Warner — a name whose resemblance to pioneering mogul Jack Warner is exploited by Wodehouse. Trout flies to London to check on his client, but quickly leaves behind the years of indoctrination in Bachelors Anonymous and falls in love himself, leaving Llewellyn open to the pursuit of Vera, until he unsuccessfully tries to hide in a hospital. There, he becomes involved with a nurse, but fortunately she is the woman affianced to Trout.

Llewellyn is simultaneously generous and an egotist — a "modern Santa Claus" who knows the pleasure his company will add to any meal.[11] Quick to anger, when threatened by matrimony he fires Joe and changes his mind about buying *Cousin Angela*, but once he is out of danger Llewellyn offers to pay Joe $250,000 for the rights to the piece.

By this point, Llewellyn's character has been considerably diluted, and he has little distinction as a movie mogul; he is simply another comic figure for whom wedding bells are the ultimate peril. The commentary on the motion picture industry in *Bachelors Anonymous* is considerably diminished from *The Plot That Thickened*, and the narrative seems rather perfunctory, failing to live up to the comic potential of its premise.

There may be more operating here than simply the dimming of his memory of Hollywood, and Wodehouse's increasing satisfaction with television adaptations of his work. Since "the Mulliners of Hollywood" and *Laughing Gas*, Wodehouse had acquired a more international experience of the film industry, after his dealings with German producers during World War II. All of these factors would have caused him to see Hollywood in a comparatively positive light. Nor were these books written in anticipation of magazine serialization, as were his previous Hollywood novels.

In 1967, "Uncle Fred Flits By," this time starring Wilfrid Hyde-White, appeared on British television on *Comedy Playhouse*, more than a dozen years after the American versions; the same series showed "The Reverent Wooing of Archibald" in 1974.

The third major British Wodehouse television series was an anthology of 20 stories developed to half-hour form as *Wodehouse Playhouse.* Most of the source material was the Mulliner stories, with a few others of golf and the Drones club. The series was broadcast in the United States over public television, and subsequently syndicated to many local PBS stations well into the 1980s, before finally appearing on home video in 2003.

The television screen naturally opened up new storytelling possibilities not available in prose. For instance, "Big Business" was able to use a recording of Paul Robeson singing "Ol' Man River" when Reginald Mulliner is supposed to have been sad enough to express it with the proper emotion, adding a new layer of comedy to what could only be hinted at in the original story. However, even when elaborating on the original, David Climie's scripts frequently used dialogue and scenes directly from the stories, and managed to create a near-seamless whole.

The first two series, of seven episodes in 1975 and another six in 1976, starred the husband-and-wife team of Pauline Collins and John Alderton, but the final series of seven episodes in 1978 featured only Alderton. Some in the British audience quibbled with the casting as reflecting the wrong accents and class sensibilities, but American audiences were oblivious to such details.[12] There was overacting in many of the episodes, however, and Collins and especially Alderton played different types of roles, which, while commendable as an acting challenge, robbed the series of continuity in character types. His often secondary part outshined the ostensible romantic lead. While Collins's roles varied considerably, Alderton demonstrated the anthological nature of the original Wodehouse stories, with an infinite number of variations possible on the same basic character premise. (A 1981 series for Jackanory Unit Productions, *Welcome to Wodehouse*, presented Alderton's readings of five stories on minimally decorated sets.)

The individual episodes varied widely in quality, with the result that the series is better when blurred in memory than when reexamined episode by episode. Of the first seven episodes in 1975, the first two were disappointments. "The Truth About George," although amusing, had as its subject matter a stutter, a subject that evokes a certain discomfort today when used for humor. The second episode, "Romance at Droitgate Spa," was a complete misfire, predictable, tiresome, and unfunny. Only Raymond Huntley was appropriately cast, while the romantic lead was dreadful. However, by the third episode, "Portrait of a Disciplinarian," the writing and acting of the series began to convey the humor of the Wodehouse stories, both in dialogue and situations. "Unpleasantness at Bludleigh Court," "Rodney Fails to Qualify," and "A Voice from the Past" were all of an equal calibre; only "The Rise of Minna Nordstrom" demonstrates weaknesses.

However, as whole, the first series failed to convey the wit of the stories, while sometimes capturing their hilarity and slapstick.

Alderton recalled that when presented with a list of the stories intended as the source, Wodehouse excused himself from the room to reexamine them. Laughs could be heard until he reemerged, smiling, saying "Some of them are *awfully* good."[13] Although he had been exhausted by the ordeal of the ninetieth-birthday interviews, saying he never wanted to see a camera again, he liked *Wodehouse Playhouse* so much that he agreed to do brief introductions that were filmed in January. He had just received his knighthood with the New Year, and sat for a waxwork for Madame Tussaud's in the fall. All this provided a further toll on his constitution, and he checked into the hospital. On Valentine's Day, 1975, he died, at age 93.[14]

The second series of *Wodehouse Playhouse*, in 1976, hoping for better results, replaced producer David Askey with Michael Mills, veteran of *The World of Wooster* and *The World of Wodehouse* a decade earlier. It was a wise decision, as the series quality notably improved. "Anselm Gets His Chance" gently tackles its subject, church formalities and piety, managing to be unobjectionable without losing any of the humor or pungence, as represented by ministers who constantly sprinkle their conversation with Biblical quotations, fully cited as to source. In "Mr. Potter Takes a Rest Cure," the madcap whirl gradually widens as beautiful but manipulative Bobbie Wickham, hoping to avoid a marriage her mother is encouraging, convinces Mr. Potter that Gandle is from a family with homicidal tendencies, while telling Gandle that Potter wants to commit suicide and must be prevented. It is slapstick, and unoriginal, but could not more accurately mirror the source.

By midpoint in the season, the series fully hit its stride, with such episodes as "Feet of Clay," "The Nodder," and "The Code of the Mulliners." The series finally conveyed the wit of the Wodehouse dialogue, the satire of the character types (such as the self-advertising adventurer Captain Jack Fosdyke and the vampish female novelist in "Feet of Clay"). Most notably, the superlative "Strychnine in the Soup" reflects the humor, satire, and manipulation of genre formula and different character types from a range of narratives. A mistaken deduction leads to the romantic conclusion while the two explorers, potential in-laws, prove to be out of their depth in a drawing room whodunit. Running through "Strychnine in the Soup" is the predicament of the lovers, united by their love of the thriller, until finally its spell wins the mother's consent for the hero to marry her daughter.

The third series of *Wodehouse Playhouse*, seven episodes produced in 1978 by Gareth Gwenlan, revealed Alderton's persona, and the repertory casting had so evolved as to be ideal. Such episodes as "The Smile That Wins," "Tangled Hearts," and "The Luck of the Stiffhams" maintained the high standard of the second season. Even those that fail to quite match their quality, such as "Big Business," are still memorable. (That episode contains a portion with Alderton in blackface, a situation that kept a later *Jeeves and Wooster* episode, "Kidnapped," from being broadcast in America.) They were uniformly well enacted, capturing the humorous nuances and situations, such as the advice-dispensing know-it-all in "Tangled Hearts" who must be humbled. On the other hand, "Trouble Down at Tudsleigh" has a riotously amusing first half but sputters with the introduction of a child performer, who has much the same effect on the viewer as she is intended to have in the story and succeeds all too well in making performance and episode quickly annoying. Perhaps the pinnacle of the series was "The Editor Regrets," ideally adapted, perfectly enacted, with every pause, nuance, and line impeccably delivered. Only the Drones played by middle-aged actors were out of sync. The situation of Bingo Little, editor of *Wee Tots*, the journal for the nursery, could not have been better brought to life.

The last dramatization, "Mulliner's Buck-u-Uppo," overcame the inherent narrative difficulty of visualizing a tonic that provides almost magical human strength and personal dominance, by combining a light balance between persuasive power with slow motion movements that resemble something out of the contemporary television series *The Six Million Dollar Man*. "Mulliner's Buck-u-Uppo" was a fitting end to an exploration of different ways of bringing various Wodehouse milieus to the screen in a range of stories, succeeding to different degrees but usually bringing his prose vividly to the screen.

The technique used by *Wodehouse Playhouse* may be instructively compared with the Stoll golf film series of 1924, despite the two series having been produced a half-century apart. They have equivalent running times of about a half-hour each, which prove an ideal length to capture the bulk of a short story on screen without either excessive compression or stretching the source material. Both are balanced delicately between the sophisticated humor of the source material and the belief that an infusion of slapstick is needed to reach their full potential on the screen. In the case of the Stoll series, it was the addition of the caddie. In the case of *Wodehouse Playhouse*, it is through small episodes added to the narrative involving the characters or excessively extending certain scenes, which at least do not provide such palpable interruptions. This causes both series to sometimes lose the sense of pacing necessary to comedy.

Wodehouse Playhouse included three golf stories, "Rodney Fails to

Qualify," "Feet of Clay," and "Tangled Hearts." Since both *Wodehouse Playhouse* and the Stoll series offered versions of "Rodney Fails to Qualify," it provides a very direct test case. Discounting the interpolations of the caddie in the Stoll version, the two works more closely resemble each other than might be expected; they dramatize a number of shared scenes, using some of the same key lines from Wodehouse for laughs. Each had scenes the other lacked, but followed the basic outline of the story and could be regarded as essentially faithful to the source. The acting styles, however, while very different, both employ overplaying as a key humorous device. Expressions and gestures accent, in the one case, the absent dialogue, and in the other, the dialogue itself. Unquestionably, the Stoll version suffers by the inability to convey the Wodehouse wording outside of the limited form of intertitles. This would not have seemed so at the time, naturally, given that audiences were habituated to the inherent limitations of silent cinema. However, not only does *Wodehouse Playhouse* enormously benefit from use of the words on its soundtrack, but the actual inflection given by the performers adds a whole further dimension.

With the novels *The Plot That Thickened* and *Bachelors Anonymous*, and the television series *Wodehouse Playhouse*, the author's last years were laced with reminders of his own Hollywood sojourn so many years before. As he wrote gently of studio figures, he had noted television providing lively yet faithful adaptations. Wodehouse must have been comforted; despite earlier disillusionment, at the end he saw the best.

And, after he had taken his own last bow, his inspiration lived on, and there was much more still to come.

IX

Posthumous Adaptations

With the end of Wodehouse's life, screen versions did more than continue apace; they increased in number. His books remain as popular as ever, and the impetus to bring them to film persists. Instead of the interview shows during his final years, there have been more retrospective documentaries on Wodehouse. Along with these was the 1989 television dramatization of his career as a lyricist, *Wodehouse on Broadway*.

After Wodehouse's death, documentaries proper became more common, but typically use the interview footage shot during his lifetime. The year 1981 saw *Thank You, P. G. Wodehouse* in England, while one of the best was the 70-minute *Bookmark: Plum*, broadcast on the BBC for Christmas 1989. These programs have gone beyond the traditional biographical format toward a more interpretive approach, such as *P. G. Wodehouse: The Long Exile* in 2002. Such shows were not confined to England and America but were also produced in other countries such as Sweden.

British adaptations of Wodehouse stories that showed on television in India prompted a version of their own from that nation. State television Doordarshan in India put on a ten-part film of *Leave It to Psmith*, titled *Isi Bahane* (*On This Excuse*), played in Hindi by an Indian cast. Psmith, one of Wodehouse's most popular characters (who introduces himself by saying, "the 'p' is silent as in 'pshrimp'"), returned to the screen for the first time in over five decades in 1988. The verdant Blandings Castle is changed to the palace of an indolent rajah in desert Rajasthan. The story is brought up to date; Freddy Threepwood has a Sony walkman. Lady Constance is the wife, rather than the sister, of Lord Emswoth, and becomes a tragic character, having been forced into marriage. "The Effici Baxter" (instead of "efficient") is a typical Indian bureaucrat, and Psmith himself was renamed Rambo. Blighted love and the need for money were two key themes. *Isi Bahane* was not popular with critics or Indian Wodehousians, who criticized the crude dialogue and production.[1]

Wodehouse had only appeared sporadically in radio broadcasts up through the 1960s. Yet radio would prove to be the most appropriate medium for Wodehouse adaptations, because the range of voices and narration allowed a closer approximation of the effect he had been able to place on the printed page. Indeed, much of the narration and dialogue could be taken directly from the Wodehouse text. This was proven by the first and most successful exemplar of this approach, the BBC series *What Ho, Jeeves* (1973–1981). Richard Briers starred as Bertie Wooster and Michael Hordern was Jeeves in multipart adaptations of seven of the novels—*Thank You, Jeeves*; *Right Ho, Jeeves*; *The Code of the Woosters*; *Joy in the Morning*; *The Mating Season*; *Jeeves and the Feudal Spirit*; and *Stiff Upper Lip, Jeeves*— as well as a number of the short stories combined as *The Inimitable Jeeves*.

This could be labeled the ideal, the pinnacle of all Wodehouse adaptations, as close to flawless as it is possible to be. The miniseries format allowed sufficient time to dramatize each novel, between three and four hours, accurately reproducing the flavor of the book. The series preserved the first-person viewpoint, with Bertie's narration and asides as well as the dialogue. Moreover, the outrageous humor is conveyed in a manner consonant with the original stories, making *What Ho, Jeeves* the most thoroughly laugh-inducing adaptation of Wodehouse ever made.

The acting conveys the pace of the stories and highlights all the inflection and characterization possible. Briers particularly was the perfect Bertie and has proven to be an ideal Wodehouse performer in other contexts (such as the films *The Girl on the Boat* and *Heavy Weather*). Much of what he brings to the role may also be accounted for by his feel for the material; he is an aficionado in his own right, active in the British Wodehouse society. While unseen, Briers and Hordern set a standard for the voices and mannerisms of Bertie and Jeeves that remains unrivaled in any medium.

A one-man stage show by Edward Duke, enacting Bertie Wooster as well as Jeeves and all the other characters, was issued on audiotape. Outside of endowing Bertie with an annoying, effeminate giggle, Duke impressively establishes the range of voices in a manner seemingly only possible with a full cast. *Jeeves Takes Charge* was issued in 1987, comprising the story of that title along with "Bertie Changes His Mind." A second tape, *Jeeves Comes to America*, appeared in 1993 and included "Jeeves and the Hard-Boiled Egg" and "The Chump Cyril" (reprinted in *The Inimitable Jeeves* as "A Letter of Introduction" and "Startling Dressiness of a Lift Attendant"). Each episode was one-half hour, and the cassettes were distributed by Buckingham Classics.

With the 1990–1993 Granada *Jeeves and Wooster* television series, for the first time a preexisting comedy team, Stephen Fry and Hugh Laurie, was chosen for the lead roles, rather than a combination of disparate stars, as in the case of David Niven and Arthur Treacher in the 1930s or Ian

Hugh Laurie and Stephen Fry in *Jeeves and Wooster*.

Carmichael and Dennis Price in the 1960s. Fry and Laurie's long experience together enabled them to elicit a natural closeness between the two characters that had not been apparent in the previous pairings. For the first time, a screen version indicated the actual similarity in age between the two characters, unlike the traditional portrayal of Jeeves as a figure whose age matched his sagacity. Laurie's various looks of befuddlement, his guilelessness and vulnerability, together with Fry's quiet superiority to the events around him, captured the Wodehouse characterizations far more accurately than the previous combinations.

The series did not use a laugh track or as much emphasis on the comedic dialogue that had been a part of *Wodehouse Playhouse*. Although like *Wodehouse Playhouse*, *Jeeves and Wooster* sometimes veered into pure slapstick, more often it was lower-key, relying on the characters and the situations into which their nature led them. Laurie's position as victim of the events surrounding him, and individuals far less likeable than he, helped to capture the necessary sympathy for his characterization, while Carmichael's stutter tended more to elicit pity (while Niven was largely marginalized).

Both Fry and Laurie brought a commitment to the roles as they were originally created, and prior to their screen portrayals had an appreciation of Wodehouse. This has continued with separate essays by Laurie and

Fry in a number of publications. Laurie admitted the seeming impossibility of bringing much of the dialogue and description to the screen with their full impact:

> Let me give you an example. Bertie is leaving in a huff: "'Tinkerty tonk,' I said, and I meant it to sting.'" I ask you: how is one to do justice of even the roughest sort to a line like that? How can any human actor, with his clumsily attached ears, and his irritating voice, and his completely misguided hair, hope to deliver a line as pure as that? It cannot be done....
>
> Naturally, one hopes there were compensations in watching Wodehouse on the screen — pleasant scenery, amusing clothes, a particular actor's eyebrows — but it can never replicate the experience of reading him.[2]

Nonetheless, *Wodehouse Playhouse* had proved this goal was nearly possible.

However, the greater difficulty was the result, as Fry noted, of Wodehouse's brilliant decision to use Bertie as first-person narrator. "It is after all through Bertie's language that we encounter Jeeves and through his eyes and ears that the stories work.... The particular joy of a Jeeves story derives from the delicious feeling one derives from being completely in Bertie's hands."[3] From this so much of the humor emanates, but only in a radio adaptation could this same first-person point of view be realized — it is all but impossible to bring to the popular screen. Hence, it was perhaps inevitable that *Jeeves and Wooster* was unable to match its radio predecessor, *What Ho, Jeeves*.

It was the quality of the scripts that convinced the stars to take on such a formidable project. The manners and banter among Bertie and his friends and other characters was often perfect. Fry noted that "Wodehouse's three great achievements are Plot, Character and Language, and the greatest of these, by far, is Language. If we were reasonably competent we could go some way towards conveying a fair sense of the narrative of the stories and revealing too a good deal of the nature of the characters." However, Fry believed the actor can never surpass what the readers hear in their own minds while reading.[4]

The supporting characterizations, unlike the lovable eccentrics of *Wodehouse Playhouse*, tended to be much more caricatured. The actors themselves were often startlingly odd-looking, whether the women feared by Bertie, or his fellow Drones. With elaborate production, the series was designed in a highly stylized, almost artificial fashion, to be as distant from any reality as possible while retaining the basic 1920s temporal period. In this way, the set design, costumes, casting, and makeup, together with Anne Dudley's original pastiches of 1920s music, crossed beyond recreation to support the never-never-land of Wodehouse's imagination.

Still, considering David Climie's achievement in scripting *Wodehouse Playhouse* a dozen years earlier, and despite the success *Jeeves and Wooster* had, it was too often a disappointment. Unlike earlier versions, each episode of *Jeeves and Wooster* lasted close to 55 minutes; at this length, new departures, combinations, and variations on the texts were tried, and some were plainly more successful than others. Following the lead of *The World of Wooster*, script writer Clive Exton frequently combined various stories, but this time no actual episode titles were given on screen, obscuring the adaptation process. Sometimes several sequential short stories were brought together, but just as often disparate plot strands from various narratives were combined. Exton was even able, in a number of instances, to extract the elements of a single novel into two separate episodes, each largely independent of the other.

At their best, the plots reflect the complexities and hare-brained schemes of the stories. The individual plot strands of the stories were disentangled and recreated according to the dramatic needs of 55 minutes of screen time. However, as the series lasted four seasons, this process increasingly began to reveal its inherently hit-or-miss nature, departing steadily further from Wodehouse and relying more on Exton's own imagination. Exton's additions noticeably lack the Wodehouse wit and are inconsistent with the remainder. *Jeeves and Wooster* succeeds, gloriously, when it dramatizes the stories, but fails when it abandons them or lapses into invention or padded interpolations. They lack the tight Wodehouse plotting that made the illogical seem, within its own world, logical, rather than just wacky and silly. The sophistication diminishes in favor of the situation comedy aspect, dissolving the narrative into dreary slapstick chases.

Only the acting of Fry and Laurie, and the direction of Robert Young, Simon Langton, and Ferdinand Fairfax, were a bulwark against these drawbacks. Fry admitted that they might only get 20 percent of Wodehouse into the programs, and that he might have protested the changes had he been on the other side of the camera.[5] The diminishing quality tended to be obscured for American audiences since the series was broadcast out of order on Public Broadcasting's *Masterpiece Theater*, and five of the 23 episodes were never shown, only released on video. Fry introduced the third series, broadcast in the United States in 1992–1993 as the second series of *Jeeves and Wooster* on *Masterpiece Theater*.

The unlikelihood of Hollywood bringing Wodehouse to the large screen in the 1980s and 1990s was demonstrated by the efforts of Curtis Armstrong and John Doolittle. They were involved with three Wodehouse big-screen adaptations, one of which almost made it to the screen. The rights to "Honeysuckle Cottage" were bought by Avenue Pictures for around $60,000, as was the script. The stars were to be Val Kilmer, Penelope Ann Miller, Rose Wells, and J.T. Walsh (as McKinnon), with Christopher Guest directing. Much of the dialogue and scenes from the story were used.

The Wodehouse story is an unusual one, more fantastic and serious than humorous. It concerns a failed romance, celebrating a character who is rescued from the threat of undesired matrimony. The cottage of the title has an almost supernatural influence, compelling its characters to behave in sentimental, romantic ways even when their heads struggle against it. The hero is a writer of hardboiled detective novels who inherits the property from his aunt, a composer of bestselling romances that he loathed. Only thanks to the interruption of the gardener's dog is he saved from proposing to a girl who is like the heroine of one of his aunt's dreadful books.

In the film, the cottage was to represent Wodehouse's world intact. It was envisioned as emphasizing the character's interior experiences, thus both enlarging upon, but remaining fundamentally faithful to, the Wodehouse milieu. Because of the supernatural aspect of the story, it was possible to go beyond a present-day setting while avoiding the trappings of a "period" story. The Wodehouse estate did not want the use of the Mr. Mulliner framing device, which was unnecessary anyway, for the adaptation. *Honeysuckle Cottage* was about to go into production in October 1990 when it was abruptly cancelled.

The next two Armstrong-Doolittle attempts had to take greater liberties with their source than "Honeysuckle Cottage," through Americanizing the settings and bringing them up to date. "Ukridge's Accident Syndicate" was given the screen title *Personal Liability* and optioned by Touchstone Pictures. In it, the character of Teddy is not resisting an accident, but is accident-prone, and the character inspired by Ukridge sees this as a way to make money. However, once Teddy becomes involved in romance, he is no longer so liable to have accidents, compelling a deliberately planned accident. An adaptation of *Cocktail Time* was also written, featuring a right-wing senator who trumpets personal morality becoming inspired to write an erotic novel by his mistress, with the ghostwriter surprised by the book's success.

Only *Honeysuckle Cottage* was sold as a Wodehouse adaptation; his name was unknown among modern Hollywood producers, perhaps explaining his absence from the American movie screen since 1956 and *Anything Goes*. Wodehouse was perhaps more fortunate when he had generated dislike as a result of his candid comments in 1931 or the lawsuit with Philip Dunne; at least then he had not been forgotten in Hollywood. At the same time, the agent for the Wodehouse estate, A.P. Watt, believed the big-screen rights were of great value, perhaps because of the simultaneous interest in the Fry-Laurie television series. There was also interest in filming Wodehouse in other countries.[6]

Sweden produced its third Wodehouse movie in 1991 with *Den Ofrivillige Golfaren* (*The Accidental Golfer*), running 100 minutes. In conjunction with producer Bo Jonsson, Lasse Aberg, one of the most popular figures in the Swedish film industry, adapted and directed and starred as well. He played a shy introvert who makes a bet that he can learn to play golf within a week; taken to Scotland, he falls in love with the daughter of the professional who teaches him. *Den Ofrivillige Golfaren* was the first Wodehouse theatrical feature in nearly three decades.

Meanwhile, there were a number of dramatizations of the Blandings saga. It appeared on the German television screen in 1974 as *Blut Floss Auf Blandings Castle* (*Blood Flowed at Blandings Castle*) and again there in 1977 with a presentation of *Oh Clarence* on the German screen as *Der Lord Und Seine Koenigin* (*A King and His Queen*).

Some of the short stories were broadcast over BBC radio in 1985, and *Heavy Weather* was serialized in 1988. In 1992, the BBC dramatized a radio version by Wodehouse biographer Richard Usborne of *Galahad at Blandings*, with former Bertie Wooster star Ian Carmichael as Gally. Three years later, in 1995, the first internationally shown Blandings television production was made, and the best overall to date.

This was a television version of *Heavy Weather*, produced by Verity Lambert and filmed on a six-week schedule using locations at Sudeley Castle, Gloucestershire. The 90-minute Cinema Verity–Jupiter Films production for BBC combined fidelity to the original text with an elegant period recreation, simultaneously recognizing that the Wodehouse characters were musical-comedy types from a make-believe realm. They were played to the hilt by a stellar cast, most notably Peter O'Toole in what he regarded as a "dream role" as an impeccably balmy Lord Emsworth.[7] Wodehouse movie and radio veteran Richard Briers costarred as the avuncular and kindly Galahad Threepwood. The script by Douglas Livingstone interweaved the conflicting and overlapping motives that was such a strength of the Wodehouse narrative. Jack Gold's direction maintained the atmosphere of genial looniness, at the same time succeeding in achieving the maximum comedic effect of many of the situations.

As the only tale of the Empress of Blandings among the surviving screen versions of the saga, *Heavy Weather* was bound to seem even more eccentric than the other, nonporcine Blandings tales that can still be viewed today. *Heavy Weather* and *Leave It to Me* offer two elegantly produced, equally amusing but fundamentally divergent interpretations of Blandings Castle, while *Lord Emsworth and the Little Friend* offers a third, more modestly scaled alternative. All three indicate the various possible treatments of the saga on screen. *Heavy Weather* shifts toward caricature, while *Leave It to Me* goes in the direction of slapstick. *Lord Emsworth and the Little Friend* did not veer excessively in either direction, instead relying purely on dialogue and situations. Each focuses on different characters the other overlooked, such as Psmith in *Leave It to Me* versus Clarence in *Lord Emsworth and the Little Friend* and *Heavy Weather.* His imperious sister Constance is key in both of the latter but a minor figure in *Leave It to Me.* The two feature films suffer from discordant, excessively dramatic scenes—Baxter's interrogation in *Leave It to Me*, and the lover's tiff in *Heavy Weather.* Gerrard's Psmith of *Leave It to Me* verges on a wacky Groucho Marx style in his reliance on one-liners and zany humor. Peter O'Toole's Emsworth in *Heavy Weather* pushes Emsworth to the brink of obsessive idiocy, perched precariously on the fine line as the farce of absent-mindedness verges on feeble-mindedness and near senility. *Lord Emsworth and the Little Friend* provides a milder view of Clarence, a deferential, tentative figure evading the world, between the self-effacement of *Leave It to Me* and the utterly daft characterization of *Heavy Weather. Lord Emsworth and the Little Friend* offers a balance between *Leave It to Me* and *Heavy Weather* that comes close to the ideal of what can be achieved with the Wodehouse characters and words. One can only wish that the lost Ralph Richardson *World of Wodehouse* series were available for comparison.

After Jeeves and Bertie Wooster, the Blandings Castle saga is the second favorite Wodehouse realm on screen, and films of Blandings have actually been produced in more countries, not only England but Sweden (*Blixt Och Dunder*), Germany, and India (*Isi Bahane*). Perhaps this was because the actual language used in a Blandings narrative is not as crucial as the situations, whereas the wording of a Jeeves story is key. Ironically, none of the Blandings stories have been filmed in Hollywood; perhaps their tone and setting is considered too inherently British, despite its appeal in other nations.

On the radio, steadily more BBC dramatizations were heard, from Ukridge short stories in 1993 to *Full Moon* in 1999, and more. A series of six golf stories was collectively titled *The Oldest Member* (with Maurice Denham in the title role) in 1996. Perhaps most memorable was *Uncle Dynamite* in 1994, in which adapter Richard Usborne merged perennial short story favorite "Uncle Fred in the Springtime" as an introduction to the novel. Richard Briers returned once more, this time as an ideal Uncle Fred, with Paul Eddington narrating and Hugh Grant in hapless support as Pongo. In 2002, BBC Radio 4 produced a series of Blandings stories read by Alan Titchmarsh, unfortunately squeezed into a mere 15-minute running time. This was followed with a series of Mulliner dramatizations allocating 30 minutes to each episode and with each actor playing multiple characters, and Richard Griffiths narrating. These were subsequently issued on CD by BBC Radio Classics.

From 1997 to 1998, two radio adaptations were produced by the City Lit Theatre Company by L.A. Theatre Works for Chicago Theatres on the Air and were distributed on audiotape. Outside the constraints of length, the second, *Thank You, Jeeves*, very nearly reached the quality of the BBC Hordern-Briers series. Almost of necessity, *Thank You, Jeeves* required the most changes to make it acceptable to a modern audience. The plot was wisely condensed to under an hour and the minstrel musicians made into hillbilly performers. Yet it still kept the Wodehouse spirit. Paxton Whitehead as Jeeves and Simon Templeton as Bertie were ideally cast under Rosalind Ayres's direction. Less auspicious but perhaps politically advisable was the inclusion of the mayor of Los Angeles as J. Washburn Stoker. Along with his off-beat casting was a scratchy-voiced Jennifer Tilly as his daughter. The first of City Lit Theatre's adaptations had been a later story, *The Code of the Woosters*, a less successful outing. This one was again adapted by Mark Richard, who directed himself as Bertie. Martin Jarvis costarred as Jeeves as well as Roderick Spode, and Ayres played Aunt Dahlia. Lasting two hours, this was the more faithful of the two, but not quite as successful in its casting as *Thank You, Jeeves*. Richard Newhouse produced *The Code of the Woosters*, while Susan Albert Loewenberg was executive producer of *Thank You, Jeeves*.

In 2001, Alan Ayckbourn's play *By Jeeves*, in a Pittsburgh stage presentation, was recorded on tape for British and Canadian video release and broadcast on Canadian television in March 2001. Starring John Scherer as Bertie, and Martin Jarvis as Jeeves, characters and situations from a variety of stories were merged. While evocative of Wodehouse, it was also far from him, with the dialogue absent, and the characters not always true to the original conception. The characterization of Jeeves owes too much to butler stereotypes, and he becomes solemn and almost sepulchral, failing to capture the knowing, sly irony with which Stephen Fry and Michael Hordern infused their interpretations. Scherer's Bertie, while slightly manic, was more in line with the canon.

By Jeeves attempts to approximate the narration as Bertie begins by telling a story. However, Jeeves corrects him, enlarging his own part in the narrative voice and placing him as a more active figure, rather than the *deus ex machina*. Departing for Totleigh Towers to present a banjo con-

Art for the stage version of *By Jeeves.*

cert, Bertie joins Honoria Glossop, Madeline Bassett, and Stiffy Byng, to the distress of Bingo Little, Gussie Fink-Nottle, and Stinker Pinker. There are adventures by the side of the road and in the country house, involving such staples as disguise and unintended romantic involvements. However, the plot becomes excessively convoluted, with a bewildering number of cases of mistaken identity. The result is Ayckbourn's carrying to the point of sheer absurdity what had been light and silly in Wodehouse's hands. In a rather crass, overlong ending, Bertie finally gets to play the banjo. However, he becomes too much the butt of humor, rather than one who perceives the absurdity, as the Wodehouse narration revealed.

Indeed, *By Jeeves* is more of a homage, a work inspired by Wodehouse, rather than an adaptation. In this respect, it builds upon the television series *Jeeves and Wooster*, with their frequent combination of elements from a number of stories in individual episodes. *By Jeeves* reveals that Ayckbourn clearly knows Wodehouse, and has lifted many bits from various stories; he melds them all into his own original but lacks the Wodehouse touch. There is an overabundance of incidence and characters, as if Ayckbourn were trying to compress the whole *oeuvre* into a single play; he would have been better advised to have adapted a single one of the books. Some of Ayckbourn's original touches, such as the wealthy romantic rival Cyrus Budge III (Jr.), are simply silly.

However, given the premise of inserting the characters in a musical comedy format, one may say *By Jeeves* succeeds, in the same way as does *Jeeves and Wooster*. Considerable change has been involved to adjust it for a unique format, different from the stories, although *By Jeeves* had a greater distance to go in shifting it to musical mode.

Andrew Lloyd Webber's music was disappointing, and the songs only partially melded with the show, failing to ideally match the mood. The title song is vaguely memorable, and only one other romantic melody, "Half a Moment," conveys any real feeling. Some songs, such as the tiresome "Travel Hopefully," seem interminable. However, even for missing the wit of the source, the play captured enough of the humorous ideas of the original to be a diverting, entertaining, and amusing show.

By Jeeves had a long history. In the early 1970s, Wodehouse and Guy Bolton had agreed to collaborate for producer Frank Loesser on a Bertie and Jeeves stage musical in the Princess Theater style, working with Robert Wright and George Forrest. It was to be titled *Betting on Bertie*, and evolved from ideas Bolton and Wodehouse had in 1954 for *Come On, Jeeves*, which had, however, not included Bertie.

In 1974, while plans for production were underway, but before the book was completed, Lloyd Webber and Ayckbourn made Wodehouse a lucrative offer to do their own play. When their production premiered in London as *Jeeves*, it was a three-hour disaster starring David Hemmings as Bertie. It was quickly shelved until Lloyd Webber finally convinced Ayckbourn to write a much more compressed book in the Princess Theater tradition. More than three-fourths of the music was rewritten. In addition to the book and lyrics, this time Ayckbourn directed as well. The result was a small-scale musical, unlike much of Lloyd Webber's other work, with an increased comedic component. For its part, *Betting on Bertie*, stalled by the deaths of Wodehouse, Bolton, and Loesser, did not premiere until after *By Jeeves* had ultimately proven successful.

Analyzing Wodehouse adaptations to the screen involves much more than merely calculating fidelity to the text. Equally important is the flavor of Wodehouse's world and its timeless frivolity. Carefree, whimsical, but essentially harmless characters are set in the period of supposed innocence before the Depression and World War II. All of this means that a Wodehouse adaptation requires not only a skilled scriptwriter to convey Wodehouse prose and narrative in screenplay form; the director and actors must also understand and be able to inhabit this seemingly flimsy and farcical brand of levity.

Hence, fidelity to the spirit and characterizations can preserve the Wodehouse flavor, even when the adaptation has rearranged or originated the plot. This was achieved in the first few seasons of *Jeeves and Wooster*, before Clive Exton replaced the interweaving of diverse Wodehouse plot strands with his own inventions. The 1936 movie of *Piccadilly Jim* essentially overlaid its own plot on Wodehouse incidents and characters. It used the novel's back story of the marriage of Eugenia and the elder Crocker, while recreating a fresh main romance in the Wodehouse style. The characters were largely preserved as they were in the novel. Such actors as Robert Montgomery, Frank Morgan, Eric Blore, Billie Burke, Cora Witherspoon, and Grant Mitchell perfectly incarnated the people Wodehouse had created, eliciting abundant humor as they did so. Together, this blend resulted in a moderately successful Wodehouse screen rendering.

The plot of the Wodehouse original is actually less essential than the mood, setting, and characterization, as was proven in the 2004 remake of *Piccadilly Jim*. Following scriptwriter Julian Fellowes's Academy Award for *Gosford Park* (2001), and its commercial success with a recreation of 1930s Britain, he was able to initiate the third film version of *Piccadilly Jim*. In itself, this was no small achievement, for the last Wodehouse movie on the English big screen had been *The Girl on the Boat* 40 years earlier. Fellowes penned a faithful adaptation, although one that lacked the wit of such Wodehouse teleplay writers as Exton or David Climie. Nonetheless, it would have been an adequate framework in the hands of Simon Langton or the other directors of *Jeeves and Wooster*.

The *Piccadilly Jim* that finally emerged from Fellowes's screenplay was an interpretation deeply at odds with Wodehouse humor, the result of the selection of a director, John McKay, who was mismatched with the story. Unlike Robert Altman's direction of *Gosford Park*, McKay found the concept of a period setting distracting and labored to undercut it in every way. McKay sought to avoid the world of Wodehouse television adaptations and their country-house weekends. In its stead, he sought to make an equivalence between the 1930s, the 1960s, and the world of 2004, asserting that they were all one and the same, and that Wodehouse, of all authors, could be made funky.

McKay was determined to find a way of doing Wodehouse that belonged firmly in 2004, rather than in the tone of "thirties comedy":

> I'd never really read Wodehouse before coming on board. In actual fact, as a Scot, I had a sort of inbuilt prejudice about him: in complete ignorance of anything he's ever written, I believed that he was some English toff who wrote silly stories about guys in plus-fours. Then I read the script of *Piccadilly Jim*, which is about a playboy, a bad boy: Jim is like the Liam Gallagher of the thirties! And I thought, "There's more to this!" So I began to read the original stories themselves and found that, actually, Wodehouse has been completely misrepresented and misserved, particularly by telly representations of his stuff that have tended to focus on a rather silly, "hooray Henry" side of some of his characters.
>
> He's actually completely anarchic and wild and tends to be taking the mickey out of posh English people as much as he is populating the world with them. *Piccadilly Jim* is a great story for that, because it's actually all about Americans: it's about this bad-boy American playboy in England, abhorring the English aristocracy, into which his stepmum is trying to buy her way. So stepmum Eugenia would like to be posh and high-toned and well-behaved, but Jim goes out drinking every night and spoils things for her.[8]

McKay noted, "I think P.G. Wodehouse inhabits a parallel universe to the period he is writing about, so we should find a parallel universe to suit this *Piccadilly Jim*. We thus decided we would make up our own 'thirties.'"[9] Every bit of decor looks less like the ostensible 1930s setting than one of the decade's science fiction visions of the world as it would shortly become. The designs attempt to evoke the satires of the sterile stylization of modernism in films by Jacques Tati or Stanley Kubrick. However, McKay has no real vision of his own; instead *Piccadilly Jim* is chock-a-block modern with anachronisms and absurd inventions. McKay's defiantly iconoclastic visuals are incongruous, their lack of internal coherence constantly preventing the viewer from becoming immersed in the world of the story. Equally at odds with any narrative unity is the singing of modern songs and the presence of twenty-first century retro automobiles.

The costumes and makeup are particularly outlandish, especially unbelievable coiffures that spike, thrust, or droop to one side. As McKay elucidated,

> In the movie, you will see that we often have original thirties things like an item of clothing next to a seventies thing, so a character will have a thirties top next to a pair of seventies trousers, and perhaps have a hat or a hairstyle or something which is completely reviving either of those times. There is a kind of time-tunnel going on in the style of the movie, because I wanted to make a strongly styled film in the way that P.G. Wodehouse wrote such strongly styled humorous prose.[10]

The actors dress in alternating degrees of outrageousness, especially the

Frances O'Connor as Ann Chester with Sam Rockwell in the title role of *Piccadilly Jim* (2005).

two sisters. The romantic leads vary scene by scene from Jim in an enormous fur coat and scarf, to Ann in modern boots, to Jim and Ann in contemporary nightclub dress with resonances to 1970s disco.

Some of this approach may have been the result of the modest $15 million budget.[11] Such exteriors as a ship at night ineptly try to conceal their inadequacy. The Mission Pictures production included nearly a month of shooting on the Isle of Man, which partially funded the film.[12]

McKay's determination to impose a chic ultramodernism on a period and genre deeply resistant to it are evident from the animated opening credits. Set to a jazzy ballad about the uncertainty of distinguishing between love and lust, the evocation is clearly of 1960s swinging, "mod" London, of Beatles and flower children. In McKay's words, "I also felt it should be disrespectful and groovy in a way that the comedies of that period — and, in fact, even P. G. Wodehouse — were quite groovy to the young people at the time."[13] Appropriately, Wodehouse receives the smallest screen lettering credit possible, in a film that has established its contradictory stance even before the first narrative frame.

Probably not since Arthur Greville Collins helmed *Thank You, Jeeves* in 1936 has a director so mangled Wodehouse, bungling or simply eliminating most of the humor. Wodehouse requires a deft sense of lightness, but McKay overwhelms the viewer by overstating and pounding home the gags in a way only appropriate for a modern comedian. He is deaf to the need for subtlety in achieving humor, so key to the Wodehouse method.

In attempting to modernize Wodehouse, McKay lacks any conception of what has made the author successful. The opening of butler Bayliss getting the morning paper ends with a surreal view of an automobile perched atop a wooded area. The next sequence provides a sharp comparison of the divergent approach between the *Piccadilly Jim* of 1936 and 2004. In the former, Bayliss wakens Jim from a late night to discover he is asleep with his feet on the pillow where his head ought to be. Such a tasteful indicator of insouciance from the 1930s is beyond the sensibility of 2004; in this version Bayliss finds Jim in bed with three scantily clad floozies. Nothing could have been farther from the harmless spirit of Wodehouse, even when he portrays marital mores and infidelity in such theatrical adaptations as *Candle-Light*.

The Piccadilly Jim of 2004 is a true wastrel, a womanizer, brawler, and drunkard who is deeply unsympathetic. Robert Montgomery, the Piccadilly Jim of 1936, might have played such a character in a likeable manner, but instead of the classical Hollywood stars who could so perfectly embody Wodehouse characters, 2004 offers the modern Sam Rockwell. His performance lacks charm or charisma; he plays the role as standard issue "bad boy."

Of course, according to contemporary romantic formula, this must be the secret wish of Ann, whose characterization is altered substantially. Instead of Nesta writing thrillers, as in the novel, it is Ann who composes them, incorporating criminal brutality that reflects her own volatile, slightly disturbed nature. Jim compares her speech to that of Sam Spade, and her devotion to murder is portrayed as the direct result of Jim's scathing review of the book of her poetry. Yet her first impression upon meeting Jim (she does not know his true identity until the end) is that he is too much of a "Mr. Nice Guy," lacking the dangerous edge for which she yearns. Frances O'Connor plays much of the role in varying tones of hysteria, and frequent, rather obvious dubbing reveal an actress having understandable difficulty with her role. While the audience cares more for the individual she etches than for Rockwell's Jim, her bitter, disillusioned demeanor, engendering her own unhappiness, renders her portrayal all the more incompatible with comedy.[14]

McKay elaborated on his conception of this plot.

> The romance of Jim and Ann is the romance of two people who are perfectly suited to each other but just can't quite get it together. There's always some very silly thing that is keeping them apart or making them angry with each other. Jim is a supremely cool, fast-talking, badly behaved, very sort of sexually hot guy.

And Ann is his equivalent: she punches his weight, she's a very capable, feisty, spunky take-no-prisoners, liberated kind of woman. In actual fact, she is a hard boiled crime writer and she can give Jim as good as he can. But the thing is that she is the one girl in the world that he can't have.

Ann has already decided that she hates Piccadilly Jim purely on the basis of his reputation, so Jim has a hard time pursuing her because he can never admit who he is. In fact, he has to pretend to be someone else entirely: he pretends to be a kind of not-drinking, not-gambling, not-smoking, not-doing-anything-naughty kind of guy. and in the end Ann wonders if really she should be attracted to him because he's so not her kind of guy: if only he was a drinking, smoking, gambling, chasing-women kind of guy!

So it's at that point that the ultimate complication happens, where she finds out that this not-Jim actually resembles Piccadilly Jim. Then she gets Jim to pretend to be Jim to help her kidnap her nephew Ogden, so Jim has to learn whole new ways of becoming himself.[15]

While the two leads are badly conceived, some of the support is strong, with an ensemble that occasionally matches the players who had graced the 1936 version. As McKay noted, "Directing *Piccadilly Jim* was a little bit like being a cattle man on a ranch, because Julian Fellowes has adapted a novel that is full of characters. There's no such thing as a minor character in a P. G. Wodehouse story: everyone somehow winds up being a main character, because they're all very funny and they all have their little bit to do."[16] Best is Tom Wilkinson as the elder Crocker, yet his scenes with Rockwell make the latter's miscasting all the more evident. Austin Pendleton as Peter Pett, and Alison Janney and Brenda Blethyn as the rival sisters, also fit their roles, although the women are not as intimidating as Wodehouse imagined.[17] Geoffrey Palmer could be perfect as Bayliss, were he given the material. By contrast, Hugh Bonneville portrays Lord Wisbeach in a bad parody of a World War II espionage movie, and Pam Ferris plays a strangely androgynous detective Trimble, as if in drag.

Most missed is Tommy Bupp, who won every ounce of humor from his interpretation of the smug child Ogden. Again, in 2004, a crucial misstep is made, introducing Rupert Simonian as Ogden, drinking as well as smoking, and leaving out the addiction to sweets with which Wodehouse had so perfectly etched this ultimate "spoiled brat."

The greatest error is in eliminating the sincerity of the remorse Jim must feel. In the novel, love changes him, and only later does Jim realize why Ann hates the man she never met: he penned a vicious review of her book of poetry. The Wodehouse style conveys this idea, as he wrote in the words of Jim to Ann in the novel:

"Be reasonable! Don't you admit the possibility of reformation? Take your own case! Five years ago you were a minor poetess. Now you are an amateur kidnapper — a bright, lovable girl, at whose approach people lock up their children and sit on the key. As for me, five years ago I was a heartless brute. Now I am a sober, serious business man, specially called in by your uncle to help jack up his tottering firm. Why not bury the dead past? Besides—I don't want to praise myself, I just want to call your attention to it—think what I have done for you! You admitted yourself that it was my influence that had revolutionized your character. But for me, you would now be doing worse than write poetry. You would be writing *vers libre*. I saved you from that, and you spurn me!"[18]

This theme was retained, according to surviving plot synopses, in the original, now-lost, faithful 1919 movie of *Piccadilly Jim*, with Owen Moore in the title role. The 1936 film of *Piccadilly Jim* had Jim pen cartoon parodies of the Pett family in retribution for their condescending treatment of his father, before Jim knew Ann was their relative. The 2004 version makes an alteration that ruins the credibility of Jim's transformation. The columns under the byline "Piccadilly Jim" were penned by a ghost writer, meaning that Jim never did actually wrong Ann. To compensate, he need do no more than punch the real writer in the nose. Without the need for contrition, Rockwell etches a Jim incapable of remorse, rendering the central conflict meaningless. All that remains is a playboy who has found an equally wild girl.

As one reviewer noted, "It's hard to ruin Wodehouse, but somehow, this film just about manages it."[19] McKay's production design lacks discipline and focus, and so does his approach to film comedy, which requires consistency and as much care in build-up and timing as Wodehouse lavished on his own prose.[20] Unable to choose between pure farce or earnest romance, McKay achieves only confusion.[21]

Piccadilly Jim is a doubtful indicator of the future of Wodehouse on screen. It is too much an experiment, and a failed one, at transferring Wodehouse into the mores of the modern cinema. This had never been done before, since Wodehouse clearly belonged to the classical era of stage and screen comedy. Ironically, Wodehouse theater adaptations, which might be open to such treatment, and formed the backbone of the author's screen adaptations through the 1950s, subsequently have been all but forgotten by audiences and producers looking solely to his stories and novels.

When Hollywood turned toward the younger audience in the 1950s and began including themes that would have been censored only a few years earlier, Wodehouse conveniently shifted from movie to television screens. And there, for the most part, it has remained, in whatever country. Comparison of the 2004 with the 1936 version of *Piccadilly Jim* provides a clear line of demarcation with the classic era of Wodehouse on screen. That movie's approach to the author was in line with previous and subsequent adaptations of Wodehouse prose and plays, right through the era of television. If Wodehouse on the twenty-first century movie screen requires characters who need to be introduced in bed with three women, there is indeed little place for this writer in theatrical feature films. Behavior from Wodehouse's time is not the same as the present, and having Ann arrange for assignations with Jim, or making him give a goodbye kiss to Bayliss, masquerading as his father, only seem crass.

Perhaps television is the best home for Wodehouse, where he need only appeal to narrower, more literary audiences, comfortable with the flavor of another, more distant time. There, the promise that was already beginning to be fulfilled during Wodehouse's lifetime has arrived at its maturity. Anthology episodes (*Wodehouse Playhouse*), television features (*Heavy Weather*), miniseries (*Jeeves and Wooster*), and recordings of stage performances (*By Jeeves*), have all proven ideal forms in which to relate his stories—and all are almost classic renderings in their respective mediums. The same, too, may be said of the radio series *What Ho, Jeeves*. As a result, the productions of Wodehouse are improving over the years, thanks to the range of forms now available. Whatever the commercial success or failure of *Piccadilly Jim*, the writing of P. G. Wodehouse has proven its durability, not only as literature, but as source material for stage, radio, movies, and television. After 90 years, the saga of Wodehouse on the screen continues apace.

Conclusion

The stage was a force in P. G. Wodehouse's writing throughout his career, as he sought to write material that could be adapted for the theater, or recycled his writing from it. Similarly, the desire to gain magazine publication was an editorial constant up until 1950, for two-thirds of his composing life.

By contrast, Wodehouse never wrote with the intention of seeing a work brought to the screen. During his first month as a screenwriter in Hollywood, he remarked that he would prefer to compose originals for the screen rather than adapt his existing stories. Many of his subsequent Hollywood satires, and other stories, novels, and plays, he probably deemed unfilmable; *The Old Reliable* used an unsold theatrical plot. Moreover, his styles of narration and dialogue were inherently literary, or best transformable to the medium of a radio play. As a result, the fact that his writing has been so readily recreated on the screen is all the more impressive.

At the time his work first appeared on film, in 1915, through the time of his script writing in the 1930s, Wodehouse was a name known to audiences for his creations for the stage, and his prolific serials, short stories, and humorous essays that appeared simultaneously in magazines and newspapers. His novels were only one facet of his reputation, and yet today, when it is through such volumes reprinted and found on bookstore shelves, he remains just as strong a presence on the screen. However, while at one time it was Hollywood that was most prolific in its output of Wodehouse adaptations, since the 1960s the American film industry has yielded that position to England and other countries.

With the coming of sound films, screenwriting offered Wodehouse a fresh challenge, especially since his stage sideline was declining since its height in the Princess Theater days. He approached the studio system fully cognizant of its perils; he wrote "Slaves of Hollywood" even before he went under contract to author scripts and experienced the very difficulties for the author that he had already chronicled. His persistence in returning to Hollywood despite discouragement gave him the rare privilege of adapting one of his own novels into a major film, *A Damsel in Distress*. Even as he did so, during the time of his second residence three adaptations by others were released, the fair *Piccadilly Jim* and the wretched *Thank You, Jeeves* and *Step Lively, Jeeves*— none of which owed much of their plot to his stories.

From his own time in Hollywood, Wodehouse gained profound inspiration, precisely because he was so frustrated at the studios. His stories reflecting these experiences are some of the most clever and intricate Hollywood satires ever written. Over more than 40 years, through articles, short stories and novels, Wodehouse created an amazing fictional map of producers, actors, and the studio system.

The record of filmmaking derived from Wodehouse demonstrates the various possibilities, whether shorts or feature films of the silent era, sound comedy, or television specials and series. The adaptations reflect the influence of his theatrical career, and in his prose Wodehouse may have also derived some previously unacknowledged ideas from his screenwriting and the cinematic adaptations by others. Television, more than the movies, has proved most suitable as a means of bringing Wodehouse to the screen, with its success best judged by its ability to keep his name before new generations who discover his writing through the small screen.

Moreover, in all but the poorest adaptations, and in all his own writings about Hollywood, Wodehouse succeeded in the greatest aim. He made us laugh.

Appendix 1

Wodehouse's Stories and Articles About Hollywood

"Came the Dawn," published in the United States in *Liberty* (June 11, 1927) and in England in *Strand Magazine* (July 1927); first anthologized in *Meet Mr. Mulliner* in England (London: Herbert Jenkins, September 27, 1927) and the United States (Garden City: Doubleday, Doran, March 2, 1928).

"Slaves of Hollywood," published in the *Saturday Evening Post* (December 7, 1929); first anthologized in modified form as "The Hollywood Scandal" in *Louder and Funnier* in England (London: Faber and Faber, March 10, 1932); also published as "The Girl in the Pink Bathing Suit" in the United States in *America, I Like You* (New York: Simon and Schuster, May 3, 1956) and in England in *Over Seventy* (London: Herbert Jenkins, October 3, 1957).

"Wodehouse Explains," Letter in *Los Angeles Times*, June 20, 1931, p. A4.

"Monkey Business," published in England in *Strand Magazine* (December 1932) and in the United States as "A Cagey Gorilla" in *American Magazine* (December 1932); first anthologized as "Monkey Business" in England in *Blandings Castle and Elsewhere* (London: Herbert Jenkins, April 12, 1935) and in the United States in *Blandings Castle* (Garden City: Doubleday, Doran, September 20, 1935).

"A Star Is Born," published in *American Magazine* (January 1933), retitled "Rise of Minna Nordstrom" in England in *Strand Magazine* (April 1933); first anthologized as "Rise of Minna Nordstrom" in England in *Blandings Castle and Elsewhere* (London: Herbert Jenkins, April 12, 1935) and in the United States in *Blandings Castle* (Garden City: Doubleday, Doran, September 20, 1935).

"Love on a Diet," published in *American Magazine* (February 1933) and in England as "The Juice of an Orange" in *Strand Magazine* (February 1933); first anthologized as "The Juice of an Orange" in England in *Blandings Castle and Elsewhere* (London: Herbert Jenkins, April 12, 1935) and in the United States in *Blandings Castle* (Garden City: Doubleday, Doran, September 20, 1935).

"The Nodder," published in England in *Strand Magazine* (January 1933) and in the United States as "Love Birds" in *American Magazine* (January 1933); first anthologized as "The Nodder" in England in *Blandings Castle and Elsewhere* (London: Herbert Jenkins, April 12, 1935) and in the United States in *Blandings Castle* (Garden City: Doubleday, Doran, September 20, 1935).

"The Castaways," published in England in *Strand Magazine* (June 1933); first anthologized as "The Castaways" in England in *Blandings Castle and Elsewhere* (London: Herbert Jenkins, April 12, 1935) and in the United States in *Blandings Castle* (Garden City: Doubleday, Doran, September 20, 1935).

The Luck of the Bodkins, serialized in England in *The Passing Show* (September 21, to November 23, 1935) and in rewritten form in the United States in *Red Book* (August 1935 to January 1936); published in these respective versions in book form in England (London: Herbert Jenkins, October 11, 1935) and in the United States (Boston: Little, Brown, January 3, 1936).

Laughing Gas, serialized in the United States in *This Week* (March 24, to April 28, 1935) and England in *Pearson's Magazine* (August to October 1935); published in book form in England (London: Herbert Jenkins, September 25, 1936) and England (Garden City: Doubleday Doran, November 19, 1936).

Review of "The Good Earth," sent by wire around the nation, appearing in the *Los Angeles Times,* February 21, 1937, p. III.4.

Phipps to the Rescue, serialized in the United States in *Collier's* (June 24, to July 22, 1950); published in book form in England as *The Old Reliable* (London: Herbert Jenkins, April 18, 1951) and the United States (Garden City: Doubleday, October 11, 1951).

Portions of chapters 2 and 3 of *Performing Flea* (London: Herbert Jenkins, October 9, 1953), retitled *Author! Author!* in the United States (New York: Simon and Schuster, June 20, 1962).

Chapter 17 of *Bring On the Girls,* by P. G. Wodehouse and Guy Bolton, published in the United States (New York: Simon and Schuster, October 5, 1953) and England (London: Herbert Jenkins, May 21, 1954).

Chapter 16, "Television," published in England in *Over Seventy* (London: Herbert Jenkins, October 3, 1957).

Pearls, Girls, and Monty Bodkin, published in England (London: Barrie and Jenkins, October 12, 1972); published in the United States as *The Plot That Thickened* (New York: Simon and Schuster, August 6, 1973).

Bachelors Anonymous, published in England (London: Barrie and Jenkins, October 15, 1973) and the United States (New York: Simon and Schuster, August 28, 1974).

"Preface," in *A Damsel in Distress* (New York: Ballantine Books, 1975).

Appendix 2

Motion Picture and Television Filmography

Note: All source material is solely by Wodehouse unless otherwise noted.

A Gentleman of Leisure (1915, U.S.)

Produced by Jesse L. Lasky Feature Play Co. Release: March 1, 1915, Paramount Pictures Corp. Copyright: Jesse L. Lasky Feature Play Co., March 2, 1915; LU4581. Length: 5 reels. Format: Silent, black and white; theatrical feature film.

Based on the play *A Gentleman of Leisure* by John Stapleton and P. G. Wodehouse, first produced in New York (The Playhouse, August 24, 1911), and as *A Thief for a Night* in Chicago (McVicker's Theater, March 30, 1913); from the novel *The Intrusion of Jimmy* by P. G. Wodehouse, serialized in magazine form in England in *Tit Bits* (ending September 3, 1910) and the United States in *Evening World* (beginning October 1914); published in book form in the United States (New York: W.J. Watt, May 11, 1910) and England as *A Gentleman of Leisure* (London: Alston Rivers Ltd., November 15, 1910).

Presenter, Jesse L. Lasky; supervisor, Cecil B. DeMille; director, George Melford; scenario, William C. DeMille; camera, Walter Stradling.

Cast: Wallace Eddinger (Robert Edgar Willoughby Pitt), Sydney Deane (Sir Thomas Blunt), Gertrude Kellar (Lady Julia Blunt), Tom Forman (Sir Spencer Dreever), Carol Hollaway (Molly Creedon), Frederick Montague (Big Phil Creedon), Billy Elmer (Spike Mullins), Frederick Vroom (Macklin, Pitt's friend), Francis Tyler (Willett, Pitt's friend), Monroe Salisbury (Stutten, Pitt's friend), Mr. Machin (Fuller, Pitt's friend), Florence Dagmar (Kate), Larry Peyton (Ole Larsen), Robert Dunbar (Jeweler), Lucien Littlefield (Clerk).

Citations: *Motography*, March 13, 1915, p. 426; *Motion Picture News*, February 27, 1915, p. 51; *Moving Picture World*, February 20, 1915, p. 1155; March 13, 1915, p. 1619; March 20, 1915, p. 1840; *New York Dramatic Mirror*, March 10, 1915, p. 33; October 28, 1916, p. 42; *Variety*, March 5, 1915, p. 21.

Rule Sixty-Three (1915, U.S.)

Produced by Essanay. Release: August 28, 1915, Essanay. Length: 2 reels. Format: Silent, black and white; theatrical short film.

Based on a story by P. G. Wodehouse.

Cast: Bryant Washburn, Jean Moyer, Hugh E. Thompson, Leota Lorraine, Royal Douglas, Charlotte Mineau.

Citation: *Moving Picture World*, September 11, 1915, p. 1833.

Uneasy Money (1918, U.S.)

Produced by Essanay Film Mfg. Co. and Perfection Pictures. Release: January 1, 1918, George Kleine System; Film Booking Office. Copyright: Essanay Film Mfg. Co., December 8, 1917; LP11835. Length: 5–6 reels. Format: Silent, black and white; theatrical feature film.

Based on *Uneasy Money*, serialized in the United States in *Saturday Evening Post* (December 4, 1916 to January 15, 1917) and in England in *Strand Magazine* (December 1916 to June 1917); published in book form in the United States (New York: D. Appleton, March 17, 1916) and in abridged book form in England (London: Methuen, October 4, 1917).

Presenter, George K. Spoor; director, Lawrence C. Windom; scenarist, Raymond E. Dakin; camera, Arthur E. Reeves.

Cast: Taylor Holmes (Lord Dawlish), Virginia Valli (Elizabeth Nutcombe), Arthur W. Bates (Nutty Nutcombe), Charles Gardner (Ira Nutcombe), Virginia Bowker (Lady Wetherby), Fred Tiden (Lord Wetherby), Lillian Drew (Claire Edmont), James F. Fulton (Mr. Pickering), Rod La Rocque (Johnny Gates).

Citations: *Exhibitor's Trade Review*, December 29, 1917, p. 372; *Motography*, December 29, 1917, p. 1349; *Motion Picture News*, December 29, 1917, p. 4582; *Moving Picture World*, December 29, 1917, p. 1955; *New York Dramatic Mirror*, December 8, 1917, back cover; December 22, 1917, p. 33; *Pictures and Picturegoer*, November 1, 1919, p. 524; *Wid's*, February 7, 1918, pp. 931–32.

Making Good with Mother (1919, U.S.)

Inspired by the "Reggie Pepper" stories.

Director, Lawrence C. Windom.

Cast: Lawrence Grossmith (Reggie Pepper), Charles Coleman (Jeeves).

Cutting Out Venus (1919, U.S.)

Inspired by the "Reggie Pepper" stories.

Director, Lawrence C. Windom.

Cast: Lawrence Grossmith (Reggie Pepper), Charles Coleman (Jeeves).

Oh, Boy! (1919, U.S.)

Produced by Albert Capellani Productions, Inc. Release: June 22, 1919, Pathé Exchange, Inc. Copyright: Pathé Exchange, Inc., June 19, 1919; LU13850. Length: 6 reels. Format: Silent, black and white; theatrical feature film.

Based on the musical comedy play *Oh, Boy!*, book and lyrics by P. G. Wodehouse and Guy Bolton, music by Jerome Kern, first produced in the United States (New York, Princess Theater, February 20, 1917), and retitled *Oh, Joy!* for performance in England (London, Kingsway Theatre, January 27, 1919).

Producer, director, and scenarist, Albert Capellani; camera, Lucien Andriot.

Cast: June Caprice (Lou Ellen Carter), Creighton Hale (George Budd), Zena Keefe (Jackie Sampson), Flora Finch (Miss Penelope Budd), W.H. Thompson (Judge Daniel Carter), Grace Reals (Mrs. Carter), Joseph Conyers (Constable Simms), J.K. Murray (Dean of Richguys College), Maurice Bennett Flynn (Lefty Flynn), Albert Capellani (Orchestra Conductor), Ben Taggart, Charles Hartley.

Citations: *Exhibitor's Trade Review*, June 21, 1919, p. 219; *Motion Picture News*, June 21, 1919, p. 4221; June 28, 1919, p. 171, 226; *Moving Picture World*, June 21,

1919, p. 1829; *New York Morning Telegraph*, June 15, 1919; *Variety*, June 13, 1919, p. 49; *Wid's*, June 15, 1919, p. 13.

A Damsel in Distress (1919, U.S.)

Produced by Albert Capellani Productions, Inc. Release: October 12, 1919, Pathé Exchange, Inc. Copyright: Pathé Exchange, Inc., March 18, 1920; LU14897. Length: 5 reels. Format: Silent, black and white; theatrical feature film.

Based on *A Damsel in Distress*, serialized in the United States in *Saturday Evening Post* (May 10, to June 28, 1919); published in book form in the United States (New York: George H. Doran, October 4, 1919) and England (London: Herbert Jenkins, October 15, 1919).

Supervisor, Albert Capellani; director, George Archainbaud; assistant director, Philip Masi; camera, Lucien Tainguy; art, Henri Menessier.

Cast: June Caprice (Maud Marsh), Creighton Hale (George Bevan), William H. Thompson (John W. Marsh), Charlotte Granville (Mrs. Caroline Byng), Arthur Albro (Reggie Byng), George Trimble (Keggs), Katherine Johnson (Alice Farraday), Mark Smith (Percy Marsh).

Citations: *Exhibitor's Trade Review*, November 1, 1919, p. 1869; *Motion Picture News*, October 25, 1919, p. 3198; *New York Morning Telegraph*, October 19, 1919; *Variety*, October 17, 1919, p. 63; *Wid's*, October 19, 1919, p. 21.

The Prince and Betty (1919, U.S.)

Produced by Jesse D. Hampton Productions. Release: December 21, 1919, Pathé Exchange, Inc. Copyright: Pathé Exchange, Inc., January 2, 1920; LU14585. Length: 5 reels. Format: Silent, black and white; theatrical feature film.

Based on the novel *The Prince and Betty*, published in four different versions: in the United States in *Ainslee's* (January 1912), serialized in *Strand Magazine* (February to April 1912), and published in book form in the United States (New York: W.J. Watt, February 14, 1912) and England (London: Mills and Boon Limited, May 1, 1912).

Presenter, Jesse D. Hampton; director, Robert Thornby; scenarist, Fred Myton; camera, Harry Gerstad.

Cast: William Desmond (John Maude), Mary Thurman (Betty Keith), Anita Kay (Mrs. Jack Wheldon), George Swann (Lord Hayling), Walter Perry (President of Mervo), Wilton Taylor (Benjamin Scobell), William Devaull (Crump), Frank Lanning (The Shepherd), Boris Karloff.

Note: Contemporary reviews mistakenly spell the name of the actor playing Crump as William Levaull.

Citations: *Exhibitor's Trade Review*, December 20, 1919, p. 269; *Motion Picture News*, December 20, 1919, p. 4503, 4532; *Moving Picture World*, December 20, 1919, pp. 1010–11; *Wid's*, December 14, 1919, p. 6.

Piccadilly Jim (1919, U.S.)

Produced by Selznick Pictures Corp. Release: December 1919 to January 1920, Select Pictures Corp. Copyright: Selznick Pictures Corp., December 4, 1919; LP14521. Length: 5 reels. Format: Silent, black and white; theatrical feature film.

Based on the serial *Piccadilly Jim*, published in the United States in *Saturday Evening Post* (September 16, to November 11, 1916); in book form in the United

States (New York: Dodd, Mead, February 24, 1917) and in England (London: Herbert Jenkins Limited, May 1918).

Director, Wesley Ruggles; camera, George Peters.

Cast: Owen Moore (James Braithwaite Crocker, also known as Piccadilly Jim), Zena Keefe (Ann Chester), George Bunny (Mr. Bingley Crocker), William T. Hays (Peter Pett), Dora Mills Adams (Mrs. Peter Pett), Alfred Hickman (Lord Wisebeach), Reginald Sheffield (Ogden Pett), Harlem Tommy Murphy (Jerry), George Howard.

Note: The name of the actor playing Peter Pett is spelled William Daze in all contemporary reviews.

Citations: *Exhibitor's Trade Review*, September 6, 1919, p. 1122 (ad insert); January 13, 1920, p. 615; *Motion Picture News*, January 10, 1920, p. 611; February 21, 1920, p. 1981; *Moving Picture World*, January 10, 1920, p. 187; January 17, 1920, pp. 464–65; *Variety*, February 6, 1920, p. 53; *Wid's*, February 8, 1920, p. 8.

Stick Around (1920, U.S.)

Producer, A.J. Van Beuren. Length: 2 reels. Format: Silent, black and white; theatrical short film.

Based on the short story "Bill the Bloodhound," published in *Century* (February 1915); first anthologized in *The Man with Two Left Feet* in England (London: Methuen, March 8, 1917) and the United States (New York: A.L. Burt, February 1, 1933).

Cast: Ernest Truex.

Citation: *Variety*, September 30, 1920, p. 42.

Their Mutual Child (1920, U.S.)

Produced by American Film Co., Inc., as a Flying "A" Special. Release: December 1920, Pathé Exchange, Inc. Copyright: American Film Co., Inc., December 13, 1920; LP15907. Length: 6 reels. Format: Silent, black and white; theatrical feature film.

Based on *The White Hope* (*Munsey's Magazine*, May 1914); published in book form as *Their Mutual Child* in the United States (New York: Boni and Liveright, August 5, 1919) and as *The Coming of Bill* in England (London: Herbert Jenkins Limited, July 1, 1920).

Producer, Jesse D. Hampton; director, George L. Cox; assistant director, Sidney Algier; scenarist, Daniel F. Whitcomb; camera, George Rizard; technical director, Sidney A. Baldridge.

Cast: Margarita Fisher (Ruth Bannister), Joseph Bennett (Bailey Bannister), Margaret Campbell (Mrs. Lora Delane Porter), Nigel Barrie (Kirk Winfield), Harvey Clark (George Pennicut), Andrew Robson (John Bannister), Beverly Travers (Mamie), Pat Moore (Baby Wm. Bannister Winfield), Thomas O'Brien (Steve Dingle), William Lloyd (Hank Jardine), William Marion (Percy Shanklyn), Stanhope Wheatcroft (Basil Millbank).

Citations: *Exhibitor's Trade Review*, February 19, 1921, p. 1159; *Moving Picture World*, November 27, 1920, pp. 487–88; *Variety*, January 21, 1921, p. 40.

Oh, Lady, Lady (1920, U.S.)

Alternate titles: *Oh, Lady, Lady!*; *Oh, Lady Lady*; *Oh Lady, Lady.* Produced by Realart Pictures Corp. Release: 1920, Realart Pictures Corp. Copyright: Realart

Pictures Corp., November 2, 1920; LP15756. Length: 5 reels; 4,212 feet. Format: Silent, black and white; theatrical feature film.

Based on the musical comedy play *Oh, Lady! Lady!!*, book and lyrics by Guy Bolton and P. G. Wodehouse, first produced in New York (Princess Theatre, February 1, 1918).

Director, Major Maurice Campbell; assistant director, Walter McLeod; scenarist, Edith Kennedy; camera, H. Kinley Martin; art, Una Nixson Hopkins.

Cast: Bebe Daniels (May Barber), Harrison Ford (Hale Underwood), Walter Hiers (Willoughby Finch), Charlotte Woods (Molly Farringdon), Lillian Langdon (Mrs. Farringdon), Jack Doud (Alec Smart).

Citations: *Motion Picture Classic*, January 1921, p. 53; *Motion Picture News*, October 9, 1920, p. 2828; January 1, 1921, p. 447; *Moving Picture World*, January 1, 1921, p. 100; January 15, 1921, p. 282; *New York Times*, December 20, 1920, p. 11; *Variety*, December 24, 1920, p. 27; *Wid's*, December 26, 1920, p. 19.

A Gentleman of Leisure (1923, U.S.)

Produced by Famous Players–Lasky. Release: July 15, 1923, Paramount Pictures. Copyright: Famous Players–Lasky, July 17, 1923; LP19213. Length: 6 reels; 5,095 or 5,695 feet. Format: Silent, black and white; theatrical feature film.

Based on the play *A Gentleman of Leisure* by John Stapleton and P. G. Wodehouse, first produced in New York (The Playhouse, August 24, 1911), and as *A Thief for a Night* in Chicago (McVicker's Theater, March 30, 1913); from the novel *The Intrusion of Jimmy* by P. G. Wodehouse, serialized in magazine form in England in *Tit Bits* (ending September 3, 1910) and in the United States in *Evening World* (beginning October 1914); published in book form in the United States (New York: W.J. Watt, May 11, 1910) and in England as *A Gentleman of Leisure* (London: Alston Rivers Ltd., November 15, 1910).

Presenter, Jesse L. Lasky; director, Joseph Henabery; adaptation, Anthony Coldeway; adaptation, Jack Cunningham; photography, Faxon M. Dean.

Cast: Jack Holt (Robert Pitt), Casson Ferguson (Sir Spencer Deever), Sigrid Holmquist (Molly Creedon), Alec Francis (Sir John Blount), Adele Farrington (Lady Blount), Frank Nelson (Spike Mullen), Alfred Allen (Big Phil Creedon), Nadeen Paul (Maid), Alice Queensberry (Chorus Girl).

The Clicking of Cuthbert (1924, UK)

Series of 6 films. Produced by Stoll Pictures Productions Limited. Length: 2 reels; circa 30 minutes. Format: Silent, black and white; theatrical short film series.

Producer, Andrew P. Wilson; editor, Charles N. Sanderson.

Cast: Harry Beasley (The Caddie).

The Clicking of Cuthbert (1924)

Based on "The Unexpected Clicking of Cuthbert," published in England in *Strand Magazine* (October 1921) and in the United States as "Cuthbert Unexpectedly Clicks" in *Elk's Magazine* (June 1922); first anthologized as "The Clicking of Cuthbert" in England in *The Clicking of Cuthbert* (London: Herbert Jenkins, February 3, 1922) and in the United States in *Golf Without Tears* (New York: George H. Doran, May 28, 1924).

Cast: Peter Haddon (Cuthbert), Helena Pickard (Adeline), Moore Marriott (Vladimir Brusiloff), Peter Upcher (Raymond).

Chester Forgets Himself (1924)

Based on "Chester Forgets Himself," published in the United States in *Saturday Evening Post* (July 7, 1923); first anthologized in England in *The Heart of a Goof* (London: Herbert Jenkins, April 15, 1926) and in the United States in *Divots* (New York: George H. Doran, May 4, 1927).

Cast: Jameson Thomas (Chester Meredith), Ena Evans (Felicia Blakeney), Nelson Ramsey (Vicar), Nell Emerald (Mrs. Blackeney).

The Long Hole (1924)

Reissue title: *The Moving Hazard.* Based on "The Long Hole," published in England in *Strand Magazine* (August 1921) and the United States in *McClure's* (March 1922); first anthologized in England in *The Clicking of Cuthbert* (London: Herbert Jenkins, February 3, 1922) and in the United States in *Golf Without Tears* (New York: George H. Doran, May 28, 1924).

Cast: Charles Courtneidge (Ralph Bingham), Roger Keyes (Arthur Jakes), Moore Marriott (Grocer).

Ordeal by Golf (1924)

Based on "Ordeal by Golf," published in the United States in *Collier's* (December 6, 1919), in England as "A Kink in His Character" in *Strand Magazine* (February 1920); first anthologized in *The Clicking of Cuthbert* (London: Herbert Jenkins, February 3, 1922) and in the United States in *Golf Without Tears* (New York: George H. Doran, May 28, 1924).

Cast: Edwin Underhill (Rupert Dixon), Jean Jay (Millicent Boyd), Moore Marriott (Reverend Heeza Jones), Jack Rowell (Mitchell Holmes).

Rodney Fails to Qualify (1924)

Based on "Rodney Fails to Qualify," published in the United States in *Saturday Evening Post* (February 23, 1924) and England in *Strand Magazine* (March 1924); first anthologized in England in *The Heart of a Goof* (London: Herbert Jenkins, April 15, 1926) and in the United States in *Divots* (New York: George H. Doran, May 4, 1927).

Cast: Victor Robson (Rodney Spelvin), Lionelle Howard (William Bates), Phyllis Lytton (June Pickard), Dallas Cairns (Major Patmore).

The Magic Plus Fours (1924)

Based on "The Magic Plus Fours," published in England in *Strand Magazine* (December 1922) and in the United States as "Plus Fours" in *Red Book* (January 1923); first anthologized in England in *The Heart of a Goof* (London: Herbert Jenkins, April 15, 1926) and in the United States in *Divots* (New York: George H. Doran, May 4, 1927).

Sally (1925, U.S.)

Produced by First National Pictures. Release: March 29, 1925, First National Pictures. Copyright: First National Pictures, March 12, 1925; LP21235. Length: 9 reels; 8,636 feet. Format: Silent, black and white; theatrical feature film.

Based on the musical play *Sally*, book by Guy Bolton and Clifford Grey (based on Bolton and P. G. Wodehouse's unproduced *The Little Thing*), music by Jerome Kern, ballet music by Victor Herbert. First produced in New York (New Amsterdam Theatre, December 21, 1920) and London (Winter Garden Theatre, September 10, 1921).

Director, Alfred E. Green; assistant director, Jack Boland; scenarist, June Mathis; comedy construction, Mervyn LeRoy; editorial supervisor, June Mathis; photography, T.D. McCord; art, E.J. Shulter; editor, George McGuire.

Cast: Colleen Moore (Sally), Lloyd Hughes (Blair Farquar), Leon Errol (Duke of Checkergovinia), Dan Mason (Pops Shendorf), John T. Murray (Otis Hooper), Eva Novak (Rosie Lafferty), Ray Hallor (Jimmy Spelvin), Carlo Schipa (Sascha Commuski), Myrtle Stedman (Mrs. Ten Brock), Capt. E.H. Calvert (Richard Farquar), Louise Beaudet (Madame Julie Du Fay).

Der Goldene Schmetterling (1926, Austria /Denmark /Germany)

UK title: *The Golden Butterfly* (Stoll Pictures Productions Ltd.). US title: *The Road to Happiness.* Produced by Phoembus-Film AG (Germany) and Sascha Film (Austria). Length: 6–7 reels. Format: Silent, black and white; theatrical feature film.

Based on the short story "The Making of Mac's," published in England in *Strand Magazine* (May 1915) and in the United States as "The Romance of 'Mac's'" in *Red Book* (May 1916); first anthologized as "The Making of Mac's" in *The Man with Two Left Feet* in England (London: Methuen, March 8, 1917) and the United States (New York: A.L. Burt, February 1, 1933).

Director, Michael Curtiz; writing, Jane Bess and Adolf Lantz; original music, Willy Schmidt-Gentner; cinematography, Gustav Ucicky and Eduard von Borsody.

Cast: Lili Damita (Lilian), Nils Asther (Andy), Karl Platen (Uncle Bill, the waiter), Jack Trevor (Teddy Abernon), Curt Bois (Andre Dubois), Ferdinand Bonn, Kurt Gerron, Hermann Leffler, Julius von Szöreghy.

The Small Bachelor (1927, U.S.)

Produced by Universal Pictures. Release: November 6, 1927, Universal-Jewel. Copyright: Universal Pictures, July 12, 1927; LP24180. Length: 7 reels; 6,218 feet. Format: Silent, black and white; theatrical feature film.

Based on *The Small Bachelor* (from the musical play *Oh, Lady! Lady!*), serialized in the United States in *Liberty* (September 18, to October 30, 1926) and England in *New* (December 1926 to July 1927); published in book form in England (London: Methuen, April 28, 1927) and the United States (New York: George H. Doran, June 17, 1927).

Presenter, Carl Laemmle; director, William A. Seiter; scenarist, John Clymer; adaptation, Rex Taylor; titles, Walter Anthony; photography, Arthur Todd.

Cast: Barbara Kent (Molly Waddington), André Beranger (Finch), William Austin (Algernon Chubb), Lucien Littlefield (Mr. Waddington), Carmelita Geraghty (Eulalia), Gertrude Astor (Fanny), George Davis (Garroway), Tom Dugan (Mullelt), Vera Lewis (Mrs. Waddington), Ned Sparks (J. Hamilton Beamish).

The Cardboard Lover (1928, U.S.)

Produced by Cosmopolitan Productions. Release: August 25, 1928, Metro-Goldwyn-Mayer Distributing Corp. Copyright: Cosmopolitan Productions, August 25, 1928; LP25928. Length: 8 reels; 7,108 feet. Format: Silent, black and white; theatrical feature film.

Based on the play *Her Cardboard Lover*, by Valerie Wyngate and P. G. Wodehouse, first produced in New York (March 21, 1927) and London (Lyric Theatre, August 21, 1928), adapted from the French play *Dans sa candeur naïve* by Jacques Deval, first produced in Paris (January 13, 1926).

Director, Robert Z. Leonard; scenarist, F. Hugh Herbert; adaptation, Carey Wilson; titles, Lucille Newmark; photography, John Arnold; editor, Basil Wrangell; settings, Cedric Gibbons.

Cast: Marion Davies (Sally), Jetta Goudal (Simone), Nils Asther (André), Andres De Segurola (Himself), Tenen Holtz (Albine), Pepe Lederer (Peppy).

Citation: *Variety*, September 5, 1928, p. 14.

Oh, Kay! (1928, U.S.)

Produced by First National Pictures. Release: August 26, 1928, First National Pictures. Copyright: First National Pictures, August 17, 1928; LP25536. Length: 6–7 reels; 6,100 feet. Format: Silent, black and white; theatrical feature film.

Based on the play *Oh, Kay!*, book by Guy Bolton and P. G. Wodehouse, music by George Gershwin, lyrics by Ira Gershwin and Howard Dietz, first produced in New York (Imperial Theatre, November 8, 1926) and London (His Majesty's Theatre, September 21, 1927).

Presenter, John McCormick; director, Mervyn LeRoy; scenarist, Carey Wilson; adaptation, Elsie Janis; titles, P. G. Wodehouse; photography, Sid Hickox; editor, Paul Weatherwax.

Cast: Colleen Moore (Lady Kay Rutfield), Lawrence Gray (Jimmy Winter), Alan Hale (Jansen), Ford Sterling (Shorty McGee), Claude Gillingwater (Judge Appleton), Julanne Johnston (Constance Appleton), Claude King (The Earl of Rutfield), Edgar Norton (Lord Braggot), Percy Williams (The Butler), Fred O'Beck (Captain Hornsby).

Citation: *Play Pictorial*, issue 309.

Sally (1929, U.S.)

Produced by First National Pictures. Release: January 12, 1929, First National Pictures; New York premiere, December 23, 1929. Copyright: First National Pictures, February 11, 1930; LP1084. Length: 12 reels; 9,277 feet. Format: Vitaphone, Technicolor; theatrical feature film.

Based on the musical *Sally*, book by Guy Bolton and Clifford Grey (based on Bolton and P. G. Wodehouse's unproduced *The Little Thing*), music by Jerome Kern, ballet music by Victor Herbert. First produced in New York (New Amsterdam Theatre, December 21, 1920) and London (Winter Garden Theatre, September 10, 1921).

Director, John Francis Dillon; screenplay and dialogue, Waldemar Young; photography, Dev Jennings; photography, C. Edgar Schoenbaum; art, Jack Stone; editor, LeRoy Stone; costumes, Edward Stevenson; music, LeoForbstein; dance, Larry Ceballos.

Songs and Music: "Sally," words and music by Al Dubin, Joe Burke and Jerome Kern; "Walking off Those Balkan Blues," "After Business Hours," "All I

Want to Do, Do, Do Is Dance," "If I'm Dreaming Don't Wake Me Up Too Soon" and "What Will I Do Without You?" words and music by Al Dubin and Joe Burke; "Wild Rose," words by Clifford Grey, music by Jerome Kern; "Look for the Silver Lining," words by B. G. De Sylva, music by Jerome Kern.

Cast: Marilyn Miller (Sally), Alexander Gray (Blair Farquar), Joe E. Brown (Connie, The Grand Duke), T. Roy Barnes (Otis Hooper), Pert Kelton (Rosie, his girl friend), Ford Sterling (Pops Shendorff), Maude Turner Gordon (Mrs. Ten Brock), Nora Lane (Marcia, her daughter), E.J. Ratcliffe (John Farquar, Blair's father), Jack Duffy (The Old Roué), Albertina Rasch Ballet.

Her Cardboard Lover (1929, UK)

Release: April 1929, British Photophone. Length: 5 minutes. Format: Sound, black and white; theatrical short film.

Based on the play *Dans sa candeur naïve* by Jacques Deval, first produced in Paris (January 13, 1926), and the play *Her Cardboard Lover* by Valerie Wyngate and P. G. Wodehouse, first produced in New York (March 21, 1927) and London (Lyric Theatre, August 21, 1928).

Director, Clayton Hutton.

Cast: Tallulah Bankhead (Simone).

Those Three French Girls (1930, U.S.)

Produced by Metro-Goldwyn-Mayer Pictures. Release: October 11, 1930, Metro-Goldwyn-Mayer Pictures. Copyright: Metro-Goldwyn-Mayer Pictures, October 23, 1930; LP1670. Length: 8 reels; 6,760 feet. Format: Movietone, black and white; theatrical feature film.

Director, Harry Beaumont; adaptation, Sylvia Thalberg and Frank Butler; story, Dale Van Every, Arthur Freed; continuity, Sylvia Thalberg and Frank Butler; dialogue, P. G. Wodehouse; photography, Merritt B. Gerstad; art, Cedric Gibbons; editor, George Hively; wardrobe, René Hubert; recording engineer, Douglas Shearer; dance, Sammy Lee.

Songs and music: "You're Simply Delish" and "Six Poor Mortals," words by Arthur Freed, music by Joseph Meyer.

Cast: Fifi D'Orsay (Charmaine), Reginald Denny (Larry), Cliff Edwards (Owly), Yola D'Avril (Diane), George Grossmith (Earl of Ippleton), Edward Brophy (Yank), Peter Gawthorne (Parker).

Citations: *Empire Theatre News*, November 21, 1930; *Variety*, October 15, 1930.

Men Call It Love (1931, U.S.)

Working title: *Among the Married*. Produced by Loew's, Inc. Shooting: January 2, to January 24, 1931. Release: March 14, 1931, Metro-Goldwyn-Mayer Distributing Corp. Copyright: Metro-Goldwyn-Mayer Distributing Corp., March 16, 1931; LP2053. Length: 8 reels, 70–72 minutes. Format: Sound, black and white; theatrical feature film.

Based on the play *Among the Married* by Vincent Lawrence, first produced in New York (October 3, 1929).

Supervisor, B.P. Fineman; director, Edgar Selwyn; assistant director, Earl Taggart; dialogue continuity, Doris Anderson; photography, Harold Rosson; art,

Cedric Gibbons; editor, Frank Sullivan; wardrobe, René Hubert; recording director, Douglas Shearer; recording engineer, Fred Morgan.

Songs and Music: "I Can't Give You Anything but Love," music by Jimmy McHugh, lyrics by Dorothy Fields.

Cast: Adolphe Menjou (Tony Minot), Leila Hyams (Connie Mills), Norman Foster (Jack Mills), Mary Duncan (Helen Robinson), Hedda Hopper (Callie Brooks), Robert Emmett Keane (Joe Robinson), Harry Northrup (Brandt).

Citations: *Film Daily*, June 21, 1931, p. 10; *Hollywood Filmograph*, January 24, 1931, p. 24; *Motion Picture Herald*, January 3, 1931, p. 88; January 10, 1931, p. 55; January 24, 1931, p. 45; February 28, 1931, p. 50; *New York Times*, June 20, 1931, p. 20; *Variety*, June 23, 1931, p. 18.

Just a Gigolo (1931, U.S.)

Working title: *Dancing Partner*; *The Princess and the Dancer.* Produced by Loew's, Inc. Shooting: March 12, to late April 1931. Release: June 6, 1931, Metro-Goldwyn-Mayer Distributing Corp. Copyright: Metro-Goldwyn-Mayer Distributing Corp., June 8, 1931; LP2281. Length: 7 reels; 66–71 minutes. Format: Sound, black and white; theatrical feature film.

Source: Based on a German play by Alexander Engel and Alfred Grünwald, adapted into English by Frederic and Fanny Hatton as *Dancing Partner*, first produced in New York, August 5, 1930).

Executive producer, Irving Thalberg; supervisor, B.P. Fineman; director, Jack Conway; assistant director, John Waters; adaptation and dialogue, Hans Kraly, Richard Schayer, Claudine West; photography, Oliver T. Marsh; art director, Cedric Gibbons; film editor, Frank Sullivan; wardrobe, René Hubert; recording director, Douglas Shearer.

Cast: William Haines (Lord Robert Brummel), Irene Purcell (Roxana Hartley), C. Aubrey Smith (Lord George Hampton), Charlotte Granville (Lady Jane Hartley), Lilian Bond (Lady Agatha Carrol), Albert Conti (A French husband), Maria Alba (A French wife), Ray Milland (Freddie), Lenore Bushman (Gwenny), Gerald Fielding (Tony), Yola d'Avril (Pauline).

Note: The play *Dancing Partner* opened in Atlantic City, New Jersey, in late July 1930 before its New York engagement. Purcell and Granville reprised their stage roles in the film.

Source citations: *Chicago Daily Tribune*, June 23, 1931, p. 19; *Film Daily*, June 14, 1931, p. 16; *Hollywood Filmograph*, March 21, 1931, p. 24; April 25, 1931, p. 24; *Los Angeles Times*, June 27, 1931, p. A7; *Motion Picture Herald*, April 25, 1931, p. 36; *New York Times*, June 13, 1931, p. 20; June 14, 1931, p. X4; *Variety*, June 16, 1931, p. 34; *Washington Post*, July 12, 1931, p. A3.

The Man in Possession (1931, US)

Produced by Loew's, Inc. Shooting, mid-April to mid-May 1931. Release: 4 July 1931 Metro-Goldwyn-Mayer Distributing Corp. Copyright: Metro-Goldwyn-Mayer Distributing Corp. 1 July 1931; LP2323. Length: 9 reels; 84 minutes. Format: Sound, black & white; theatrical feature film.

Source: Based on the play *The Man in Possession* by H.M. Harwood, first produced in London (22 January 1930) and on Broadway (1 November 1930).

A Sam Wood Production; producer, Harry Rapf; director, Sam Wood; assistant director, Don Waters; adaptation, Sarah Y. Mason; additional dialogue, Sarah Y. Mason, P. G. Wodehouse; photography, Oliver T. Marsh; art, Cedric Gibbons; editor, Ben Lewis; gowns, Adrian; recording director, Douglas Shearer; recording engineer, Karl Zint.

Cast: Robert Montgomery (Raymond Dabney), Charlotte Greenwood (Clara), Irene Purcell (Crystal Wetherby), C. Aubrey Smith (Mr. Dabney), Beryl Mercer (Mrs. Dabney), Reginald Owen (Claude Dabney), Alan Mowbray (Sir Charles Cartwright), Maude Eburne (Esther), Forrester Harvey (A Bailiff), Yorke Sherwood (A Butcher), Nora Gregor.

Note: Montgomery recreated the role of Raymond for an August 12, 1935 *Lux Radio Theater* broadcast.

Citations: *Film Daily*, July 19, 1931, p. 10; September 6, 1931, p. 17; *Hollywood Filmograph*, April 25, 1931, p. 24; May 23, 1931, p. 32; *Motion Picture Herald*, January 10, 1931, p. 47; June 13, 1931, p. 31; *New York Times*, July 18, 1931, p. 16; *Picture Show*, March 5, 1932, p. 18; *Screen Stories*, December 5, 1931, pp. 3–9, 26–27; *Variety*, July 21, 1931, p. 34.

The Passionate Plumber (1932, U.S.)

Alternate Title: *Her Cardboard Lover.* Produced by Loew's, Inc. Shooting began early December 1931. Release: February 6, 1932, Metro-Goldwyn-Mayer Distributing Corp. Copyright: Metro-Goldwyn-Mayer Distributing Corp., February 8, 1932; LP2826. Length: 8 reels; 73–74 minutes. Format: Sound, black and white; theatrical feature film.

Based on the play *Her Cardboard Lover*, by Valerie Wyngate and P. G. Wodehouse, first produced in New York (March 21, 1927) and London (Lyric Theatre, August 21, 1928), adapted from the French play *Dans sa candeur naïve* by Jacques Deval, first produced in Paris (January 13, 1926).

A Buster Keaton production; director, Edward Sedgwick; assistant director, Al Shenberg; adaptation, Laurence E. Johnson; dialogue, Ralph Spence; photography, Norbert Brodine; art, Cedric Gibbons; editor, William S. Gray; recording director, Douglas Shearer.

Cast: Buster Keaton (Elmer E. Tuttle), Jimmy Durante (Julius J. McCracken), Polly Moran (Albine), Irene Purcell (Patricia Jardine), Gilbert Roland (Tony Lagorce), Mona Maris (Nina Estrados), Maude Eburne (Aunt Charlotte), Henry Armetta (Bouncer), Paul Porcasi (Paul Le Maire), Jean Del Val (Chauffeur), August Tollaire (General Bouschay), Edward Brophy (Man on Street) , Rolfe Sedan (Man at Duel).

Citations: *Film Daily*, October 19, 1931, p. 8; March 13, 1932, p. 10; *Hollywood Filmograph*, December 5, 1931, p. 12; August 7, 1931, p. 3; September 10, 1931, p. 3; September 14, 1931, p. 2; September 17, 1931, p. 3; September 21, 1931, p. 2; September 25, 1931, p. 3; September 30, 1931, p. 1; October 5, 1931, p. 3; January 13, 1932, p. 3; *Motion Picture Herald*, March 19, 1932, p. 42; *New York Times*, March 12, 1932, p. 19; *Variety*, March 15, 1932, p. 14.

Le Plombier Amoureux (1932, U.S.; French)

Produced by Metro-Goldwyn-Mayer Corp. Release by Metro-Goldwyn-Mayer Distributing Corp. Format: Sound, black and white; theatrical feature film.

Based on the play *Her Cardboard Lover*, by Valerie Wyngate and P. G. Wodehouse, first produced in New York (March 21, 1927) and London (Lyric Theatre, August 21, 1928), adapted from the French play *Dans sa candeur naïve* by Jacques Deval, first produced in Paris (January 13, 1926).

A Buster Keaton production; producer, Buster Keaton; director, Claude Autant-Lara; screenplay, Laurence E. Johnson.

Cast: Buster Keaton, Jimmy Durante, Jeannette Ferney, Polly Moran, Barbara Léonard, Irene Purcell, Maude Eburne, Jean Del Val, George Davis, Fred Perry.

Note: A French-language version of *The Passionate Plumber.*

Brother Alfred (1932, UK)

Produced by British International Pictures. Release: April 1932, Wardour Films Ltd. Length: 6,333 feet; 77 minutes. Format: Silent, black and white; theatrical feature film.

Based on the play by P.G. Wodehouse and Herbert Westbrook, first produced in London (Savoy Theatre, April 8, 1913); from the story, "Rallying Round Old George," by Wodehouse and Westbrook, published in England in *Strand Magazine* (December 1912) and as "Brother Alfred" in the United States in *Collier's* (September 27, 1913); first anthologized in *The Man with Two Left Feet* in England (London: Methuen, March 8, 1917) and the United States (New York: A.L. Burt, February 1, 1933).

Director, Henry Edwards; adaptation and scenario, Henry Edwards and Claude Guerney; cinematography, Walter Harvey and Horace Wheddon; design, David Rawnsley; editor, A.S. Bates; musical director, Idris Lewis; music, Vivian Ellis.

Cast: Gene Gerrard (George Lattaker), Molly Lamont (Stella), Bobbie Comber (Billy Marshall), Elsie Randolph (Mamie), Clifford Heatherley (Prince Sachsberg), Hal Gordon (Harold Voles), Henry Wenman (Uncle George), Hugh E. Wright (Sydney), Toni Edgar Bruce (Mrs. Vandaline), Harvey Braban (Denis Sturgis), Maurice Colbourne (Equerry), James Carew (Mr. Marshall), Blanche Adele (Pilbeam).

Citation: *Picturegoer Weekly*, August 13, 1932, p. 20.

Leave It to Me (1933, UK)

Produced by British International Pictures Ltd. Release: April 1933, Wardour Films Ltd. Length: 6,884 feet; 76 minutes. Format: Sound, black and white; theatrical feature film.

Based on the play *Leave It to Psmith* by Ian Hay and P.G. Wodehouse (London: Samuel French, August 1932), first produced in London (Shaftesbury Theatre, September 29, 1930), from the book *Leave It to Psmith* by P.G. Wodehouse, serialized in the United States in *Saturday Evening Post* (February 3, to March 17, 1923) and England in *Grand* (began June 1923); published in book form in England (London: Herbert Jenkins, November 30, 1923) and the United States (New York: George H. Doran, March 14, 1924).

Producer, John Maxwell; director, Monty Banks; scenario, Gene Gerrard, Frank Miller and Cecil Lewis.

Cast: Gene Gerrard (Sebastian Help), Olive Borden (Peavey), Molly Lamont (Eve Halliday), George K. Gee (Coots), Gus McNaughton (Baxter), Clive Currie

(Lord Emsworth), Toni Bruce (Lady Constance), Peter Godfrey (Siegfied Velour), Syd Crossley (Beach), Melville Cooper (Honorable Freddie), Wylie Watson (Client), Monty Banks.

Citations: *Film Weekly*, August 18, 1933, p. 34; *Variety*, May 2, 1933.

Summer Lightning (1933, UK)

Produced by British & Dominions. Release: May 1933, United Artists. Reissued: 1937, Equity British. Length: 7,004 feet; 78 minutes. Format: Sound, black and white; theatrical feature film.

Based on *Summer Lightning*, serialized in England in *Pall Mall* (March to August 1929) and in the United States in *Collier's* (April 6, 1929 to June 22, 1929); published in book form as *Fish Preferred* in the United States (Garden City: Doubleday, Doran, July 1, 1929) and as *Summer Lightning* in England (London: Herbert Jenkins, July 19, 1929).

Producer, Herbert Wilcox; director, Maclean Rogers; writing, Miles Malleson; cinematography, Freddie Young.

Cast: Ralph Lynn (Hugo Carmody), Winifred Shotter (Millicent Keable), Chili Bouchier (Sue Brown), Horace Hodges (Lord Emsworth), Helen Ferrers (Lady Emsworth), Esme Percy (Baxter), Miles Malleson (Beach), Gordon James (Pillbream), Joe Monkhouse (Pigman).

Citation: *Film Pictorial*, October 21, 1933, p. 19.

By Candlelight (1933, U.S.)

Produced by Universal Pictures Corp. Shooting began October 21, 1933. Release: December 18, 1933, Universal Pictures Corp. Copyright: Universal Pictures Corp., December 13, 1933; LP4328. Length: 7 reels; 68 or 70 minutes. Format: Sound, black and white; theatrical feature film.

Based on the play *Kleine Komoedie* by Siegfried Geyer and the English-language adaptation *Candle-Light* by P. G. Wodehouse (New York: Samuel French, June 8, 1934), first staged in New York (Empire Theatre, September 30, 1929).

Presenter, Carl Laemmle; producer, Carl Laemmle, Jr.; associate producer, Julius Bernheim; directors, James Whale and Robert Wyler; screenplay, Hans Kraly, Karen De Wolf, F. Hugh Herbert, and Ruth Cummings; camera, John J. Mescall; art, Charles D. Hall; editors, Ted Kent and David Berg; editing supervisor, Maurice Pivar; music score, W. Franke Harling; sound supervisor, Gilbert Kurland.

Cast: Elissa Landi (Marie), Paul Lukas (Josef), Nils Asther (Prince Alfred von Rommer), Esther Ralston (Baroness Louise von Ballin), Lawrence Grant (Count von Rischenheim), Dorothy Revier (Countess von Rischenheim), Warburton Gamble (Baron von Ballin), Lois January (Ann).

Note: More than a year after the release, the play was also adapted on a *Lux Radio Theater* broadcast of June 9, 1935, with Robert Montgomery, Irene Purcell, and Alfred Shirley in the roles of the valet, the lady, and the prince.

Citations: *Daily Variety*, December 16, 1933, p. 3; *Film Daily*, August 18, 1933, p. 4; August 19, 1933, p. 1; January 6, 1934, p. 6; *Hollywood Reporter*, September 5, 1933, p. 4; September 9, 1933, p. 3; September 25, 1933, p. 2; October 23, 1933, p. 2; December 16, 1933, p. 2; *Motion Picture Daily*, January 6, 1934, p. 4; *Motion Picture Herald*, December 23, 1933, p. 46; *New York Times*, January 6, 1934, p. 18, January 14, 1934, p. X5; *Variety*, January 9, 1934, p. 17.

Dizzy Dames (1935, U.S.)

Produced by Liberty Pictures Corp. Shooting began early January 1935 at RKO Pathé Studios. Release: May 1, 1935, Liberty Pictures Corp. Copyright: Liberty Pictures Corp., May 20, 1935; LP5560. Length: 9 reels; 65 or 73 minutes. Format: Sound, black and white; theatrical feature film.

Suggested by the short story "The Watch Dog," published in the United States in *Hampton's Magazine* (July 1910), reprinted as "A Dog-Eared Romance" (*The Home Magazine*, August 1931), and similar to "Love Me, Love My Dog," published in England by *Strand Magazine* (August 1910).

Presenter, M.H. Hoffman; director, William Nigh; screenplay, George Waggner; photography, Harry Neumann; editor, Mildred Johnston; music score, Howard Jackson; process photography, Lawrence Gray.

Songs and Music: "The Martinique," words and music by George Waggner and Louis Alter; "I Was Taken by Storm," words and music by Edward Heyman and Louis Alter; "Love Is the Thing," words and music by Harry Tobias and Neil Moret; "Let's Be Frivolous," words and music by Howard Jackson and George Waggner.

Cast: Marjorie Rambeau (Lillian Bennett), Florine McKinney (Helen Bennett), Lawrence Gray (Terry), Inez Courtney (Arlette), Berton Churchill (Dad Hackett), Fuzzy Knight (Buzz), Kitty Kelly (La Vere), Lillian Miles (Gloria), John Warburton (Rodney Stokes), Mary Forbes (Mrs. Stokes), Christine Marston (Rhumba dancer), Edward Heyman, Howard Jackson, Kosloff Dancers.

Citations: *Daily Variety*, May 29, 1935, p. 3; *Film Daily*, January 3, 1935, p. 23; May 31, 1935, p. 2; July 18, 1936, p. 7; *Hollywood Reporter*, May 29, 1935, p. 3; *Motion Picture Daily*, June 6, 1935, p. 11; *Variety*, July 22, 1936, p. 17.

Anything Goes (1936, U.S.)

Television title: *Tops Is the Limit*. Produced by Paramount Productions, Inc. Release: January 24, 1936, Paramount Productions, Inc. Copyright: Paramount Productions, Inc., January 30, 1936; LP6100. Length: 10 reels; 90 or 92 minutes. Format: Sound, black and white; theatrical feature film.

Based on the musical play *Anything Goes*, book by Guy Bolton and P. G. Wodehouse, revised by Howard Lindsay and Russel Crouse, music and lyrics by Cole Porter (New York: Samuel French, August 14, 1936), first produced in New York (Alvin Theatre, November 21, 1934) and London (Palace Theatre, June 14, 1935).

Presenter, Adolph Zukor; producer, Benjamin Glazer; director, Lewis Milestone; assistant director, Nate Watt; screenplay, Benjamin Glazer and Morrie Ryskind; photography, Karl Struss; art, Hans Dreier and Ernst Fegte; editor, Eda Warren; interior decoration, A.E. Freudeman; costume designer, Travis Banton; sound recording, Jack Goodrich and Don Johnson; special photographic effects, Farciot Edouart and Gordon Jennings; dance ensembles staged by LeRoy Prinz; production advisor, Vinton Freedley.

Songs and Music: "Anything Goes," "I Get a Kick out of You," "You're the Top" and "There'll Always Be a Lady Fair," music and lyrics by Cole Porter; "Moonburn," music by Hoagy Carmichael, lyrics by Edward Heyman; "My Heart and I," music by Frederick Hollander, lyrics by Leo Robin; "Sailor Beware," music and lyrics by Richard A. Whiting and Leo Robin; "Shanghai-dee-ho," music and lyrics by Frederick Hollander, Richard A. Whiting and Leo Robin.

Cast: Bing Crosby (Billy Crockett); Ethel Merman (Reno Sweeney); Charlie Ruggles (Rev. Dr. Moon, also known as Moonface Martin); Ida Lupino (Hope Harcourt); Grace Bradley (Bonnie Le Tour); Arthur Treacher (Sir Evelyn Oakleigh); Robert McWade (Elisha J. Whitney); Richard Carle (Bishop Dobson); Margaret Dumont (Mrs. Wentworth); Jerry Tucker (Junior); Matt Moore (Captain McPhail); Pat Collins (Executive Officer); Edward Gargan (First Detective); Matt McHugh (Second Detective); Jack Mulhall (Purser); Avalon Boys (Quartette); Harry Wilson, Bud Fine (Pug Uglies); Rolfe Sedan (Bearded Man); Billy Dooley (Ship's Photographer); George Cooper, Sam Ash, Eddie Borden (Stewards); Jane Buckingham (Dress Woman); Louise Bennett (Girl at Table); J. Gunnis Davis (Still Cameraman); Frank Baker, James Aubrey (Cameramen); Neil Fitzgerald (Sound Man); Snub Pollard (Driver of Sound Truck); Ben Erway (Plumber); Oscar Rudolph (Page Boy); Lotus Liu (Chinese Dancer); Keye Luke, Philip Ahn (Chinese Boys); Phil Tead (First Cameraman); Tammany Young (Second Cameraman); Monte Carter (Third Cameraman); Fredric Santly, Heinie Conklin, Franklin Parker (Reporters); Guy Usher (First Federal Man); Jack Adair (Second Federal Man); Monty Collins (Deck Steward); John Carradine (Ballet Master); Laura Treadwell (Middle-aged Lady); George Andre Beranger (Gaylord); G. Pat Collins (Purser); Jack Norton (Drunk).

Citations: *Daily Variety*, July 3, 1935, p. 2; January 4, 1936, p. 3; *Film Daily*, February 6, 1936, p. 9; *Hollywood Reporter*, August 24, 1935, p. 5; January 4, 1936, p. 3; *Motion Picture Daily*, January 6, 1936, p. 6; *Motion Picture Herald*, November 16, 1935, p. 52; February 22, 1936, p. 62, 64; *New York Times*, February 6, 1936, p. 23; *Variety*, February 12, 1936, p. 16.

Piccadilly Jim (1936, U.S.)

Produced by Loew's, Inc. Shooting: June 9, to July 16, 1936. Release: August 14, 1936, Loew's Inc. Copyright: Metro-Goldwyn-Mayer Corp., August 10, 1936; LP6562. Length: 10 reels; 87, 90, 95, 98 or 100 minutes. Format: Sound, black and white; theatrical feature film.

Based on *Piccadilly Jim*, serialized in the United States in *Saturday Evening Post* (September 16, to November 11, 1916); published in book form in the United States (New York: Dodd, Mead, February 24, 1917) and England (London: Herbert Jenkins Limited, May 1918).

A Robert Z. Leonard Production; producer, Harry Rapf; director, Robert Z. Leonard; assistant director, Sandy Roth; screenplay, Charles Brackett and Edwin Knopf; contributors to dialogue, Lynn Starling and Samuel Hoffenstein; photography, Joseph Ruttenberg; art, Cedric Gibbons; art director associate, Joseph Wright, Edwin B. Willis; editor, William S. Gray; wardrobe, Dolly Tree; music score, Dr. William Axt; recording director, Douglas Shearer; sound, James Brock.

Cast: Robert Montgomery (Jim Crocker, also known as Jim Bayliss), Frank Morgan (Mr. James Crocker, also known as Count Olav Osrio), Madge Evans (Ann Chester), Eric Blore (Bayliss), Billie Burke (Eugenia Willis), Robert Benchley (Bill Macon), Ralph Forbes (Lord Freddie Priory), Cora Witherspoon (Nesta Pett), Tommy Bupp (Ogden Pett), Aileen Pringle (Paducah), Grant Mitchell (Herbert Pett), E.E. Clive (Editor), Billy Bevan (Taxi Driver), Grayce Hampton (Mrs. Brede), Stanley Morner (Band Singer), Bud Flanagan (Petie McGregor), Sidney Miller (Messenger Boy), Torben Meyer (Butler).

Note: The production was "shelved" in 1935, then rescheduled for late 1935, when writers Brian Marlow and Edwin Knopf were assigned to write the script. Harlan Ware was then added to the writing staff, followed by Manny Seff, who was to polish the script with Knopf after Marlow and Ware completed their work. All writers left the project in early September 1935, with the exception of Knopf, who received credit for the screenplay with Charles Brackett.

Citations: *Daily Variety*, August 3, 1936, p. 3; *Film Daily*, August 6, 1936, p. 14; *Hollywood Reporter*, October 26, 1934, p. 3; November 3, 1934, p. 4; November 16, 1934, p. 4; August 8, 1935, p. 3; August 20, 1935, p. 1; August 27, 1935, p. 2; September 6, 1935, p. 3; June 10, 1936, p. 9; June 15, 1936, p. 15; August 3, 1936, p. 3; *Motion Picture Daily*, August 4, 1936, p. 6; *Motion Picture Herald*, July 18, 1936, p. 60; August 15, 1936, p. 59; *New York Times*, August 31, 1936, p. 19; *Variety*, September 2, 1936, p. 18.

Thank You, Jeeves! (1936, U.S.)

Alternate title: *P. G. Wodehouse's Thank You, Jeeves!*; *Thank You, Mr. Jeeves*. Produced by Twentieth Century Fox Film Corp. Shooting: July 7, to late July 1936. Release: October 23, 1936, Twentieth Century Fox Film Corp. Copyright: Twentieth Century Fox Film Corp., October 2, 1936; LP7960. Length: 6 reels; 5,135 feet; 55 or 57 minutes. Format: Sound, black and white; theatrical feature film.

Based on *Thank You, Jeeves*, serialized in England in *Strand Magazine* (August 1933 to January 1934) and the United States in *Cosmopolitan* (January to February 1934); published in book form in England (London: Herbert Jenkins, March 16, 1934) and the United States (Boston: Little, Brown, April 23, 1934).

Executive producer, Sol M. Wurtzel; director, Arthur Greville Collins; assistant director, Aaron Rosenberg; screenplay, Joseph Hoffman and Stephen Gross; contributing writers, Allen Rivkin, Edward T. Lowe and Lou Breslow; contributor to screenplay construction, Harry Sauber; photography, Barney McGill; art, Duncan Cramer; editor, Nick De Maggio; costumes, Herschel; music, Samuel Kaylin; sound, Joseph Aiken and Harry M. Leonard.

Cast: Arthur Treacher (Jeeves), Virginia Field (Marjorie Lowman), David Niven (Bertie Wooster), Lester Matthews (Elliott Manville), Colin Tapley (Tom Brock), John Graham Spacey (Jack Stone), Ernie Stanton (Mr. Snelling), Gene Reynolds (Bobby Smith), Douglas Walton (Edward McDermott), Willie Best (Drowsy), Paul McVey (Mr. Brown), Colin Kenny (Crook), Jimmie Aubrey (Cab Driver), Joe North (Butler), Dorothy Phillips (Mrs. Brown), Ed Dearing (Motor Officer).

Note: The title card in the opening credits reads: "P. G. Wodehouse's Thank You, Jeeves!" *Thank You, Jeeves!* was retitled *Thank You, Mr. Jeeves* when it was reedited for television release in 1955 as a 45-minute episode of the series *TV Hour of the Stars*, hosted by John Conte.

Citations: *Box Office*, September 19, 1936; *Daily Variety*, July 7, 1936, p. 8; September 10, 1936, p. 3; *Film Daily*, September 17, 1936, p. 8; *Hollywood Reporter*, October 18, 1935, p. 3; July 20, 1936, p. 14; September 10, 1936, p. 3; *Motion Picture Daily*, September 11, 1936, p. 4; *Motion Picture Herald*, August 8, 1936, p. 52; September 19, 1936, p. 48; *New York Times*, July 19, 1936; October 5, 1936, p. 25; *Variety*, September 23, 1936, p. 16.

Personal Property (1937, U.S.)

Working titles: *Man in Possession*; *Man in Her House*. Produced by Loew's, Inc. Shooting: January 5, to February 15, 1937. Release: March 19, 1937, Loew's Inc. Copyright: Metro-Goldwyn-Mayer Corp., May 15, 1937; LP6994. Length: 8 reels; 84–85 or 88 minutes. Format: Sound, black and white; theatrical feature film.

Based on the play *Man in Possession* by H.M. Harwood (London, January 22, 1930; Broadway, November 1, 1930).

Producer, John W. Considine, Jr.; director, W.S. Van Dyke, II; assistant director, Dolph Zimmer; screenplay, Hugh Mills and Ernest Vajda; contributor to dialogue, Harold Goldman; contributing writer, Bradbury Foote; photography, William Daniels; art, Cedric Gibbons; art director associates, Harry McAfee and Edwin B. Willis; editor, Ben Lewis; wardrobe, Dolly Tree; music score, Franz Waxman; recording director, Douglas Shearer.

Cast: Jean Harlow (Crystal Wetherby); Robert Taylor (Raymond Dabney); Reginald Owen (Claude Dabney); Una O'Connor (Clara); Henrietta Crosman (Mrs. Dabney); E.E. Clive (Mr. Dabney); Cora Witherspoon (Mrs. Burns); Marla Shelton (Catherine Burns); Forrester Harvey (Bailiff Herbert Jenkins); Lionel Braham (Lord Carstairs); Barnett Parker (Arthur Trevelyan); William Stack (Policeman); Jimmy Aubrey, Leyland Hodgson, Douglas Gordon (English Cabbies); Arthur Stuart Hull, Charles Requa (English Businessmen); Robert Cory, Herbert Evans, John Powers, Bobby Hale (English Moving Van Men); Thomas A. Braidon (English Minister); Frederick Sewell (Opera Attendant); Billy Bevan (Frank, the waiter); Tom Ricketts (Elderly Man).

Note: A remake of the 1931 film for which Wodehouse wrote additional dialogue.

Citations: *Box Office*, March 27, 1937; *Daily Variety*, March 11, 1937, p. 3; *Film Daily*, March 16, 1937, p. 12; *Hollywood Reporter*, January 5, 1937, p. 2; *Hollywood Reporter*, January 11, 1937, p. 10; *Hollywood Reporter*, January 30, 1937, p. 74; *Motion Picture Daily*, March 12, 1937, p. 2; *Motion Picture Herald*, March 6, 1937, p. 49; March 20, 1937, p. 44, 49; *New York Times*, April 16, 1937, p. 27; *Picture Show*, July 31, 1937, pp. 7–8, 10; *Variety*, April 21, 1937, p. 3.

Step Lively, Jeeves! (1937, U.S.)

Produced by Twentieth Century Fox Film Corp. Shooting: early December 1936 to early January 1937. Release: April 9, 1937, Twentieth Century Fox Film Corp. Copyright: Twentieth Century Fox Film Corp., April 9, 1937; LP7110. Length: 7 reels; 6,160 feet; 67 or 69 minutes. Format: Sound, black and white; theatrical feature film.

Inspired by the character Jeeves, created by P. G. Wodehouse.

Producer, Sol M. Wurtzel; associate producer, John Stone; director, Eugene Forde; assistant director, William Eckhardt; screenplay, Frank Fenton and Lynn Root; original story, Frances Hyland; contributor to screenplay construction, Saul Elkins; photography, Daniel Clark; art, Duncan Cramer; editor, Fred Allen; costumes, Herschel; music, Samuel Kaylin; sound, S.C. Chapman; sound, Harry M. Leonard.

Cast: Arthur Treacher (Jeeves); Patricia Ellis (Patricia Westley); Robert Kent (Gerry Townsend); Alan Dinehart (Hon. Cedric B. Cromwell); George Givot (Prince Boris Caminov); Helen Flint (Babe); John Harrington (Barney Ross);

George Cooper (Slug); Arthur Housman (Max); Max Wagner (Joey); Franklin Pangborn (Gaston); Joe Brown (Dutch); George Cowl (Inspector); Phyllis Barry (Mrs. Tremaine); Larry Dodds (Bobby); Vernon Steele (Lord Fenton); Charles Bennett (Steward); Tom Herbert (Bartender); Allen Fox, Sherry Hall, Creighton Hale, Dick French (Reporters); Frank Fanning (Cop); Frank Marlowe (Gangster); Nora Lane (Lady in Black); Edith Kingdon (Thin Woman); Betty Stokes (Stout Woman); Lloyd Whitlock, Landers Stevens, Laura Treadwell (Guests).

Citations: *Box Office*, January 23, 1937; *Daily Variety*, January 18, 1937, p. 3; *Film Daily*, April 5, 1937, p. 6; *Hollywood Reporter*, December 14, 1936, p. 11; January 4, 1937, p. 35; January 18, 1937, p. 3; *Motion Picture Daily*, January 19, 1937, p. 13; *Motion Picture Herald*, January 30, 1937, p. 50; *New York Times*, April 2, 1937, p. 19; *Variety*, April 7, 1937, p. 14

A Damsel in Distress (1937, U.S.)

Produced by RKO Radio Pictures, Inc. Shooting: July 22, to October 16, 1937. Release: November 19, 1937, RKO Radio Pictures, Inc. Copyright: RKO Radio Pictures, Inc., November 19, 1937; LP7730. Length: 11 reels; 98 or 100 minutes. Format: Sound, black and white; theatrical feature film.

Based on *A Damsel in Distress*, serialized in the United States in *Saturday Evening Post* (May 10, to June 28, 1919), published in book form in the United States (New York: George H. Doran, October 4, 1919) and England (London: Herbert Jenkins, October 15, 1919); and the play *A Damsel in Distress*, by Ian Hay and P. G. Wodehouse (London: Samuel French, April 1930), first produced in London (New Theatre, August 13, 1928).

A Pandro S. Berman production; executive producer, Samuel J. Briskin; director, George Stevens; assistant director, Argyle Nelson; screenplay, P. G. Wodehouse, Ernest Pagano and S.K. Lauren; contributing writers, P.J. Wolfson and William Burns; photography, Joseph H. August; camera, J. Roy Hunt; art, Van Nest Polglase; art director associate, Carroll Clark; editor, Henry Berman; set dresser, Darrell Silvera; wardrobe, Claire Cramer; music, Victor Baravalle; orchestral arrangement, Russell Bennett; additional arrangement, Ray Noble and George Bassman; recording, Earl A. Wollcott; sound technician, J.O. Aalberg; special effects, Vernon L. Walker; dance, Hermes Pan; production manager, J.R. Crone; unit manager, Al Rogell.

Songs and Music: "Nice Work If You Can Get It," "The Jolly Tar and the Milk Maid," "Sing of Spring," "A Foggy Day in London Town," "I Can't Be Bothered Now," "Things Are Looking Up" and "Keep a Stiff Upper Lip," music by George Gershwin, lyrics by Ira Gershwin.

Cast: Fred Astaire (Jerry Halliday); George Burns (George); Gracie Allen (Gracie); Joan Fontaine (Lady Alyce Marshmorton); Reginald Gardiner (Keggs); Ray Noble (Reggie); Constance Collier (Lady Caroline); Montagu Love (Lord John Marshmorton); Harry Watson (Albert); Jan Duggan (Miss Ruggles); Charles Bennett (Barker); Frank Benson (Attendant); Thelma Hart (Ticket Seller); Max Linder, Jack Wynn (Footmen); Mary Gordon (Maid); Violet Seaton (Alice's Maid); Ben Jacobs (Bus Driver); Mae Beatty (Landlady); William O'Brien (Chauffeur); Monte Blue, Jack Carson, Mary Dean, Joe Niemeyer, Jim Clemons, Jim Walklin, Betty Rome, Charles Daugherty, Robert Tate, Marie Marks, Angie Blue, Peggy Carroll, Cynthia Westlake, Cleo Ridgley, Fred Kelsey, John Blood, Buster Slavin, Bobbie Smith, Elsa Peterson, Starrett Ford, Charles Darwin, Major Sam Harris,

Gertrude Carr, Hans Tansler, Kathleen Ellis, Ralph Brooks, Myrta Bonillas, Eugene Beday, Eleanor Vandeveer, Clive Morgan, Leonard Mudie, Pearl Amatore, Jac George (Madrigal singers); Stand-ins for Fred Astaire, Harry Cornbleth, Harry Matthews; Stand-in for George Burns, Bruce Preston; Stand-in for Gracie Allen, Jessie Lee; Stand-ins for Joan Fontaine, Charlotte Hoag, Dorothy Panter; Stand-in for Constance Collier, Olive Hatch; Stand-in for Reginald Gardner, Ben Jacobs; Stand-in for Montagu Love, Fred Fuller; Stand-in for Ray Noble, John Dawson; Stand-in Frank Hemphill.

Note: On November 5, 1937, a one-hour radio version was presented over CBS on the weekly series *Hollywood Hotel* starring Astaire, Fontaine, and Burns and Allen. Hermes Pan won an Academy Award for his choreography on the picture's "funhouse" sequence, which was performed in the carnival setting by Astaire, Burns and Allen. Ira Gershwin's lyrics to one song, "Put Me to the Test," were dropped, but the song's music was used in one of the dance numbers. (In 1944, the lyrics were used in the Columbia film *Cover Girl*, set to music revised by Jerome Kern.) Determined that at least some of his music would be performed by proficient singers, George Gershwin composed two songs, "The Jolly Tar and the Milkmaid" and "Sing of Spring," for madrigal singers.

Citations: *Daily Variety*, November 18, 1937, p. 3; *Film Daily*, November 20, 1937, p. 7; November 22, 1937, pp. 13–17; *Hollywood Reporter*, July 26, 1937, p. 11; July 29, 1937, p. 14; August 30, 1937, p. 18; November 18, 1937, p. 3; *Motion Picture Herald*, November 27, 1937, p. 52, 54; December 11, 1937, p. 87; *Movie Story Magazine*, December 1937, pp. 34–35, 82–83; *New York Times*, November 25, 1937, p. 37; *Variety*, November 24, 1937, p. 16.

Rosalie (1937, U.S.)

Working title: *The Merry Princess.* Produced by Loew's, Inc. Shooting: August 30, to November 6, 1937. Release: December 24, 1937, Loew's Inc. Copyright: Metro-Goldwyn-Mayer Corp., December 20, 1937; LP 7706. Length: 13 reels; 122 minutes. Format: Sound, black and white; theatrical feature film.

Based on the musical *Rosalie*, book by William Anthony McGuire and Guy Bolton, music by George Gershwin and Sigmund Romberg, lyrics by P. G. Wodehouse and Ira Gershwin, first produced in New York (New Amsterdam Theatre, January 10, 1928).

A William Anthony McGuire Production; director, W.S. Van Dyke, II; assistant directors, William Scully and George Yohalem; screenplay, William Anthony McGuire; photography, Oliver T. Marsh; second camera, Leonard Smith; assistant camera, John Greer; art, Cedric Gibbons; art director associates, Joseph Wright and Edwin B. Willis; editor, Blanche Sewell; wardrobe, Dolly Tree; music, Herbert Stothart; music conductor, Georgie Stoll; music presentation, Merrill Pye; music arrangement, Roger Edens; orchestration and vocal arrangement, Leo Arnaud, Murray Cutter, Leonid Raab and Paul Marquardt; recording director, Douglas Shearer; sound, William Steinkamp and William Edmondson; music recording, Mike McLaughlin; montage effects, Slavko Vorkapich; dances and ensembles, created by Albertina Rasch; dance director for Cadet routines, Dave Gould; assistant to Dave Gould for Cadet routines, Frank Floyd; assistant dance director, George King; technical advisor, Count Andrey Tolstoy; production manager, Frank Messenger; chief electrician, Ted Wurtenberg; head grip, Pop Arnold; still photographer, William Grimes.

Songs and Music: "In the Still of the Night," "Close," "Rosalie," "Show Me the Town," "Why Should I Care?" "I've a Strange New Rhythm in My Heart," "On, Brave Old Army Team," "To Love or Not to Love," "Spring Love Is in the Air," "Who Knows," "National Anthem" and "It's All Over but the Shouting," words and music by Cole Porter.

Cast: Nelson Eddy (Dick Thorpe); Eleanor Powell (Rosalie); Frank Morgan (King); Edna May Oliver (Queen); Ray Bolger (Bill Delroy); Ilona Massey (Brenda); Billy Gilbert (Oloff); Reginald Owen (Chancellor); Tom Rutherford (Prince Paul); Clay Clement (Captain Banner); Virginia Grey (Mary Callahan); George Zucco (General Maroff); Oscar O'Shea (Mr. Callahan); Jerry Colonna (Joseph); Janet Beecher (Miss Baker); William Demarest (Army Coach); Tommy Bond (Mickey); Gene Conklin, Tudor Williams (Soloists); Joe Marks (Puck); Alexander Canepari (Town Crier); Camille Soray, Lois Clements, the Esquires Singers (singers in "Who Knows"); George Boyce, Harry Masters, Dave White (dancers in specialty number); Marie Arbuckle, Bernice Alstock, Elinor Coleson, Grace Neilson, Barbara Whitson (soloists in Vassar number); Al Shean (Herman Schmidt); Katharine Aldridge (Lady in Waiting); Singing voice double for Eleanor Powell, Marjorie Lane.

Note: Frank Morgan recreated his role from the Broadway production of the play, which was produced by Florenz Ziegfeld and starred Marilyn Miller in the title role.

Citations: *Daily Variety*, December 17, 1937, p. 3; *Film Daily*, December 15, 1937, p. 7; December 22, 1937, p. 5; *Hollywood Filmograph*, May 24, 1930, p. 24; *Hollywood Reporter*, June 17, 1937, p. 1; July 6, 1937, p. 3; August 30, 1937, p. 1; September 3, 1937, p. 8; September 19, 1937, p. 2; December 17, 1937, p. 3; December 20, 1937, p. 2; December 24, 1937, p. 7; January 5, 1938, p. 1; *International Photographer*, January 1938, pp. 24–26; *Motion Picture Daily*, December 18, 1937, p. 3; *Motion Picture Herald*, November 6, 1937, pp. 34–35; December 25, 1937, pp. 38–39; *New York Times*, November 21, 1936, p. 21; December 31, 1937, p. 9; *Variety*, February 22, 1937, p. 16.

Blixt och Dunder (1938, Sweden)

(*Thunder and Lightning*)

Produced by Svensk Filmindustri. Release: March 21, 1938. Length: 2493 meters. Format: Sound, black and white; theatrical feature film.

Based on *Summer Lightning*, serialized in England in *Pall Mall* (March to August 1929) and in the United States in *Collier's* (April 6, 1929 to June 22, 1929); published in book form as *Fish Preferred* in the United States (Garden City: Doubleday, Doran, July 1, 1929) and as *Summer Lightning* in England (London: Herbert Jenkins, July 19, 1929).

Director, Anders Henrikson; writing, Hasse Ekman.

Cast: Olof Winnerstrand (Magnus Gabriel Hägerskiöld), Nils Wahlbom (Pontus Hägerskiöld), Frida Winnerstrand (Charlotta Hägerskiöld), Åke Söderblom (Claes-Ferdinande Hägerskiöld), Marianne Aminoff (Inga), Hasse Ekman (Bertil Bendix), Sickan Carlsson (Pyret), Eric Abrahamsson (Härman), Torsten Winge (Axel Hjalmar Stencloo), Weyler Hildebrand (Charlie Blomberg), Alice Babs (Flower Girl), Julia Cæsar (Telegraph Operator), David Erikson (Driver), Emil Fjellström (Anderson).

Her Cardboard Lover (1942, U.S.)

Working titles: *Love Me Not*; *Slightly Platonic*. Produced by Metro-Goldwyn-Mayer Corp. Shooting: January 15, to March 12, additional scenes began April 13, 1942. Release: June 1942, Loew's Inc. Copyright: Loew's Inc., May 26, 1942; LP11416. Length: 9 reels; 8,348 feet; 90 or 93 minutes. Format: Sound, black and white; theatrical feature film.

Based on the play *Dans sa cadeur naïve* by Jacques Deval, first produced in Paris (January 13, 1926), and the play *Her Cardboard Lover* by Valerie Wyngate and P.G. Wodehouse, first produced in New York (March 21, 1927) and London (Lyric Theatre, August 21, 1928).

Producer, J. Walter Ruben; director, George Cukor; assistant director, Edward Woehler; screenplay, Jacques Deval, John Collier, Anthony Veiller and William H. Wright; photography, Harry Stradling and Robert Planck; exterior photography, Harold Marzorati; art, Cedric Gibbons; associate, Randall Duell; editor, Robert J. Kern; set design, Edwin B. Willis; associate, Jack Moore; gowns, Kalloch; music score, Franz Waxman; recording director, Douglas Shearer; unit manager, Arthur Rose.

Song: "I Dare You," music by Burton Lane, lyrics by Ralph Freed.

Cast: Norma Shearer (Consuelo Croyden); Robert Taylor (Terry Trindale); George Sanders (Tony Barling); Frank McHugh (Chappie Champagne); Elizabeth Patterson (Eva); Chill Wills (Judge Sam); Donald Meek (Pawnbroker); Jill Esmond (Lizzie Hartwell); Roger Moore (Simpson, Chauffeur); Bud Jamison (Doorman); Frank Elliott (Croupier); Olin Howland (Frank); Richard Crane (Page); Arthur Loft (Tom); Ottola Nesmith, Winifred Harris (Players); Alec Craig (Danny); Dudley Dickerson (Porter); Tom Herbert (Drunk); Johnnie Berkes (Waiter); Rex Evans (Night Clerk, Mr. Dolgar); Gertrude Short (Operator); Ben Carter (Elevator Boy); Dick Rich (Policeman); Fred Kelsey (House Detective); Raymond Hatton (Bailiff); Louis Mason (Clerk); Thurston Hall (Mr. Garthwaite, Tony's lawyer); Harry Hayden (Attorney for Hotel); Heinie Conklin (Drunk in Courtroom); Hobart Cavanaugh (Police Detective); Florence Shirley.

Note: The onscreen writing credit reads: "Screen Play by Jacques Deval, John Collier, Anthony Veiller and William H. Wright, based upon a play by Jacques Deval, first English Dramatization and Title by Valerie Wyngate, Later Revisions by P.G. Wodehouse."

Citations: *Box Office*, May 30, 1942; *Daily Variety*, May 26, 1942, p. 3; *Film Daily*, May 27, 1942, p. 8; *Hollywood Reporter*, December 5, 1934, p. 7; January 16, 1942, p. 14; January 30, 1935, p. 1; February 7, 1935, p. 1; March 12, 1935, p. 2; March 16, 1935, p. 1; November 6, 1941, p. 2; January 6, 1942, p. 4; January 12, 1942, p. 6; January 14, 1942, p. 9; January 16, 1942, p. 4; February 3, 1942, p. 3; March 10, 1942, p. 2; March 13, 1942, p. 10; April 14, 1942, p. 6; April 16, 1942, p. 6; May 27, 1942, p. 3; July 20, 1942, p. 3; December 28, 1942, p. 4; *Motion Picture Herald Product Digest*, May 30, 1942, p. 686; *New York Times*, July 17, 1942, p. 19; *New Yorker*, July 25, 1942; *Variety*, May 27, 1942, p. 8.

Gomorron Bill! (1945, Sweden)

(*Good Morning Bill!*). Svensk Talfilm. Length: 2239 meters. Format: Sound, black and white; theatrical feature film.

Based on the play *Good Morning Bill*, from the Hungarian of Ladislaus Fodor

(London: Methuen, 1928), first produced in London (Duke of York's Theatre, November 28, 1927), becoming the serial *The Medicine Girl*, in the United States in *Collier's* (July 4, to August 1, 1931); first published in England as the novel *Doctor Sally* (London: Methuen, April 7, 1932) and anthologized in *The Crime Wave at Blandings* in the United States (Garden City: Doubleday, Doran, June 25, 1937).

Director, Lauritz Falk, Peter Winner; writing, Torsten Lundqvist and Lars Tessing.

Cast: Lauritz Falk (Bill Bärnfelt), Gaby Stenberg (Dr. Birgit Andersson), Stig Järrel (Julle Spant), Doris Söderström (Lilly Bergström), Marianne Löfgren (Isabella), Hilda Borgström (Augusta), Olof Winnerstrand (Prof. Widman), Douglas Håge (Squire), Börje Mellvig (Receptionist), Harry Ahlin.

Till the Clouds Roll By (1947, U.S.)

Working title: *As the Clouds Roll By*. Produced by Metro-Goldwyn-Mayer Corp. Shooting: October 8, to November 8, 1945; mid-December 1945 to early January 1946; mid-March to early May 1946; retakes, May 23, 1946. Release: January 1947, Loew's Inc.; Hollywood premiere, January 16, 1947. Copyright: Loew's Inc., December 4, 1946; LP764. Length: 15 reels; 120 minutes. Format: Sound, Technicolor; theatrical feature film.

Producer, Arthur Freed; director, Richard Whorf; musical numbers staged and directed by Robert Alton; Judy Garland's numbers directed by Vincente Minnelli; assistant director, Wally Worsley; screenplay, Myles Connolly and Jean Holloway; story, Guy Bolton; adaptation, George Wells; director of photography, Harry Stradling; director of photography, George J. Folsey; art, Cedric Gibbons and Daniel B. Cathcart; editor, Albert Akst; set decoration, Edwin B. Willis; associate, Richard Pefferle; costume supervisor, Irene; costume designer, Helen Rose; men's costumes, Valles; music, Lennie Hayton; orchestration, Conrad Salinger; vocal arrangement, Kay Thompson; recording director, Douglas Shearer; special effects, Warren Newcombe; montage, Peter Ballbusch; hair styles, Sydney Guilaroff; makeup, Jack Dawn.

Songs and Music: "Cotton Blossom," "Make Believe," "Life upon the Wicked Stage," "Can't Help Lovin' Dat Man," "Ol' Man River," "Why Was I Born?" "All the Things You Are" and "The Last Time I Saw Paris," music by Jerome Kern, lyrics by Oscar Hammerstein II; "How'd You Like to Spoon with Me?" music by Jerome Kern, lyrics by Edward Laska; "They Didn't Believe Me," music by Jerome Kern, lyrics by Herbert Reynolds; "Till the Clouds Roll By" and "Leave It to Jane," music by Jerome Kern, lyrics by Guy Bolton and P. G. Wodehouse; "Cleopatterer" and "The Land Where the Good Songs Go," music by Jerome Kern, lyrics by P. G. Wodehouse; "Look for the Silver Lining," music by Jerome Kern, lyrics by B. G. De Sylva; "Sunny" and "Who," music by Jerome Kern, lyrics by Otto Harbach and Oscar Hammerstein II; "One More Dance," music by Jerome Kern, lyrics by Leonard Joy; "I Won't Dance," music by Jerome Kern, lyrics by Dorothy Fields, Oscar Hammerstein II, Otto Harbach and Jimmy McHugh; "She Didn't Say Yes," "Yesterdays" and "Smoke Gets in Your Eyes," music by Jerome Kern, lyrics by Otto Harbach; "Long Ago and Far Away," music by Jerome Kern, lyrics by Ira Gershwin; "A Fine Romance," music by Jerome Kern, lyrics by Dorothy Fields.

Cast: June Allyson (Guest Star); Lucille Bremer (Sally Hessler); Judy Garland (Marilyn Miller); Kathryn Grayson (Magnolia in Show Boat number); Van Heflin

(James I. Hessler); Lena Horne (Julie in Show Boat number); Van Johnson (Band Leader); Tony Martin (Ravenal in Show Boat number); Dinah Shore (Julia Sanderson); Frank Sinatra (specialty performer in finale); Robert Walker (Jerome Kern); Gower Champion and Cyd Charisse (dance specialties); Harry Hayden (Charles Frohman); Paul Langton (Oscar Hammerstein); Angela Lansbury (Guest Star); Paul Maxey (Victor Herbert); Ray McDonald (Guest Star); Mary Nash (Mrs. Muller); Virginia O'Brien (Ellie); Dorothy Patrick (Mrs. Jerome Kern); Caleb Peterson (Joe); Wm. Bill Phillips (Hennessey); Joan Wells (Sally, as a girl); the Wilde Twins (specialty act); Esther Williams (Movie Star); Rex Evans (Cecil Keller); Maurice Kelly (dance specialty); Ray Teal (Orchestra Conductor); Byron Foulger (Frohman's Secretary); William Halligan (Captain Andy in Show Boat number); Bruce Cowling (Steve); Johnnie Johnston (specialty performer in finale); Herschel Graham, Fred Hueston, Dick Earle, Larry Steers, Reed Howes, Hazard Newberry, Ed Biby, Lew Smith, Larry Williams, James Flato, Leonard Mellin, James Darrell, Tony Merlo, Charles Madrin, and Charles Griffin (Opening Night Critics); Lee Phelps and Ralph Dunn (Moving Men); Lucille Casey, Mary Jane French, Beryl McCutcheon, Alice Wallace, Irene Vernon, Gloria Joy Arden, Mickey Malloy, Alma Carroll, and Wesley Brent (Showgirls); George Peters, Harry Denny, Bob MacLean, Frank McClure, George Murray, John Alban, and Lee Bennett (Stage Door Johnnies); Jean Andren (Secretary); John Albright (Call Boy); Margaret Bert and Elspeth Dudgeon (Maids); Claire McDowell (Ward Woman); Herbert Heywood (Stagehand); Armand Tanny, George Bruggeman, and Rube Schaeffer (Trapeze Men); Thomas Louden (Rural Postman); Ann Codee (Miss Laroche); James Finlayson (Candy Vendor); Tom Stevenson (Genius); Lilyan Irene (Barmaid); Robert Cory, George Kirby, Bobby Hale, Tom Pilkington, and Al Duval (Barkers); Penny Parker (Punch and Judy Operator); Robert Emmet O'Connor (Clerk); Stanley Andrews (Doctor); Ernest Galon (German Spectator); Russell Hicks (Motion Picture Producer); William Forrest (Motion Picture Director); Roger Cole (Cameraman); Charles Bradstreet, Don Anderson, and Bert Moorhouse (Men in Café); Reginald Simpson (Headwaiter); Gordon Dumont (Theatrical Agent in montage); Harold Miller (Nightclub Owner in montage); Don Wayson and Howard Mitchell (Detectives in montage); Paul Gordon (Unicycle Clown); Herbert Weber and Chatita Weber (Wire Walkers); Tiny Kline (Swivel Chair Lady); Louis Manley (Fire Eater); Jim Grey and Douglas Wright (Bull Clowns); Dennis Plooster, LeRoy Hart, Loren Hicks, Richard Mather, and Eugene Dunn (Hick Family Tumbling Act); Arnaut Brothers (Bird Act); Paula Ray and Peggy Remington (Riding Doubles for Judy Garland), Grace Hanneford (Dance Double for Judy Garland), Helen McAllister.

Citations: *Box Office*, November 23, 1946; *Daily Variety*, November 12, 1946, p. 3, 13; *Film Daily*, November 12, 1946, p. 7; *Hollywood Reporter*, May 19, 1944, p. 1; March 7, 1945, p. 3; April 24, 1945, p. 2; August 30, 1945, p. 13; September 20, 1945, p. 7; October 2, 1945, p. 5; October 9, 1945, p. 3; October 17, 1945, p. 1; October 19, 1945, p. 14; November 2, 1945, p. 12; November 9, 1945, p. 7; November 12, 1945, pp. 1–2, 9; December 12, 1945, p. 11; December 21, 1945, p. 16; December 28, 1945, p. 14; January 15, 1946, p. 2; March 29, 1946, p. 22; May 3, 1946, p. 12; May 23, 1946, p. 3; July 12, 1946, p. 2; July 18, 1946, p. 1; November 26, 1946, p. 10; January 6, 1947, p. 4; *Motion Picture Herald Product Digest*, April 27, 1946, p. 2963; November 16, 1946, p. 3309; *New York Times*, December 6, 1946, p. 27; April 4, 1948; *Variety*, November 13, 1946, p. 16.

By Candlelight (1949, UK)

Produced by BBC. Length: 105 minutes. Format: Sound, black and white; television special.

Based on the play *Kleine Komoedie* by Siegfried Geyer and the English-language adaptation, *Candle-Light*, by P. G. Wodehouse (New York: Samuel French, June 8, 1934), first staged in New York (Empire Theatre, September 30, 1929).

Producer, Harold Clayton; adaptor, Harry Graham.

Cast: Robert Flemying, Clive Morton, Luise Rainer, Anthony Shaw.

The Philco Television Playhouse: Uncle Dynamite (1950, U.S.)

Produced by NBC. Original broadcast: January 29, 1950, NBC. Length: 60 minutes. Format: Sound, black and white; television anthology episode.

Based on *Uncle Dynamite*, published in England (London: Herbert Jenkins, October 22, 1948) and the United States (New York: Didier, November 29, 1948).

Cast: Arthur Treacher.

Musical Comedy Time: Anything Goes (1950, U.S.)

Produced by NBC and Procter & Gamble. Original broadcast: October 2, 1950, NBC. Length: 60 minutes. Format: Sound, black and white; television anthology episode.

Based on the musical play *Anything Goes*, book by Guy Bolton and P. G. Wodehouse, revised by Howard Lindsay and Russel Crouse, music and lyrics by Cole Porter (New York: Samuel French, August 14, 1936), first produced in New York (Alvin Theatre, November 21, 1934) and London (Palace Theatre, June 14, 1935).

Producer, director, Richard H. Berger; adapters, John Whedon and Sam Moore; Harry Sosnik orchestra.

Cast: Martha Raye (Reno Sweeney), John Conte (Harry Dane), Billy Lynnn (Public Enemy No. 13), Kathryn Mylroie, Helen Raymond, Fred Wayne, Gretchen Hauser, A.J. Herbert, Larry Haynes, and Wirlie Birch.

Citation: *Variety*, October 4, 1950.

Broadway Television Theatre: By Candlelight (1953, U.S.)

Original broadcast: February 16, 1953 (syndicated). Length: 90 minutes. Format: Sound, black and white; television anthology episode.

Based on the play *Kleine Komoedie* by Siegfried Geyer and the English-language adaptation, *Candle-Light*, by P. G. Wodehouse (New York: Samuel French, June 8, 1934), first staged in New York (Empire Theatre, September 30, 1929).

Produced by Warren Wade.

Cast: Clare Luce (Marie), Rex O'Malley (Josef), Ian Keith (Prince Rudolf).

Hollywood Opening Night: Uncle Fred Flits By (1953, U.S.)

Produced by NBC and Pearson Pharmseal. Original broadcast: March 15, 1953, NBC. Length: 30 minutes. Format: Sound, black and white; television anthology episode.

Based on "Uncle Fred Flits By," published in the United States in *Red Book*

(July 1935) and in England in *Strand Magazine* (December 1935); first anthologized in *Young Men in Spats* in England (London: Herbert Jenkins, April 3, 1936) and the United States (Garden City: Doubleday, Doran, July 24, 1936).

Producer and director, William Corrigan; associate producer, Marylyn Evans; teleplay, Montgomery Ford.

Cast: David Niven, Robert Nichols, James Lilburn, Dawn Addams, Margaret Dumont, Eric Snowden, Mollie Glessing.

Host: Jimmie Fidler.

Announcer: Jimmy Wellington.

Citation: *Variety*, March 17, 1953.

Kraft Television Theatre: Candlelight (1953, U.S.)

Produced by ABC. Original broadcast: December 31, 1953, ABC. Length: 60 minutes. Format: Sound, black and white; television anthology episode.

Based on the play *Kleine Komoedie* by Siegfried Geyer and the English-language adaptation, *Candle-Light*, by P. G. Wodehouse (New York: Samuel French, June 8, 1934), first staged in New York (Empire Theatre, September 30, 1929).

Producer and director, Fiedler Cook.

Cast: Leueen McGrath (Marie), Bramwell Fletcher (Josef), Mary Sinclair (Baroness).

The Colgate Comedy Hour—The Ethel Merman Show: Anything Goes (1954, U.S.)

Produced by NBC. Original broadcast: February 28, 1954, NBC. Length: 60 minutes. Format: Sound, black and white; television anthology episode.

Based on the musical play *Anything Goes*, book by Guy Bolton and P. G. Wodehouse, revised by Howard Lindsay and Russel Crouse, music and lyrics by Cole Porter (New York: Samuel French, August 14, 1936), first produced in New York (Alvin Theatre, November 21, 1934) and London (Palace Theatre, June 14, 1935).

Supervisor for NBC Pete Barnum; executive producer, Leland Hayward; producer, Jule Styne; director, Sid Smith; written for television by Herbert Baker; musical director, Al Goodman; choreography, Bob Sidney; production design, Furth Ullman; production staged by David Alexander.

Cast: Ethel Merman (Reno Sweeney), Frank Sinatra (Harry Dane), Bert Lahr (Moonface), Sheree North (Bounce).

Citations: *Daily Variety*, March 1, 1954; *Variety*, March 3, 1954.

TV Hour of the Stars: Thank You, Mr. Jeeves (1955, U.S.)

Length: 45 minutes.

Host: John Conte.

Note: Reedited television release of the movie *Thank You, Jeeves* (1936).

Pond's Theatre: Candle Light (1955, U.S.)

Produced by ABC. Original broadcast: May 5, 1955, ABC. Length: 60 minutes. Format: Sound, black and white; television anthology episode.

Based on the play *Kleine Komoedie* by Siegfried Geyer and the English-language adaptation, *Candle-Light*, by P. G. Wodehouse (New York: Samuel French, June 8, 1934), first staged in New York (Empire Theatre, September 30, 1929).

Cast: Eva Gabor (Marie), Michael Evans (Josef), John Baragrey (Prince Rudolf), Rebecca Sand (Anna), Stiano Braggiotti (Papa), Joan Wetmore (Liserl).

Four Star Playhouse: Uncle Fred Flits By (1955, U.S.)

Produced by Four Star Productions for Singer Sewing and Bristol-Myers (Y&R). Original broadcast: May 5, 1955, CBS Length: 30 minutes. Format: Sound, black and white; television anthology episode.

Based on "Uncle Fred Flits By," published in the United States in *Red Book* (July 1935) and England in *Strand Magazine* (December 1935); first anthologized in *Young Men in Spats* in England (London: Herbert Jenkins, April 3, 1936) and the United States (Garden City: Doubleday, Doran, July 24, 1936).

Executive producer, Don W. Sharpe; producer, David Niven; director, Roy Kellino; teleplay, Oscar Millard; director of photography, George E. Diskant; editor, Samuel E. Beetley; art director, Duncan Cramer.

Cast: David Niven (Uncle Fred), Robert Nichols (Pongo), Norma Varden (Mrs. Tarmigan), Jennifer Raine (Julia), Leon Tyler (Robinson), Alex Frazer (Mr. Tarmigan), Tudor Owen (Roddis), Marjorie Bennett (Charwoman), Charlott Knight (Receptionist).

Citation: *Daily Variety*, May 10, 1955.

Lord Emsworth and the Little Friend (1956, UK)

Original broadcast: March 20, 1956. Length: 28 minutes. Format: Sound, black and white; television special.

Based on "Lord Emsworth and the Girl Friend," published in the United States in *Liberty* (October 6, 1928) and in England in *Strand Magazine* (November 1928); first anthologized in England in *Blandings Castle and Elsewhere* (London: Herbert Jenkins, April 12, 1935) and in the United States in *Blandings Castle* (Garden City: Doubleday, Doran, September 20, 1935).

Producer, Rex Tucker; dramatization, C.E. Webber.

Cast: Raymond Rollett (Beach), Rufus Cruikshank (MacAllister), Joan Sanderson (Lady Constance), John Miller (Clarence), Margaret McCourt (Gladys).

Anything Goes (1956, U.S.)

Produced by Paramount Pictures Corp. Shooting: early April to late June 1955. Release: Paramount Pictures Corp., April 1956; New York opening, March 21, 1956. Copyright Paramount Pictures Corp., March 21, 1956; LP6234. Length: 106 minutes. Format: Sound, Technicolor, VistaVision; theatrical feature film.

Based on the musical play *Anything Goes*, book by Guy Bolton and P. G. Wodehouse, revised by Howard Lindsay and Russel Crouse, music and lyrics by Cole Porter (New York: Samuel French, August 14, 1936), first produced in New York (Alvin Theatre, November 21, 1934) and London (Palace Theatre, June 14, 1935).

Producer, Robert Emmett Dolan; director, Robert Lewis; assistant director, John Coonan; second assistant director, James Rosenberger; production manager, Curtis Mick; story and screenplay, Sidney Sheldon; screenplay supervisor, Stanley

Scheuer; director of photography, John F. Warren; art directors, Hal Pereira and Joseph MacMillan Johnson; film editor, Frank Bracht; set decorations, Sam Comer and Grace Gregory; costumes, Edith Head; ballet costumes, Tom Keogh; costumes for Bing Crosby and Donald O'Connor, Sy Devore; music numbers arrangement and conductor, Joseph J. Lilley; special orchestra arrangement, Van Cleave; sound recording, Gene Merritt, Gene Garvin; special photography effects, John P. Fulton; process photography, Farciot Edouart; music numbers staged by Nick Castle; Jeanmaire ballet and "I Get a Kick out of You" staged by Roland Petit; "Anything Goes" dance number staged by Ernie Flatt; makeup supervisor, Wally Westmore.

Songs: "Anything Goes," "You're the Top," "I Get a Kick out of You," "All Through the Night," "It's Dee-Lovely" and "Blow, Gabriel, Blow," music and lyrics by Cole Porter; "You Can Bounce Right Back," "A Second-Hand Turban and a Crystal Ball" and "You Gotta Give the People Hoke," music and lyrics by Sammy Cahn and Johnny Van Heusen.

Cast: Bing Crosby (Bill Benson); Donald O'Connor (Ted Adams); Jeanmaire (Gaby Duval); Mitzi Gaynor (Patsy Blair); Phil Harris (Steve Blair); Kurt Kasznar (Victor Lawrence); Richard Erdman (Ed Brent); Walter Sande (Alex Todd); Archer MacDonald (Otto); Argentina Brunetti (Suzanne); Alma Macrorie (French Baroness); Dorothy Neumann (German Woman); James Griffith (Paul Holiday); Tracey Roberts (Blanche); Marcel Dalio (Ship's Captain); Alberto Morin (Captain of Waiters); Don Megowan (Henri); Torben Meyer (French Waiter); Jean Del Val (French Luggage Man); Nancy Kulp, Paul Wexler, Alma Ann Holguin, Dee Pollock, Mary Ann Harmon, John Erman, and Betty Rhodes (Bobby Soxers); Tom Hernandez (Frenchman); Nancy Lee Davis, Lucille Knox, and Autumn Russell (Girls at Party); Ruta Lee and Jann Darlyn (Girls); Doris Packer (English Woman in Audience); Virginia McDowall (English Usherette); Craig Hill (Marty); Albert Carrier (Assistant Purser); Emily Heath (Young American Girl); Linda Bennett (Ann); Edward Manouk and Tony Russo (French Sailors); Buzz Miller and Marc Wilder (Specialty Dancers); Dick Humphries and Ernie Flatt (Choreographers); Jack Pepper, John Benson.

Citations: *Box Office*, January 21, 1956; *Daily Variety*, January 8, 1954; December 6, 1954; January 23, 1956, p. 3; *Film Daily*, January 23, 1956, p. 10; *Hollywood Reporter*, January 3, 1955, p. 1; January 5, 1955, p. 4; January 17, 1955, p. 5; February 16, 1955, p. 8; March 30, 1955, p. 9; April 4, 1955, p. 4, 9; April 8, 1955, p. 8; April 11, 1955, p. 8; April 19, 1955, p. 6; May 18, 1955, p. 7; June 23, 1955, p. 8; January 23, 1956, p. 3; *Motion Picture Daily*, January 23, 1956; *Motion Picture Herald Product Digest*, January 28, 1956, p. 761; *New York Times*, March 22, 1956, p. 38; *Screen Hits Annual 1956*, pp. 19–22; *Variety*, January 25, 1956, p. 6.

Ford Startime: Dear Arthur (1960, U.S.)

Produced by NBC. Original broadcast: March 22, 1960, NBC. Length: 60 minutes. Format: Sound, black and white; television anthology episode.

Based on the unproduced play *Arthur*, an adaptation of a Ferenc Molnar play, published in *Molnar's Romantic Comedies* (New York: Crown, 1952).

Directors, Bretaigne Windust and Gordon Rigsby; adapter, Gore Vidal.

Cast: Rex Harrison, Sarah Marshall, Angela Baddeley, Nicholas Pryor, Robert Dryden, Gaby Rodgers, Guy Repp, Olga Fabian, and John Garson.

Citations: *Daily Variety*, March 24, 1960; *Variety*, March 30, 1960.

The Girl on the Boat (1961, UK)

A Knightsbridge Production. Filmed at Shepperton Studios. Release: January 1961, United Artists. Length: 91 minutes. Format: Sound, black and white; theatrical feature film.

Based on *Three Men and a Maid*, serialized in England in *Pan* (February to September 1921) and in the United States as *Three Men and a Maid* in *Woman's Home Companion* (October to December 1921); published in book form in the United States as *Three Men and a Maid* (New York: George H. Doran, April 30, 1922) and in England as *The Girl on the Boat* (London: Herbert Jenkins, June 15, 1922).

Producer, John Bryan; associate producer, Jack Rix; director, Henry Kaplan; assistant director, Colin Brewer; screenplay, Reuben Ship; music composed and conducted by Kenneth V. Jones; director of photography, Denys Coop; editor, Noreen Ackland; art direction, Tony Masters; assistant art director, Geoffrey Tozer; titles designer, James Baker; costume designer, James Ffolkes; set decoration, Scott Slimon.

Cast: Norman Wisdom (Sam Marlowe), Millicent Martin (Billie Bennett), Richard Briers (Eustace Hignett), Sheila Hancock (Jane), Bernard Cribbins (Peters), Athene Seyler (Mrs. Hignett), Philip Locke (Bream Mortimer), Noel Willman (Webster), William Sherwood (Mr. Bennett), Patience Collier, Reginald Beckwith (Barman), Martin Wyldeck (J.P. Mortimer), Timothy Bateson (Purser), Georgina Cookson (Passenger), Peter Bull (Blacksmith), Ronald Fraser (Colonel), Dick Bentley (American).

The World of Wooster (1965–1967, UK)

Produced by BBC. Length: Twenty 30-minute episodes. Format: Sound, black and white; television series.

Producers, Michael Mills, Peter Coates, and Frank Muir; writing, Richard Waring and Michael Mills; original music, Sandy Wilson.

Cast: Ian Carmichael (Bertie Wooster), Dennis Price (Jeeves), Fabia Drake (Aunt Agatha), Derek Nimmo (Bingo Little), Tracy Reed (Bobbie Wickham), Eleanor Summerfield (Aunt Dahlia), Paul Whitsun-Jones (Sir Roderick Glossop), Deborah Stanford (Mrs. Little).

Series 1

"Jeeves and the Dog Mcintosh" Original UK broadcast: May 30, 1965.

Based on "The Borrowed Dog," published in the United States in *Cosmopolitan* (October 1929) and as "Jeeves and the Dog McIntosh" in England in *Strand Magazine* (October 1929); first anthologized in *Very Good, Jeeves*, published in book form in the United States (Garden City: Doubleday, Doran, June 20, 1930) and in England (London: Herbert Jenkins, July 4, 1930).

"Jeeves, the Aunt and the Sluggard" Original UK broadcast: June 6, 1965.

Based on "The Aunt and the Sluggard," published in the United States in *Saturday Evening Post* (April 22, 1916) and England in *Strand Magazine* (August 1916); first anthologized in book form in England in *My Man Jeeves* (London: George

Newnes, May 1919) and in the United States in *Carry On, Jeeves* (New York: George H. Doran, October 7, 1927).

"Jeeves and the Great Sermon Handicap" Original UK broadcast: June 13, 1965.

Based on "The Great Sermon Handicap," published in the United States in *Cosmopolitan* (June 1922) and England in *Strand Magazine* (June 1922); first anthologized in *The Inimitable Jeeves*, published in book form in England (London: Herbert Jenkins, May 17, 1923) and in the United States as *Jeeves* (New York: George H. Doran, September 28, 1923).

"Jeeves and the Song of Songs" Original UK broadcast: June 20, 1965.

Based on "Jeeves and the Song of Songs," published in England in *Strand Magazine* (September 1929); first anthologized in *Very Good, Jeeves*, published in book form in the United States (Garden City: Doubleday, Doran, June 20, 1930) and in England (London: Herbert Jenkins, July 4, 1930).

"Jeeves and the Hero's Reward" Original UK broadcast: June 27, 1965.

Based on "Scoring Off Jeeves," published in England in *Strand Magazine* (February 1922); first anthologized in book form in *The Inimitable Jeeves* in England (London: Herbert Jenkins, May 17, 1923) and as "The Pride of the Woosters is Wounded" and "The Hero's Reward" in the United States in *Jeeves* (New York: George H. Doran, September 28, 1923).

"Jeeves and the Inferiority Complex of Old Sippy" Original UK broadcast: July 4, 1965.

Based on "The Inferiority Complex of Old Sippy," published in England in *Strand Magazine* (April 1926) and in the United States in *Liberty* (April 17, 1926); first anthologized in *Very Good, Jeeves*, published in book form in the United States (Garden City: Doubleday, Doran, June 20, 1930) and in England (London: Herbert Jenkins, July 4, 1930).

SERIES 2

"Jeeves and the Delayed Exit of Claude and Eustace" Original UK broadcast: January 4, 1966.

Based on two stories: "Sir Roderick Comes to Lunch," published in England in *Strand Magazine* (March 1922) and in the United States as "Jeeves and the Blighter" in *Cosmopolitan* (April 1922); and "The Delayed Exit of Claude and Eustace," published in England in *Strand Magazine* (October 1922) and in the United States in *Cosmopolitan* (November 1922); first anthologized in book form in *The Inimitable Jeeves* in England (London: Herbert Jenkins, May 17, 1923) and in the United States as "Introducing Claude and Eustace," "Sir Roderick Comes to Lunch," and "The Delayed Exit of Claude and Eustace" in *Jeeves* (New York: George H. Doran, September 28, 1923).

"Jeeves and the Change of Mind" Original UK broadcast: January 11, 1966.

Based on "Bertie Changes His Mind," published in the United States in *Cosmopolitan* (August 1922) and in England as "Bertie Gets His Chance" in *Strand Magazine* (August 1922); first anthologized in book form in *Carry On, Jeeves* in

England (London: Herbert Jenkins, October 9, 1925) and the United States (New York: George H. Doran, October 7, 1927).

"Jeeves and the Spot of Art" Original UK broadcast: January 18, 1966.

Based on "Jeeves and the Spot of Art," published in the United States in *Cosmopolitan* (December 1929) and in England in *Strand Magazine* (December 1929); first anthologized in *Very Good, Jeeves*, published in book form in the United States (Garden City: Doubleday, Doran, June 20, 1930) and England (London: Herbert Jenkins, July 4, 1930).

"Jeeves Exerts the Old Cerebellum" Original UK broadcast: January 25, 1966.

Based on "Jeeves in the Spring-Time," published in the United States in *Cosmopolitan* (December 1921) and in England in *Strand Magazine* (December 1921); first anthologized in book form in *The Inimitable Jeeves* in England (London: Herbert Jenkins, May 17, 1923) and in the United States as "Jeeves Exerts the Old Cerebellum" in *Jeeves* (New York: George H. Doran, September 28, 1923).

"Jeeves and the Purity of the Turf" Original UK broadcast: February 1, 1966.

Based on "The Purity of the Turf," published in the United States in *Cosmopolitan* (July 1922) and in England in *Strand Magazine* (July 1922); first anthologized in book form in *The Inimitable Jeeves* in England (London: Herbert Jenkins, May 17, 1923) and in the United States in *Jeeves* (New York: George H. Doran, September 28, 1923).

"Jeeves and the Clustering Around Young Bingo" Original UK broadcast: February 8, 1966.

Based on "Clustering Round Young Bingo," published in the United States in the *Saturday Evening Post* (February 21, 1925) and in England in *Strand Magazine* (April 1925); first anthologized in book form in *Carry On, Jeeves* in England (London: Herbert Jenkins, October 9, 1925) and the United States (New York: George H. Doran, October 7, 1927).

"Jeeves and the Indian Summer of an Uncle" Original UK broadcast: February 15, 1966.

Based on "The Indian Summer of an Uncle," published in the United States in *Cosmopolitan* (March 1930) and in England in *Strand Magazine* (March 1930); first anthologized in *Very Good, Jeeves*, published in book form in the United States (Garden City: Doubleday, Doran, June 20, 1930) and England (London: Herbert Jenkins, July 4, 1930).

Series 3

"Jeeves and the Greasy Bird" Original UK broadcast: October 6, 1967.

Based on "Jeeves and the Greasy Bird," published in the United States in *Playboy* (December 1965) and in England in *Argosy* (January 1967); first anthologized in book form in *Plum Pie* in England (London: Herbert Jenkins, September 22, 1966) and the United States (New York: Simon and Schuster, December 1, 1967).

"Jeeves and the Stand-in for Sippy" Original UK broadcast: October 13, 1967.

Probably based on "Without the Option," published in England in *Strand Magazine* (July 1925) and in the United States in the *Saturday Evening Post* (June 27,

1925); first anthologized in book form in *Carry On, Jeeves* in England (London: Herbert Jenkins, October 9, 1925) and the United States (New York: George H. Doran, October 7, 1927).

"Jeeves and the Old School Chum" Original UK broadcast: October 20, 1967.

Based on "Jeeves and the Old School Chum," published in the United States in *Cosmopolitan* (February 1930) and in England in *Strand Magazine* (February 1930); first anthologized in *Very Good, Jeeves*, published in book form in the United States (Garden City: Doubleday, Doran, June 20, 1930) and England (London: Herbert Jenkins, July 4, 1930).

"Jeeves and the Impending Doom" Original UK broadcast: October 27, 1967.

Based on "Jeeves and the Impending Doom," published in England in *Strand Magazine* (December 1926) and in the United States in *Liberty* (January 8, 1927); first anthologized in *Very Good, Jeeves*, published in book form in the United States (Garden City: Doubleday, Doran, June 20, 1930) and England (London: Herbert Jenkins, July 4, 1930).

"Jeeves and the Hard-Boiled Egg" Original UK broadcast: November 3, 1967.

Based on "Jeeves and the Hard-Boiled Egg," published in the United States in the Saturday Evening Post (March 3, 1917) and in England in Strand Magazine (August 1917); first anthologized in book form in England in My Man Jeeves (London: George Newnes, May 1919) and in the United States in Carry On, Jeeves (New York: George H. Doran, October 7, 1927).

"Jeeves and the Love That Purifies" Original UK broadcast: November 10, 1967.

Based on "Jeeves and the Love That Purifies," published in the United States in *Cosmopolitan* (November 1929) and in England in *Strand Magazine* (November 1929); first anthologized in *Very Good, Jeeves*, published in book form in the United States (Garden City: Doubleday, Doran, June 20, 1930) and England (London: Herbert Jenkins, July 4, 1930).

"Jeeves and the Fixing of Freddie" Original UK broadcast: November 17, 1967.

Based on "Fixing It for Freddie," anthologized in book form in *Carry On, Jeeves* in England (London: Herbert Jenkins, October 9, 1925) and the United States (New York: George H. Doran, October 7, 1927).

The World of Wodehouse (1967–1968, UK)

BBC. Length: Thirteen 30-minute episodes. Format: Sound, black and white; television series. Producers: Michael Mills and Frank Muir.

SERIES 1

Blandings Castle (1967)

Length: Six 30-minute episodes. Writing: John Chapman.

Cast: Ralph Richardson (Clarence, ninth Earl of Emsworth), Stanley Holloway (Beach, the butler), Meriel Forbes (Lady Constance), Jack Radcliffe (McAllister), Jimmy Edwards (Sir Gregory Parsloe-Parsloe), Fred Emney (Mr. Eustace Chalfont), Derek Nimmo (Frederick).

Citation: *Variety*, March 8, 1967.

"Lord Emsworth and the Girl Friend" Original UK broadcast: February 24, 1967.

Based on "Lord Emsworth and the Girl Friend," published in the United States in *Liberty* (October 6, 1928) and in England in *Strand Magazine* (November 1928); first anthologized in England in *Blandings Castle and Elsewhere* (London: Herbert Jenkins, April 12, 1935) and in the United States in *Blandings Castle* (Garden City: Doubleday, Doran, September 20, 1935).

Cast: Gaynor Jones (Gladys).

"The Great Pumpkin Crisis" Original UK broadcast: March 3, 1967.

Based on "The Custody of the Pumpkin," published in the United States in the *Saturday Evening Post* (November 29, 1924) and in England in *Strand Magazine* (December 1924); first anthologized in England in *Blandings Castle and Elsewhere* (London: Herbert Jenkins, April 12, 1935) and in the United States in *Blandings Castle* (Garden City: Doubleday, Doran, September 20, 1935).

"Lord Emsworth and the Crime Wave at Blandings" Original UK broadcast: March 10, 1967.

Based on "The Crime Wave at Blandings," published in the United States in the *Saturday Evening Post* (October 10, to October 17, 1936) and in England in *Strand Magazine* (January 1937); first anthologized in England in *Lord Emsworth and Others* (London: Herbert Jenkins, March 19, 1937) and in the United States in *The Crime Wave at Blandings* (New York: Doubleday, Doran, June 25, 1937).

"Lord Emsworth Acts for the Best" Original UK broadcast: March 17, 1967.

Based on "Lord Emsworth Acts for the Best," published in England in *Strand Magazine* (June 1926) and in the United States in *Liberty* (June 5, 1926); first anthologized in England in *Blandings Castle and Elsewhere* (London: Herbert Jenkins, April 12, 1935) and in the United States in *Blandings Castle* (Garden City: Doubleday, Doran, September 20, 1935).

"Pig Hoo-oo-ey!" Original UK broadcast: March 24, 1967.

Based on "Pig-Hoo-o-o-o-ey!," published in the United States in *Liberty* (9 July 1927) and in England in *Strand Magazine* (August 1927); first anthologized in England in *Blandings Castle and Elsewhere* (London: Herbert Jenkins, April 12, 1935) and in the United States in *Blandings Castle* (Garden City: Doubleday, Doran, September 20, 1935).

"Lord Emsworth and the Company for Gertrude" Original UK broadcast: March 31, 1967.

Based on "Company for Gertrude," published in England in *Strand Magazine* (September 1928) and in the United States in *Cosmopolitan* (October 1928); first anthologized in England in *Blandings Castle and Elsewhere* (London: Herbert Jenkins, April 12, 1935) and in the United States in *Blandings Castle* (Garden City: Doubleday, Doran, September 20, 1935).

Series 2

Ukridge (1968)

Length: Seven 30-minute episodes.

Producer Joan Kemp-Welch; writing Richard Waring.

Cast: Anton Rodgers (Stanley Featherstonehaugh Ukridge), Julian Holloway (Corky), Marian Spencer (Aunt Julia).

"The Home from Home" Original UK broadcast: July 15, 1968.

Based on "Ukridge and the Home from Home," published in the United States in *Cosmopolitan* (February 1931) and in England in *Strand Magazine* (June 1931); first anthologized in England in *Lord Emsworth and Others* (London: Herbert Jenkins, March 19, 1937) and in the United States in *Young Men in Spats* (New York: Doubleday, Doran, May 10, 1940).

"The Dog College" Original UK broadcast: July 22, 1968.

Based on "Ukridge's Dog College," published in the United States in *Cosmopolitan* (April 1923) and in England in *Strand Magazine* (May 1923); first anthologized in England in *Ukridge* (London: Herbert Jenkins, June 3, 1924) and in the United States in *He Rather Enjoyed It* (New York: George H. Doran, July 30, 1925).

"The Debut of Battling Billson" Original UK broadcast: July 29, 1968.

Based on "The Debut of Battling Billson," published in the United States in *Cosmopolitan* (June 1923) and in England in *Strand Magazine* (July 1923); first anthologized in England in *Ukridge* (London: Herbert Jenkins, June 3, 1924) and in the United States in *He Rather Enjoyed It* (New York: George H. Doran, July 30, 1925).

"The Accident Syndicate" Original UK broadcast: August 5, 1968.

Based on "Ukridge's Accident Syndicate," published in the United States in *Cosmopolitan* (May 1923) and as "Ukridge, Teddy Weeks, and the Tomato" in England in *Strand Magazine* (June 1923); first anthologized as "Ukridge's Accident Syndicate" in England in *Ukridge* (London: Herbert Jenkins, June 3, 1924) and in the United States in *He Rather Enjoyed It* (New York: George H. Doran, July 30, 1925).

"The Comeback of Battling Billson" Original UK broadcast: August 12, 1968

Based on "The Come-back of Battling Billson," published in the United States in *Cosmopolitan* (June 1935) and in England in *Strand Magazine* (July 1935); first anthologized in England in *Lord Emsworth and Others* (London: Herbert Jenkins, March 19, 1937) and in the United States in *Young Men in Spats* (New York: Doubleday, Doran, May 10, 1940).

"The Nasty Corner" Original UK broadcast: August 19, 1968.

Based on "Ukridge Rounds a Nasty Corner," published in the United States in *Cosmopolitan* (January 1924) and in England in *Strand Magazine* (February 1924); first anthologized in England in *Ukridge* (London: Herbert Jenkins, June 3, 1924) and in the United States in *He Rather Enjoyed It* (New York: George H. Doran, July 30, 1925).

"The Wedding Bells" Original UK broadcast: August 26, 1968.

Based on "No Wedding Bells for Him," published in the United States in *Cosmopolitan* (October 1923) and in England in *Strand Magazine* (November 1923); first anthologized in England in *Ukridge* (London: Herbert Jenkins, June 3, 1924) and in the United States in *He Rather Enjoyed It* (New York: George H. Doran, July 30, 1925).

Blut Floss auf Blandings Castle (1967, West Germany)

(*Blood Flowed at Blandings Castle*)

Original West German broadcast: March 29, 1967. Format: Sound; television.

Comedy Playhouse: Uncle Fred Flits By (1967, UK)

Original UK broadcast: June 16, 1967. Format: Sound, black and white; television anthology episode.

Based on "Uncle Fred Flits By," published in the United States in *Red Book* (July 1935) and in England in *Strand Magazine* (December 1935); first anthologized in England in *Young Men in Spats* (London: Herbert Jenkins, April 3, 1936) and England (Garden City: Doubleday, Doran, July 24, 1936).

Cast: Wilfrid Hyde-White (Uncle Fred).

Comedy Playhouse: The Reverent Wooing of Archibald (1974, UK)

Original UK broadcast: July 9, 1974. Format: Sound, color; television anthology episode.

Based on "The Reverent Wooing of Archibald," published in England in *Strand Magazine* (August 1928) and in the United States in *Cosmopolitan* (September 1928); first anthologized in *Mr. Mulliner Speaking*, published in England (London: Herbert Jenkins, April 30, 1929) and the United States (Garden City: Doubleday, Doran, February 21, 1930).

Wodehouse Playhouse (1975–1978, UK)

A BBC Time Life Television Co-production. US first broadcast in syndication on Public Broadcasting Service stations. Length: Twenty-one 30-minute episodes. Format: Sound, color; television series.

Adaptation, David Climie; Signature tune composed and conducted by Raymond Jones.

Cast: John Alderton; Pauline Collins (series 1 and 2).

Series 1

Producer: David Askey. Introductions: P. G. Wodehouse.

"The Truth About George" Original UK broadcast: April 23, 1975.

Based on "The Truth About George," published in England in *Strand Magazine* (July 1926) and in the United States in *Liberty* (July 23, 1926); first anthologized in *Meet Mr. Mulliner* in England (London: Herbert Jenkins, September 27, 1927) and the United States (Garden City: Doubleday, Doran, March 2, 1928).

Cast: John Alderton (George Mulliner), Anna Wing (Mrs. Barnaby), Pauline Collins (Susan Blake), Anthony Sharp (Specialist), Patrick Newell (Fierce Man), Mike Lewin (Porter), Colin Jeavons (Stranger), Geraldine Newman (Lady on Train).

"Romance at Droitgate Spa" Original UK broadcast: April 30, 1975.

Based on "The Romance at Droitgate Spa," published in the United States in the *Saturday Evening Post* (February 20, 1937) and in England in *Strand Magazine* (August 1937); first anthologized in the United States in *The Crime Wave at Blandings* (Garden City: Doubleday, Doran, June 25, 1937) and in England in *Eggs, Beans and Crumpets* (London: Herbert Jenkins, April 26, 1940).

Cast: John Alderton (Mortimer Rackstraw), Pauline Collins (Annabel Purvis), Julian Holloway (Freddie Fitch-Fitch), Raymond Huntley (Sir Aylmer Bastable), Mark Dignam (Lord Rumbelow), Graham Armitage (Parkin), Leslie Dwyer (Joe Boffin).

"Portrait of a Disciplinarian" Original UK broadcast: May 7, 1975.

Based on "Portrait of a Disciplinarian," published in the United States in *Liberty* (September 24, 1927) and in England in *Strand Magazine* (October 1927); first anthologized in *Meet Mr. Mulliner* in England (London: Herbert Jenkins, September 27, 1927) and the United States (Garden City: Doubleday, Doran, March 2, 1928).

Cast: John Alderton (Reginald Mulliner), Marcia King (Receptionist), William Gaunt (Dr. Joe Mulliner), Daphne Heard (Nanny Wilks), Pauline Collins (Jane Oliphant), Vicki Woolf (Lottie Latour), Robert Prince (Dillingwater).

"Unpleasantness at Bludleigh Court" Original UK broadcast: May 14, 1975.

Based on "Unpleasantness at Bludleigh Court," published in England in *Strand Magazine* (February 1929) and in the United States in *Liberty* (February 2, 1929); first anthologized in *Mr. Mulliner Speaking*, published in England (London: Herbert Jenkins, April 30, 1929) and the United States (Garden City: Doubleday, Doran, February 21, 1930).

Cast: John Alderton (Aubrey Bassinger), Pauline Collins (Charlotte Mulliner), Ballard Berkeley (Sir Alexander), Shelagh Fraser (Lady Bassinger), David Allister (Horatio Ballister), Michael Kemp (Wilfred Bassinger), John Sharp (Colonel Pashley-Drake), Michael Logan (Benson).

"The Rise of Minna Nordstrom" Original UK broadcast: May 21, 1975.

Based on "A Star Is Born," published in the *American Magazine* (January 1933), retitled "Rise of Minna Nordstrom" in England in *Strand Magazine* (April 1933); first anthologized as "Rise of Minna Nordstrom" in England in *Blandings Castle and Elsewhere* (London: Herbert Jenkins, April 12, 1935) and in the United States in *Blandings Castle* (Garden City: Doubleday, Doran, September 20, 1935).

Cast: John Alderton (Jacob J. Schnellenhamer); Pauline Collins (Minna Nordstrom); Michael Burrell (Waldo Winkler); Sydney Tafler (Isadore Q. Fishbein); Peter Jones (Ben F. Zizzbaum); Maggie Fitzgibbon (Helga Schnellenhamer); Harry Tierney (Hemingway, the Butler); James Smilie (Police Sergeant); Paul McDowell (First Cop); Blain Fairman (Second Cop); Barbara Bermel (Mother); Susan Finch, Dale Jackley, Deirdre Laird, and Susan Ritman (Dancers).

"Rodney Fails to Qualify" Original UK broadcast: May 28, 1975.

Based on "Rodney Fails to Qualify," published in the United States in the *Saturday Evening Post* (February 23, 1924) and in England in *Strand Magazine* (March 1924); first anthologized in England in *The Heart of a Goof* (London: Herbert Jenkins, April 15, 1926) and in the United States in *Divots* (New York: George H. Doran, May 4, 1927).

Cast: John Alderton (William Bates), Pauline Collins (Jill Packard), William Mervyn (Oldest Member), Andrew Downie (Gerald McLaren), Geoffrey Whitehead (Rodney Spelvin), Billy John (Waiter), Josephine Tewson (Mabel Potts).

"A Voice from the Past" Original UK broadcast: June 4, 1975.

Based on "A Voice from the Past," published in the United States in *American Magazine* (November 1931) and as "The Voice from the Past" in England in *Strand Magazine* (December 1931); first anthologized in *Mulliner Nights* in England (London: Herbert Jenkins, January 17, 1933) and the United States (Garden City: Doubleday, Doran, February 15, 1933).

Cast: Pauline Collins (Muriel Branksome), Therese McMurray (Poppy Tremayne), John Alderton (Sacheverell Mulliner), John Phillips (Sir Redvers Branksome), Philip Daniels (Office Boy), Astro Morris (Mr. Philbrick), Robert Prince (Bernard), Cyril Luckham (Bishop of Bognor).

Series 2

Producer: Michael Mills.

"Anselm Gets His Chance" Original UK broadcast: March 26, 1976.

Based on "Anselm Gets His Chance," published in England in *Strand Magazine* (July 1937) and in the United States in the *Saturday Evening Post* (July 3, 1937); first anthologized in *Eggs, Beans and Crumpets* in England (London: Herbert Jenkins, April 26, 1940) and the United States (Garden City: Doubleday, Doran, May 10, 1940).

Cast: John Alderton (Rev. Anselm Mulliner), Pauline Collins (Myrtle Jellaby), Thorley Walters (Sir Leopold Jellaby), Desmond Llewelyn (Rev. Sidney Gooch), Paul Curran (Joe Beamish).

"Mr. Potter Takes a Rest Cure" Original UK broadcast: April 2, 1976.

Based on "The Rest Cure," published in the United States in *Liberty* (January 23, 1926) and as "Mr. Potter Takes a Rest Cure" in England in *Strand Magazine* (February 1926); first anthologized in England in *Blandings Castle and Elsewhere* (London: Herbert Jenkins, April 12, 1935) and in the United States in *Blandings Castle* (Garden City: Doubleday, Doran, September 20, 1935).

Cast: Alan MacNaughtan (J.H. Potter), John Alderton (Clifford Gandle), Pauline Collins (Bobbie Wickham), Margaret Courtenay (Lady Wickham), Timothy Carlton (Algy Crufts).

"Strychnine in the Soup" Original UK broadcast: April 9, 1976.

Based on "A Missing Mystery," published in the United States in *American Magazine* (December 1931) and as "Strychnine in the Soup" in England in *Strand Magazine* (March 1932); first anthologized as "Strychnine in the Soup" in *Mulliner*

Nights in England (London: Herbert Jenkins, January 17, 1933) and the United States (Garden City: Doubleday, Doran, February 15, 1933).

Cast: John Alderton (Cyril Mulliner), Pauline Collins (Amelia Bassett), Joan Sanderson (Lady Bassett), Dorothy Frere (Theater Barmaid), Jeanne Collings (Teashop Waitress), Ben Aris (Lester Mapledurham), Gerald Case (Sir Mortimer Wingham), Mary Barclay (Lady Wingham), Michael Angrave (Mr. Simpson), John Dunbar (Butler), Elisabeth Day (Parlourmaid).

"Feet of Clay" Original UK broadcast: April 23, 1976.

Based on "A Slightly Broken Romance," published in the United States in *This Week* (June 18, 1950); first anthologized as "Feet of Clay" in *Nothing Serious* in England (London: Herbert Jenkins, July 21, 1950) and the United States (New York: Doubleday, May 24, 1951).

Cast: Pauline Collins (Agnes Flack), Simon Williams (Sidney McMurdo), John Alderton (Jack Fosdyke), Cyd Hayman (Cora McGuffy Spottsworth), David Shaw (Holidaymaker), Lucy Fenwick (Lulubelle Sprockett), Budemoor Yang-T'se Tong (Himself, a dog).

"The Nodder" Original UK broadcast: April 30, 1976.

Based on two stories:

"The Nodder," published in England in *Strand Magazine* (January 1933) and in the United States as "Love Birds" in *American Magazine* (January 1933); first anthologized as "The Nodder" in England in *Blandings Castle and Elsewhere* (London: Herbert Jenkins, April 12, 1935) and in the United States in *Blandings Castle* (Garden City: Doubleday, Doran, September 20, 1935).

"Monkey Business," published in England in *Strand Magazine* (December 1932) and in the United States as "A Cagey Gorilla" in *American Magazine* (December 1932); first anthologized as "Monkey Business" in England in *Blandings Castle and Elsewhere* (London: Herbert Jenkins, April 12, 1935) and in the United States in *Blandings Castle* (Garden City: Doubleday, Doran, September 20, 1935).

Cast: John Alderton (Wilmot Mulliner); Pauline Collins (Mabel Ridgway); Sydney Tafler (I.Q. Fishbein); David Healy (L.O. Levitsky); Jonathan Cecil (King Boola); Don Fellows (George Pybus); Paul McDowell (Studio Guide); Richard Dennis (A Writer); Angus A. McInnes, Jay Neill, Roger Salter, and Michael Dynan (Yes Men); Wendy Gilmore (Baby's Mother); Bill Reimbold (Clergyman).

"The Code of the Mulliners" Original UK broadcast: May 7, 1976.

Based on "The Code of the Mulliners," published in the United States in *Cosmopolitan* (February 1935) and in England in *Strand Magazine* (April 1935); first anthologized in *Young Men in Spats* in England (London: Herbert Jenkins, April 3, 1936) and in the United States (Garden City: Doubleday, Doran, July 24, 1936).

Cast: John Alderton (Archibald Mulliner), Pauline Collins (Yvonne Maltravers), Gabrielle Drake (Aurelia Cammerleigh), David Quilter (Tuppy Glossop), Walter Gotell (Sir Rackstraw Cammerleigh), Hazel Bainbridge (Lady Mulliner), Daphne Oxenford (Lady Cammerleigh), Kenneth Benda (Bagshot, the Butler), Peter MacKriel (Waiter).

Series 3

Producer: Gareth Gwenlan.

"The Smile That Wins" Original UK broadcast: October 31, 1978.

Based on "The Smile That Wins," published in the United States in *American Magazine* (October 1931) and in England in *Strand Magazine* (February 1932); first anthologized in *Mulliner Nights* in England (London: Herbert Jenkins, January 17, 1933) and the United States (Garden City: Doubleday, Doran, February 15, 1933).

Cast: John Alderton (Adrian Mulliner), Judy Buxton (Lady Millicent Shipton-Bellinger), Robert Dorning (Lord Brangbolton), Fulton Mackay (Mr. Widgery), Anthony Sharp (Specialist), Anthony Howard (Sir Sutton Hartley-Wesping), Arthur Cox (Sir Jasper Addleton), Michael Bilton (Butler), Hugh Morton (Bishop), David Rowlands (Lord Knubble).

"Trouble down at Tudsleigh" Original UK broadcast: November 7, 1978.

Based on "Trouble down at Tudsleigh," published in the United States in *Cosmopolitan* (May 1939) and in England in *Strand Magazine* (May 1935); first anthologized in England in *Young Men in Spats* (London: Herbert Jenkins, April 3, 1936) and in the United States in *Eggs, Beans and Crumpets* (Garden City: Doubleday, Doran, May 10, 1940).

Cast: John Alderton (Freddie Widgeon), Anna Fox (April Carroway), Tony Mathews (Captain Bradbury), Bernadette Windsor (Prudence Carroway), Sally Lahee (Lady Carroway), Nicholas McArdle (Ted), William Moore (Butler).

"Tangled Hearts" Original UK broadcast: November 14, 1978.

Based on "I'll Give You Some Advice," published in the United States in *Cosmopolitan* (September 1948); first anthologized as "Tangled Hearts" in *Nothing Serious* in England (London: Herbert Jenkins, July 21, 1950) and the United States (New York: Doubleday, May 24, 1951).

Cast: John Alderton (Smallwood Bessemer), Richard Caldicot (Angus McWhirter), David Troughton (Carter Muldoon), Sue Nicholls (Esme Rampling), Sally Thomsett (Celia Todd), Laura Prebble (Julia Collins).

"The Luck of the Stiffhams" Original UK broadcast: November 21, 1978.

Based on "The Luck of the Stiffams," published in the United States in *Cosmopolitan* (November 1933) and in England in *Strand Magazine* (March 1934); first anthologized in *Young Men in Spats* in England (London: Herbert Jenkins, April 3, 1936) and the United States (Garden City: Doubleday, Doran, July 24, 1936).

Cast: John Alderton (Adolphus "Stiffy" Stiffham), Leslie Sands (the Earl of Wivelscombe), Liza Goddard (Lady Geraldine Spettisbury), David Healy (Bellhop), Paul McDowell (Hotel Manager), John Rudling (Butler), Joseph Iles (Mortuary Macabre).

"The Editor Regrets" Original UK broadcast: November 28, 1978.

Based on "The Editor Regrets," published in the United States in the *Saturday Evening Post* (July 1, 1939) and in England in *Strand Magazine* (September 1939); first anthologized in *Eggs, Beans and Crumpets* in England (London: Herbert Jenkins, April 26, 1940) and the United States (Garden City: Doubleday, Doran, May 10, 1940).

Cast: John Alderton (Bingo Little), Susan Jameson (Bella Mae Jobson), Bernard Archard (Purkiss), David Quilter (Tuppy Glossop), Jane Cussons (Rosie Little), William Hayland (Stilton Cheesewright), Joan Harsant (Gladys).

"Big Business" Original UK broadcast: December 5, 1978.

Based on "Big Business," published in the United States in *Collier's* (December 13, 1952) and in England in *Lilliput* (March/April 1953); first anthologized in *A Few Quick Ones* in the United States (New York: Simon and Schuster, April 13, 1959) and England (London: Herbert Jenkins, June 26, 1959).

Cast: John Alderton (Reginald Mulliner), Derek Francis (Sir Jethro Mott), Maggie Henderson (Amanda Biffen), Gerald Sim (Vicar), Terence Conoley (Jarvis), Damaris Hayman (Miss Frisby), Norman Mitchell (P.C. Popjoy), David Rowlands (Lord Knubble).

"Mulliner's Buck-U-Uppo" Original UK broadcast: December 12, 1978.

Based on "Mulliner's Buck-U-Uppo," published in the United States in *Liberty* (September 4, 1926) and in England in *Strand Magazine* (November 1926); first anthologized in *Meet Mr. Mulliner* in England (London: Herbert Jenkins, September 27, 1927) and the United States (Garden City: Doubleday, Doran, March 2, 1928).

Cast: John Alderton (Augustine Mulliner), Cyril Luckham (Bishop), John Barron (Reverend Stanley Brandon), Avis Bunnage (Mrs. Wardle), Belinda Carroll (Jane Brandon), Beatrix Mackey (Lady Bishopess).

Der Lord und Seine Koenigin (1977, West Germany)

(*A King and His Queen*)

Original West German broadcast: June 21, 1977. Format: Sound; television.

Based on the play *Oh, Clarence!* by John Chapman, adapted from *Blandings Castle* and other Lord Emsworth stories (London: Theatre Guild, 1969), first produced in London (Lyric Theatre, August 29, 1968).

Diener und Andere Herren (1978, West Germany)

(*Butlers and Other Gentlemen*)

Length: 57 minutes. Format: Sound, color; television.

Director Wolfgang Glück; Based on Maria Matray, W. Somerset Maugham, Lida Winiewicz, and P. G. Wodehouse.

Cast: Werner Eichhorn, Regine Lutz, Bruni Löbel, Ferdy Mayne, Kurd Pieritz, Christian Reiner, Heinz Rühmann.

Welcome to Wodehouse (1982, UK)

BBC, Jackanory Unit Productions. Length: Five 30-minute episodes. Format: Sound, color; television series. Narrator: John Alderton.

"Jeeves and the Impending Doom" Original UK broadcast: January 8, 1982.

Based on "Jeeves and the Impending Doom," published in England in *Strand Magazine* (December 1926) and in the United States in *Liberty* (January 8, 1927); first anthologized in *Very Good, Jeeves*, published in book form in the United States (Garden City: Doubleday, Doran, June 20, 1930) and England (London: Herbert Jenkins, July 4, 1930).

"Pig Hoo-o-o-o-ey!" Original UK broadcast: January 15, 1982.

Based on "Pig-Hoo-o-o-o-ey!," published in the United States in *Liberty* (9 July 1927) and in England in *Strand Magazine* (August 1927); first anthologized in England in *Blandings Castle and Elsewhere* (London: Herbert Jenkins, April 12, 1935) and in the United States in *Blandings Castle* (Garden City: Doubleday, Doran, September 20, 1935).

"Open House" Original UK broadcast: January 22, 1982.

Based on "Open House," published in *American Magazine* (April 1932) and England in *Strand Magazine* (April 1932); first anthologized in *Mulliner Nights* in England (London: Herbert Jenkins, January 17, 1933) and the United States (Garden City: Doubleday, Doran, February 15, 1933).

"Sir Agravaine" Original UK broadcast: January 29, 1982.

Based on "Sir Agravaine," published in the United States in *Collier's* (June 29, 1912) and in England in *Pearson's Magazine* (December 1912); first anthologized as "Sir Agravaine, a Tale of King Alfred's Round Table" in England in *The Man Upstairs and Other Stories* (London: Methuen, January 23, 1914).

"Goodbye to All Cats" Original UK broadcast: February 5, 1982.

Based on "Goodbye to All Cats," published in the United States in *Cosmopolitan* (November 1934) and in England in *Strand Magazine* (December 1934); first anthologized in England in *Young Men in Spats* (London: Herbert Jenkins, April 3, 1936) and the United States (Garden City: Doubleday, Doran, July 24, 1936).

Isi Bahane (1988, India)

(*On This Excuse*)

Producer: Doordarshan. Hindi language. Length: Ten episodes. Format: Sound, color; television miniseries.

Based on *Leave It to Psmith*, serialized in the United States in the *Saturday Evening Post* (February 3, to March 17, 1923) and England in *Grand* (began June 1923); published in England (London: Herbert Jenkins, November 30, 1923) and the United States (New York: George H. Doran, March 14, 1924).

Citation: *Harpers and Queen*, June 1988, pp. 114–115.

Tales from the Hollywood Hills: The Old Reliable (1988, US/UK)

Producers: Zenith Prods. and WNET New York. Original U.S. broadcast: November 4, 1988 on *Great Performances*. Length: 60 minutes. Format: Sound, color; television anthology episode.

Based on *Phipps to the Rescue*, serialized in the United States in *Collier's* (June 24, to July 22, 1950); published in book form in England as *The Old Reliable* (London: Herbert Jenkins, April 18, 1951) and the United States (Garden City: Doubleday, October 11, 1951).

Executive producer, David Loxton; producer, Kimberly Myers; co-producer, Nancy Israel; director, Michael Blakemore; writer, Robert Mundy; music, Dick Hyman; photography, Bernd Heinl; editor, Rod Stephens.

Cast: Rosemary Harris (Adela Shannon), Ray Reinhardt (Alfred Cork),

Joseph Maher (Smedley Cork), Paxton Whitehead (Phipps), Lynn Redgrave ("Bill" Shannon), Russ Marin (Cab), Lori Loughlin (Kay Cork), Tom Isbell (Joe), Suzy Sharp (Secretary), Lou Jacobi (Jacob Glutz), F. William Parker (Arnold Le Borg), John C. Moskoff (Sidney Conway), Alan Oppenheimer (Monty Gladstone), John Ingle (Jerome Estabrook), John DiSanti (Sergeant), Donovan Scott.

Citations: *New York Times*, November 4, 1988; *Variety*, November 23, 1988.

Wodehouse on Broadway (1989, UK)

A Plymouth Theatre Royal Production in association with KPMG Peat Marwick McLintock BBC Bristol 1989. Length: 90 minutes. Format: Sound, color; television special.

Written and produced by Tony Staveacre; director, Keith Cheetham; stage managers, Michael Mansfield, Jayne Ross, and Cliff White; production manager, Andrew Hollett; assistant designer, Leonard Birchenall; make-up designer, Lucy Hutchinson; costume and tableaux designer, Ian Adley; camera supervisor, Geoff Vian; vision mixer, Martyn Suker; videotape editor, Frank Riches; video effects designer, Dave Jervis; technical coordinator, John Neal; sound, Peter Rose and Andrew Lawrence; lighting, Tim Mitchell and Derek Fawley; production assistant, Kate Slattery; script consultants, Edward Cazalet and Lee Davis; orchestrations, Jim Parker and Ian MacPherson; choreography, Brad Graham; musical director, Gary Yershon.

Cast: Peter Woodward (P. G. Wodehouse), Tony Slattery, Gary Yershon, Kelly Hunter, Charlotte Avery, Nicolas Colicos, Michael Crossman, Brad Graham, Margaret Houston, Julia Hampson, Nicola Dewdney.

Jeeves and Wooster (1990–1993, UK)

U.S.: Presented on *Masterpiece Theater*. Length: Twenty-three circa-55-minute episodes. Format: Sound, color; television series.

Executive producer, Sally Head; producer, Brian Eastman; dramatized by Clive Exton; music, Anne Dudley.

Cast: Stephen Fry (Reginald Jeeves), Hugh Laurie (Bertram "Bertie" Wilberforce Wooster).

UK Series I; matched U.S. Series I

Director: Robert Young.

"Jeeves Takes Charge" UK title: "In Court after the Boat Race" (aka "Jeeves' Arrival"). Original broadcast dates: UK, April 22, 1990; U.S., November 11, 1990.

Based on three stories:

"Jeeves Takes Charge," published in the United States in the *Saturday Evening Post* (November 18, 1916) and in England in *Strand Magazine* (April 1923); first anthologized in book form in *Carry On, Jeeves* in England (London: Herbert Jenkins, October 9, 1925) and the United States (New York: George H. Doran, October 7, 1927).

"Scoring Off Jeeves," published in England in *Strand Magazine* (February1922); first anthologized in book form in *The Inimitable Jeeves* in England (London: Herbert Jenkins, May 17, 1923) and as "The Pride of the Woosters is

Wounded" and "The Hero's Reward" in the United States in *Jeeves* (New York: George H. Doran, September 28, 1923).

"Sir Roderick Comes to Lunch," published in England in *Strand Magazine* (March 1922) and as "Jeeves and the Blighter" in the United States in *Cosmopolitan* (April 1922); first anthologized in book form in *The Inimitable Jeeves* in England (London: Herbert Jenkins, May 17, 1923) and in the United States as "Introducing Claude and Eustace" and "Sir Roderick Comes to Lunch" in *Jeeves* (New York: George H. Doran, September 28, 1923).

Cast: Mary Wimbush (Aunt Agatha), Michael Siberry (Bingo Little), Elizabeth Kettle (Honoria Glossop), Roger Brierley (Sir Roderick Glossop), Jane Downs (Lady Glossop), Alistair Haley (Oswald Glossop), John Woodnutt (Sir Watkyn Bassett), Jason Calder (Lord Rainsby), Ian Jeffs (Eustace Wooster), Hugo E. Blick (Claude Wooster), Adam Blackwood (Barmy Fotheringay Phipps), Justine Glenton (Daphne Braithwaite), Robert Daws (Tuppy Glossop), Richard Stirling (Boko Fittleworth), Richard Dixon (Oofy Prosser), John Duval (Freddie Chalk-Marshall), Michael Ripper (Drones Porter), Tim Barker (Cabbie).

"Tuppy and the Terrier" UK title: "Bertie Is in Love" (aka "Golf Tournament"). Original broadcast dates: UK, April 29, 1990; U.S., November 18, 1990

Based on three stories:

"Jeeves and the Yuletide Spirit," published in England in *Strand Magazine* (December 1927) and in the United States in *Liberty* (December 24, 1927); first anthologized in *Very Good, Jeeves*, published in book form in the United States (Garden City: Doubleday, Doran, June 20, 1930) and England (London: Herbert Jenkins, July 4, 1930).

"The Borrowed Dog," published in the United States in *Cosmopolitan* (October 1929) and as "Jeeves and the Dog McIntosh" in England in *Strand Magazine* (October 1929); first anthologized in *Very Good, Jeeves*, published in book form in the United States (Garden City: Doubleday, Doran, June 20, 1930) and England (London: Herbert Jenkins, July 4, 1930).

"Jeeves and the Song of Songs," published in England in *Strand Magazine* (September 1929); first anthologized in *Very Good, Jeeves*, published in book form in the United States (Garden City: Doubleday, Doran, June 20, 1930) and England (London: Herbert Jenkins, July 4, 1930).

Cast: Mary Wimbush (Aunt Agatha), Brenda Bruce (Aunt Dahlia), Robert Daws (Tuppy Glossop), Nina Botting (Bobbie Wickham), Adam Blackwood (Barmy Fotheringay Phipps), Rosemary Martin (Lady Wickham), Brian Haines (Sir Cuthbert Wickham), Constance Novis (Cora Bellinger), Michael Poole (Professor Cluj), Zulema Dene (Aneta Cluj), Billy Mitchell (Mr. Blumenfield), Anatol Yusef (Sydney Blumenfield), David Blake Kelly (Enoch Simpson), Owen Brenman (Rev. Beefy Bingham), Michael Ripper (Drones Porter), Scilla Stewart (Pianist).

"The Purity of the Turf" UK title: "The Village Sports Day at Twing" (aka "The Gambling Event"). Original broadcast dates: UK, May 6, 1990; U.S., November 25, 1990.

Based on two stories:

"The Indian Summer of an Uncle," published in the United States in *Cos-*

mopolitan (March 1930) and in England in *Strand Magazine* (March 1930); first anthologized in *Very Good, Jeeves*, published in book form in the United States (Garden City: Doubleday, Doran, June 20, 1930) and England (London: Herbert Jenkins, July 4, 1930).

"The Purity of the Turf," published in the United States in *Cosmopolitan* (July 1922) and in England in *Strand Magazine* (July 1922); first anthologized in book form in *The Inimitable Jeeves* in England (London: Herbert Jenkins, May 17, 1923) and in the United States in *Jeeves* (New York: George H. Doran, September 28, 1923).

Cast: Mary Wimbush (Aunt Agatha), Nicholas Selby (Uncle George), Paula Jacobs (Maud Wilberforce), Michael Siberry (Bingo Little), Richard Braine (Rupert Steggles), Charles Millham (Freddie Widgeon), Jack Watling (Lord Wickhammersley), Richenda Carey (Lady Wickhammersley), Helena Michell (Cynthia), Cheryl Pay (Mavis), Georgia Allen (Hildegarde), Kelly Cryer (Myrtle), Ruth Burnett (Beryl), Jack May (Vicar), Ben Davis (Harold Harmsworth), James Patten (Ted Tucker), Michael Ripper (Drones Porter), Norman Lumsden (Buffers Porter), Richard Dixon (Oofy Prosser), Richard Stirling (Boko Fittleworth), John Duval (Freddie Chalk- Marshall), Beryl King (Mrs. Penworthy), Deddie Davies (Serving Lady), Margaret Lawley (Serving Lady).

"The Hunger Strike" UK title: "How Does Gussie Woo Madeline?" Original broadcast dates: UK, May 13, 1990; U.S., December 2, 1990.

Part 1 of 2.

Based on *Right Ho, Jeeves*, serialized in the United States in the *Saturday Evening Post* (December 23, 1933, to January 27, 1934) and in England in *Grand Magazine* (April to September 1934); published in book form in England (London: Herbert Jenkins, October 5, 1934) and in the United States as *Brinkley Manor* (Boston: Little, Brown, October 15, 1934).

Cast: Brenda Bruce (Aunt Dahlia), Ralph Michael (Tom Travers), Amanda Elwes (Angela Travers), Richard Garnett (Gussie Fink Nottle), Robert Daws (Tuppy Glossop), Francesca Folan (Madeline Bassett), John Barrard (Anatole), Adam Blackwood (Barmy Fotheringay Phipps), Richard Dixon (Oofy Prosser), Michael Ripper (Drones Porter).

"Brinkley Manor" UK title: "Will Anatole Return to Brinkley Court?" (aka "The Matchmaker"). Original broadcast dates: UK, May 20, 1990; U.S., December 9, 1990.

Part 2 of 2.

Based on *Right Ho, Jeeves*, serialized in the United States in the *Saturday Evening Post* (December 23, 1933, to January 27, 1934) and England in *Grand Magazine* (April to September 1934); published in book form in England (London: Herbert Jenkins, October 5, 1934) and in the United States as *Brinkley Manor* (Boston: Little, Brown, October 15, 1934).

Cast: Brenda Bruce (Aunt Dahlia), Ralph Michael (Tom Travers), Amanda Elwes (Angela Travers), Francesca Folan (Madeline Bassett), Robert Daws (Tuppy Glossop), Richard Garnett (Gussie Fink Nottle), Adam Blackwood (Barmy Fotheringay Phipps), Richard Dixon (Oofy Prosser), John Barrard (Anatole), Peter Hughes (Headmaster), Neil Hallett (Seppings), Joan White (Old Woman), Henry Power (G. G. Simmons), Declan Traynor (P.K. Purvis).

UK Series II — in U.S. partially shown as series IV, out of sequence

U.S. video release title: *P. G. Wodehouse's Jeeves and Wooster.*
Director: Simon Langton.

"Jeeves Saves the Cow Creamer" UK title: "The Silver Jug." Original broadcast dates: UK, April 14, 1991; U.S., January 29, 1995 (became IV.4).

Based on *The Code of the Woosters*, serialized in the United States in the *Saturday Evening Post* (July 16, to September 3, 1938) and England in the *Daily Mail* (September 8, to October 21, 1938); published in the United States (New York: Doubleday, Doran, October 7, 1938) and England (London: Herbert Jenkins, October 7, 1938).

Cast: John Turner (Spode), John Woodnutt (Sir Watkyn), Charlotte Attenborough (Stiffy), Diana Blackburn (Madeline), Richard Garnett (Gussie), Simon Treves (Stinker), Vivian Pickles (Aunt Dahlia), Campbell Morrison (Oates), Martin Clunes (Barmy), Harry Landis (Proprietor), Michael Ripper (Porter), Catherine Livesey (Housemaid), Alan Gilchrist (Constable), John Atkinson (President), Richard Bebb (Member), Neville Phillips (Member), Ian Price (Member).

"A Plan for Gussie" UK title: "The Bassetts' Fancy Dress Ball." Original broadcast dates: UK, April 21, 1991; U.S., February 5, 1995 (became IV.5).

Based on *The Code of the Woosters*, serialized in the United States in the *Saturday Evening Post* (July 16, to September 3, 1938); published in the United States (New York: Doubleday, Doran, October 7, 1938) and England (London: Herbert Jenkins, October 7, 1938).

Cast: John Turner (Spode), John Woodnutt (Sir Watkyn), Diana Blackburn (Madeline), Charlotte Attenborough (Stiffy), Richard Garnett (Gussie), Campbell Morrison (Oates), Simon Treves (Stinker), Martin Clunes (Barmy), Richard Dixon (Oofy), Michael Irwin (Footman).

"Pearls Mean Tears" UK title: "The Con." Original broadcast dates: UK, April 28, 1991; U.S., January 8, 1995 (became IV.1).

Based on two stories:

"Aunt Agatha Takes the Count," published in England in *Strand Magazine* (April 1922) and as "Aunt Agatha Makes a Bloomer" in the United States in *Cosmopolitan* (October 1922); first anthologized in book form in *The Inimitable Jeeves* in England (London: Herbert Jenkins, May 17, 1923) and in the United States as "Aunt Agatha Speaks Her Mind" and "Pearls Mean Tears" in *Jeeves* (New York: George H. Doran, September 28, 1923).

"The Rummy Affair of Old Biffy," published in the United States in the *Saturday Evening Post* (September 27, 1924) and in England in *Strand Magazine* (October 1924); first anthologized in book form in *Carry On, Jeeves* in England (London: Herbert Jenkins, October 9, 1925) and the United States (New York: George H. Doran, October 7, 1927).

Cast: Mary Wimbush (Aunt Agatha), Graham Seed (Sidney), Rebecca Saire (Aline), Philip Shelley (Biffy), Roger Brierley (Sir Roderick), Jane Downs (Lady Glossop), Liz Kettle (Honoria), Martin Clunes (Barmy), Richard Dixon (Oofy), John Duval (Freddie), Robert Aldous (Manager), Steph Bramwell (Thompson), Phillip Reader (Superintendent), Christopher Whittingham (Sergeant), Natalie Abbott (Chambermaid), Jenny Whiffen (Mabel), Lucy Blair (Chorus Girl), Colette Forbes (Chorus Girl), Salli Randi (Chorus Girl), Joanna Riding (Chorus Girl).

"Jeeves in the Country" UK title: "Chuffy." Original broadcast dates: UK, May 5, 1991; U.S., January 15, 1995 (became IV.2).

Based on *Thank You, Jeeves,* serialized in England in *Strand Magazine* (August 1933 to January 1934) and in the United States in *Cosmopolitan* (January to February 1934); published in book form in England (London: Herbert Jenkins, March 16, 1934) and the United States (Boston: Little, Brown, April 23, 1934).

Cast: Matthew Solon (Chuffy), Sharon Holm (Pauline), Manning Redwood (Stoker), Fred Evans (Brinkley), Fidelis Morgan (Myrtle), Edward Holmes (Seabury), James Holland (Dwight), Dave Atkins (Vaules), William Waghorn (Dobson), John Leavitt (Mangelhoffer), John Rutland (Henberry), Merelina Kendall (Miss Daly).

"Kidnapped!" UK title: "The Mysterious Stranger." Original broadcast dates: UK, May 12, 1991; U.S., not broadcast; video release only.

Based on *Thank You, Jeeves,* serialized in England in *Strand Magazine* (August 1933 to January 1934) and in the United States in *Cosmopolitan* (January to February 1934); published in book form in England (London: Herbert Jenkins, March 16, 1934) and the United States (Boston: Little, Brown, April 23, 1934).

Cast: Matthew Solon (Chuffy), Sharon Holm (Pauline), Manning Redwood (Stoker), Roger Brierley (Sir Roderick), Jane Downs (Lady Glossop), Fidelis Morgan (Myrtle), Edward Holmes (Seabury), James Holland (Dwight Stoker), Martin Clunes (Barmy), Richard Dixon (Oofy), Dave Atkins (Voules), William Waghorn (Constable Dobson), Cynthia Grenville (Aunt Hilda), Gordon Salkilld (Stationmaster), Raymond Young (Porter), Michael Ripper (Drones Porter), Marlene Sidaway (Pub Landlady), Colin Pinney (Butler).

"Jeeves the Matchmaker" UK title: "Wooster with a Wife." Original broadcast dates: UK, May 19, 1991; U.S., January 22, 1995 (became IV.3).

Based on four stories:

"Bertie Changes his Mind," published in the United States in *Cosmopolitan* (August 1922) and in England as "Bertie Gets His Chance" in *Strand Magazine* (August 1922); first anthologized in book form in *Carry On, Jeeves* in England (London: Herbert Jenkins, October 9, 1925) and the United States (New York: George H. Doran, October 7, 1927).

"Jeeves and the Kid Clementina," published in the United States in *Cosmopolitan* (January 1930) and England in *Strand Magazine* (January 1930); first anthologized in *Very Good, Jeeves,* published in book form in the United States (Garden City: Doubleday, Doran, June 20, 1930) and England (London: Herbert Jenkins, July 4, 1930).

"Tuppy Changes His Mind," published in the United States in *Liberty* (April 1930) and in England in *Strand Magazine* (April 1930); first anthologized in *Very Good, Jeeves,* published in book form in the United States (Garden City: Doubleday, Doran, June 20, 1930) and in England as "The Ordeal of Young Tuppy" in *Very Good, Jeeves* (London: Herbert Jenkins, July 4, 1930).

"Jeeves in the Spring-Time," published in the United States in *Cosmopolitan* (December 1921) and England in *Strand Magazine* (December 1921); first anthologized in book form in *The Inimitable Jeeves* in England (London: Herbert Jenkins, May 17, 1923) and in the United States as "Jeeves Exerts the Old Cerebellum" and "No Wedding Bells for Bingo" in *Jeeves* (New York: George H. Doran, September 28, 1923).

Cast: Robert Daws (Tuppy), Michael Siberry (Bingo), Niamh Cusak (Bobbie), Geoffrey Toone (Bittlesham), Hubert Rees (Sir Reginald), Sonia Graham (Lady Dalgleish), Catherine McQueen (Daisy), Janet Henfrey (Miss Mapleton), Charlotte Avery (Mabel), Hermione Eyre (Clementina), Marissa Dunlop (Margaret), Alex Leppard (Sergeant).

UK Series III — in U.S. partially shown as series II

U.S. video release title: *P. G. Wodehouse's More Jeeves and Wooster.*
Director: Ferdinand Fairfax.

"Bertie Sets Sail" UK title: "Safety in New York." Original broadcast dates: UK, March 29, 1992; U.S., not broadcast; video release only.

Based on "Jeeves and the Unbidden Guest," published in the United States in the *Saturday Evening Post* (December 9, 1916) and in England in *Strand Magazine* (March 1917); first anthologized in book form in England in *My Man Jeeves* (London: George Newnes, May 1919) and in the United States in *Carry On, Jeeves* (New York: George H. Doran, October 7, 1927).

Cast: Robert Daws (Tuppy), John Fitzgerald-Jay (Rocky), Ronan Vibert (Wilmot), Moyra Fraser (Lady Malvern), Don Fellows (Stoker), Kymberley Huffman (Pauline), Ricco Ross (Liftman), Gordon Sterne (Diner), Ellen Sheean (Diner), Daniel Andre Pageon (Captain), Tessa Churchard (Girl on Boat), Nick Simons (Warden), Morgan Deare (Taxi Driver).

"The Full House" UK title: "Bertie Ensures Bicky Can Continue to Live in Manhattan." Original broadcast dates: UK, April 5, 1992; U.S., not broadcast; video release only.

Based on two stories:

"Jeeves and the Hard-Boiled Egg," published in the United States in the *Saturday Evening Post* (March 3, 1917) and in England in *Strand Magazine* (August 1917); first anthologized in book form in England in *My Man Jeeves* (London: George Newnes, May 1919) and in the United States in *Carry On, Jeeves* (New York: George H. Doran, October 7, 1927).

"The Aunt and the Sluggard," published in the United States in the *Saturday Evening Post* (April 22, 1916) and in England in *Strand Magazine* (August 1916); first anthologized in book form in England in *My Man Jeeves* (London: George Newnes, May 1919) and in the United States in *Carry On, Jeeves* (New York: George H. Doran, October 7, 1927).

Cast: Julian Firth (Bicky), John Fitzgerald-Jay (Rocky), John Savident (Chiswick), Heather Canning (M. Rockmotteller), Lou Hirsch (Jimmy Mundy), Ricco Ross (Liftman), Deirdre Harrison (Waitress), Sam Douglas (Corrigan), Mary Ellen Ray (Landlady), Matt Zimmerman (Birdsburger), Bill Reimbold (Birdsburger), Douglas W. Iles (Birdsburger), Mac McDonald (Birdsburger), Paul Springer (Cabbie).

"Introduction on Broadway" UK title: "Cyril and the Broadway Musical." Original broadcast dates: UK, April 12, 1992; U.S., December 27, 1992 (became II.1).

Based on two stories:

"Leave It to Jeeves," published in the United States in the *Saturday Evening*

Post (February 5, 1916) and in England in *Strand Magazine* (June 1917); first anthologized in book form in England in *My Man Jeeves* (London: George Newnes, May 1919) and in the United States as "The Artistic Career of Corky" in *Carry On, Jeeves* (New York: George H. Doran, October 7, 1927).

"Jeeves and the Chump Cyril," published in the United States in the *Saturday Evening Post* (June 8, 1918) and in England in *Strand Magazine* (August 1918); first anthologized in book form in *The Inimitable Jeeves* in England (London: Herbert Jenkins, May 17, 1923) and in the United States as "A Letter of Introduction" and "Startling Dressiness of a Lift Attendant" in *Jeeves* (New York: George H. Doran, September 28, 1923).

Cast: Mary Wimbush (Aunt Agatha); Nicholas Hewetson (Cyril); Greg Charles (Corky); Dena Davis (Muriel); David Crean (George Caffyn); Bill Bailey (Worple); Billy J. Mitchell (Blumenfield); John Cassady (Prysock); Ricco Ross (Liftman); Sam Douglas (Corrigan); Joel Cutrara (Tradesman); Elaine English (Secretary); Anatol Yusef (Sidney); John Boulter (Flowerdew); Leigh Miles, Claire Alexander, Jane Sturdy, Di Cooke, Diane Holmes, Kim Barrand, Nola Haynes, and Colette Forbes (Chorus Girls).

"Right Ho! Jeeves" UK title: "Bertie Takes Gussie's Place at Deverill Hall." Original broadcast dates: UK, April 19, 1992; U.S., January 3, 1993 (became II.2).

Based on *The Mating Season*, published in book form in England (London: Herbert Jenkins, September 9, 1949) and the United States (New York: Didier, November 29, 1949).

Cast: Mary Wimbush (Aunt Agatha), Richard Braine (Gussie), Elizabeth Morton (Madeline), Chloe Annett (Gertrude), Rosalind Knight (Dame Daphne), Hilary Sesta (Emmeline), Harriet Reynolds (Harriet), Celia Gore-Booth (Myrtle), Sheila Mitchell (Charlotte), John Elmes (Catsmeat), Harriet Bagnall (Hilda), Llewellyn Rees (Magistrate), Peter Mair (Butler).

"Hot Off the Press" UK title: "Sir Watkyn Bassett's Memoirs." Original broadcast dates: UK, April 26, 1992; U.S., January 10, 1993 (became II.3).

Based on two stories:

"Jeeves Takes Charge," published in the United States in the *Saturday Evening Post* (November 18, 1916) and in England in *Strand Magazine* (April 1923); first anthologized in book form in *Carry On, Jeeves* in England (London: Herbert Jenkins, October 9, 1925) and the United States (New York: George H. Doran, October 7, 1927).

The Mating Season, published in book form in England (London: Herbert Jenkins, September 9, 1949) and the United States (New York: Didier, November 29, 1949).

Cast: John Turner (Spode), John Woodnutt (Sir Watkyn), Richard Braine (Gussie), Fiona Gillies (Lady Florence), Elizabeth Morton (Madeline), Amanda Harris (Stiffy), Simon Treves (Stinker), Stewart Harwood (Oates), Lucy Parker (Receptionist), David Rolfe (Butterfield), Diana Cummings (Mrs. Blockett).

"Comrade Bingo" UK title: "Aunt Dahlia, Cornelia and Madeline." Original broadcast dates: UK, May 3, 1992; U.S., January 17, 1993 (became II.4).

Based on two stories:

"Comrade Bingo," published in the United States in *Cosmopolitan* (May 1922) and in England in *Strand Magazine* (May 1922); first anthologized in book form in *The Inimitable Jeeves* in England (London: Herbert Jenkins, May 17, 1923) and in the United States in *Jeeves* (New York: George H. Doran, September 28, 1923).

"Jeeves Makes an Omelette," published in England in *Lilliput* (February 1959); first anthologized in *A Few Quick Ones* in the United States (New York: Simon and Schuster, April 13, 1959) and England (London: Herbert Jenkins, June 26, 1959).

Cast: John Turner (Spode), Patricia Lawrence (Aunt Dahlia), Pip Torrens (Bingo), Elizabeth Morton (Madeline), Rachel Robertson (Charlotte), Peter Benson (Mr. Rowbotham), Colin Higgins (Comrade Butt), Geoffrey Toone (Lord Bittlesham), Brenda Kempner (Lady Bittlesham), Ann Queensbury (Cornelia), Bev Wills (Everard), Chris Banks (Edward), Stewart Porter, Roger Frost (Speakers), David Peart (Footman).

UK Series IV — in U.S. partially shown as series III, out of sequence

U.S. video release title: *P. G. Wodehouse's A Tad More Jeeves and Wooster.*

Director: Ferdinand Fairfax.

"Return to New York" Original broadcast dates: UK, May 16, 1993; U.S., October 10, 1993 (became III.1).

Based on three stories:

"Jeeves and the Spot of Art," published in the United States in *Cosmopolitan* (December 1929) and in England in *Strand Magazine* (December 1929); first anthologized in *Very Good, Jeeves,* published in book form in the United States (Garden City: Doubleday, Doran, June 20, 1930) and England (London: Herbert Jenkins, July 4, 1930).

"The Delayed Exit of Claude and Eustace," published in England in *Strand Magazine* (October 1922) and in the United States in *Cosmopolitan* (November 1922); first anthologized in book form in *The Inimitable Jeeves* in England (London: Herbert Jenkins, May 17, 1923) and in the United States in *Jeeves* (New York: George H. Doran, September 28, 1923).

"Fixing It for Freddie," anthologized in book form in *Carry On, Jeeves* in England (London: Herbert Jenkins, October 9, 1925) and the United States (New York: George H. Doran, October 7, 1927).

Cast: Elizabeth Spriggs (Aunt Agatha), Robert Daws (Tuppy), Joss Brook (Eustace), Jeremy Brook (Claude), Deirdre Strath (Gwladys), Briony Glassco (Elizabeth), Marcus D'Amico (Lucius Pim), Harry Ditson (Slingsby), Marcia Layton (Mrs. Slingsby), Janan Kubba (Marion), Joseph Mydell (Coneybear), Devon Scott (May Prysock), Jack Johnson, Thomas Johnson (Tootles).

"The Once and Future Ex" UK title: "Lady Florence Craye Arrives in New York." Original broadcast dates: UK, May 23, 1993; U.S., not broadcast; video release only.

Based on *Joy in the Morning,* published in book form in the United States (Garden City: Doubleday, August 22, 1946) and England (London: Herbert Jenkinks, June 2, 1947).

Cast: Nicholas Palliser (Stilton); Francesca Folan (Florence); Nigel Whitmey (George); Jennifer Gibson (Nobby); Frederick Treves (Worplesden); John Cater (Clam); Sam Douglas (Corrigan); Joseph Mydell (Coneybear); Peter Carlisle (Bookseller); Michael Crossman (Billy); Thomasine Heiner (Secretary); Gregory

Sweeney, Amy Tolsky, Richard Brake (Reporters); John Alexander (Gorilla); Kristopher Milnes (Edwin); Kim Barrand, Kim McCarthy, Di Cooke, Alison Jenkins, Nola Haynes, Sue Hadleigh (Chorus Girls).

"Bridegroom Wanted" UK title: "Honoria Glossop Turns Up." Original broadcast dates: UK, May 30, 1993; U.S., October 17, 1993 (became III.2).

Based on two stories:

"Jeeves and the Greasy Bird," published in the United States in *Playboy* (December 1965) and in England in *Argosy* (January 1967); first anthologized in book form in *Plum Pie* in England (London: Herbert Jenkins, September 22, 1966) and the United States (New York: Simon and Schuster, December 1, 1967).

"Bingo and the Little Woman," published in England in *Strand Magazine* (November 1922) and in England in *Cosmopolitan* (December 1922); first anthologized in book form in *The Inimitable Jeeves* in England (London: Herbert Jenkins, May 17, 1923) and in *Jeeves* in the United States (New York: George H. Doran, September 28, 1923).

Cast: Pip Torrens (Bingo), Anastasia Hille (Rosie M. Banks), Philip Locke (Glossop), Liz Kettle (Honoria), Geoffrey Toone (Lord Bittlesham), Veronica Clifford (Myrtle Snap), Otto Jarman (Blair), David Healy (Waterbury), Serretta Wilson (Trixie), Paul Kynman (Porky Jupp), Edmund Dring (Dobson), Peter Carlisle (Bookseller), Joseph Mydell (Coneybear).

"The Delayed Arrival" UK title: "Arrested in a Night Club." Original broadcast dates: UK, June 6, 1993; U.S., October 24, 1993 (became III.3).

Based on *Jeeves and the Feudal Spirit*, published in book form in England (London: Herbert Jenkins, October 15, 1954) and in the United States as *Bertie Wooster Sees It Through* (New York: Simon and Schuster, February 23, 1955).

Cast: Jean Heywood (Aunt Dahlia); Francesca Folan (Florence); Nicholas Palliser (Stilton); Walter James (Percy Gorringe); Ralph Michael (Uncle Tom); Sylvia Kay (Mrs. Trotter); John Rapley (Mr. Trotter); Peter Howell (Magistrate); James Ottaway (Mr. Burwash); Ian Collier (Seppings); Richard Dixon (Oofy); Rex Doyle (Pawnbroker); Jon Croft, Peter Diamond, Jim Barclay (Policemen).

"Trouble at Totleigh Towers" UK title: "Totleigh Towers." Original broadcast dates: UK, June 13, 1993; U.S., not broadcast; video release only.

Based on *Stiff Upper Lip, Jeeves*, serialized in the United States in *Playboy* (February to March 1963); published in book form in the United States (New York: Simon and Schuster, March 22, 1963) and England (London: Herbert Jenkins, August 16, 1963).

Cast: John Turner (Spode), John Woodnutt (Sir Watkyn), Elizabeth Morton (Madeline), Charlotte Attenborough (Stiffy), Richard Braine (Gussie), Simon Treves (Stinker), Norman Rodway (Major Plank), Sidney Livingstone (Oates), Emma Hewitt (Emerald), Colin McFarlane (Toto), Preston Lockwood (Butterfield).

"The Ties That Bind" UK title: "The Ex's Are Nearly Married Off." Original broadcast dates: UK, June 20, 1993; U.S., October 31, 1993 (became III.4).

Based on the book published in England as *Much Obliged, Jeeves* (London: Barrie and Jenkins, October 15, 1971) and in the United States as *Jeeves and the Tie That Binds* (New York: Simon and Schuster, October 15, 1971).

Cast: Elizabeth Spriggs (Aunt Agatha), John Turner (Spode), John Woodnutt (Sir Watkyn), Robert Daws (Tuppy), Elizabeth Morton (Madeline), Francesca Folan (Florence), Julian Gartside (Ginger), Fred Evans (Brinkley), Selina Cadell (Mrs. McCorkadale), Sidney Livingstone (Oates), Fiona Christie (Magnolia), Preston Lockwood (Butterfield), Geoffrey Drew (Vicar).

Den Ofrivillige Golfaren (1991, Sweden)

Alternate titles: *The Accidental Golfer*; *The Involuntary Golfer*. A Svensk Filmindustri presentation of a Viking Film production in cooperation with SF, Smart Egg Pictures and Cinema Art. Length: 107 minutes. Format: Sound, color; theatrical feature film.

Inspired by the golf stories of P. G. Wodehouse.

Producer, Bo Jonsson; director, Lasse Åberg; screenplay, Lasse Åberg, Bo Jonsson; camera, Rune Ericson.

Cast: Lasse Åberg (Stig-Helmer Olsson), Jon Skolmen (Ole Bramserud), Mats Bergman (Bruno Anderhage), Hege Schøyen (Mette Gulbrandsen), Ulf Eklund (Tom), Marianne Scheja (Pyttan), Jimmy Logan (Roderic McDougall), Margo Gunn (Fiona McDougall), Lasse Haldenberg (Bärsen), Annalisa Ericson (Alice), Ingvar Kjellson (Rutger), Claes Månsson (Distr. Antiqarian Berglund), Bertil Norström (Ivar Olofsson, farmer), Margreth Weivers (Mrs. Olofsson), Pia Oscarsson (Carina Anderhage).

Heavy Weather (1995, UK)

Alternate title: *P. G. Wodehouse's Heavy Weather*. BBC, Cinema Verity, Juniper Films, WGBH Boston. Original broadcast dates: UK, December 24, 1995; U.S., February 18, 1996 on *Masterpiece Theater*. Length: 95 minutes. Format: Sound, color; television feature film.

Based on *Heavy Weather*, serialized in the United States in the *Saturday Evening Post* (May 27, to July 15, 1933); published in book form in the United States (Boston: Little, Brown, July 28, 1933) and England (London: Herbert Jenkins, August 10, 1933).

Producer, Verity Lambert; director, Jack Gold; screenplay, Douglas Livingstone; cinematography, Ernest Vincze; editing, Ralph Sheldon; original music, Denis King; production design, Jane Martin.

Cast: Peter O'Toole (Clarence, Earl of Emsworth), Richard Briers (The Hon. Galahad Threepwood), Roy Hudd (Beach), Judy Parfitt (Lady Constance Keeble), Richard Johnson (Lord Tilbury), Samuel West ("Monty" Bodkin), Benjamin Soames (Ronnie Fish), Rebecca Lacey (Sue Brown), David Bamber (P. Frobisher Pilbeam), Ronald Fraser (Sir Gregory Parsloe), Bryan Pringle (Pirbright), Denyse Alexander (Miss Gutteridge), Matthew Byam-Shaw (Hugo Carmody), Tony Spooner (Sir Gregory's Pig Man), James Horne (Voules), Sarah Badel (Lady Julia Fish), Charles Pemberton (Porter), Anne Caroll (Barmaid), Gertrude of Tiverton (the Empress of Blandings), Alma-Rose of Iver (the Pride of Matchingham).

By Jeeves (2001, Canada)

Canadian Broadcasting Company, Really Useful Films, and Tapestry Pictures. Length: 120 min. Format: Sound, color; television feature film.

Based on the Alan Ayckbourn and Andrew Lloyd Webber musical play based on the Jeeves stories.

Executive producers, Heather Goldin and Austin Shaw, producer, Mary Young Leckie; directors, Alan Ayckbourn and Nick Morris; Libretto, Alan Ayckbourn; music, Andrew Lloyd Webber; choreographer, Sheila Carter; editor, Nick Morris; production design, Roger Glossup; costume design, Louise Belson.

Cast: John Scherer (Bertie Wooster), Martin Jarvis (Jeeves), Donna Lynne Champlin (Honoria Glossup), James Kall (Gussie Fink- Nottle), Ian Knauer (Rev. Harold "Stinker" Pinker), Heath Lamberts (Sir Watkin Bassett), Emily Loesser (Stiffy Bing), Don Stephenson (Bingo Little), Becky Watson (Madeline Bassett), Steve Wilson (Cyrus Budge III).

Piccadilly Jim (2006, UK)

Produced by Mission Pictures; Inside Track; Isle of Man Film Ltd. Shot in 2004. Release: 2006 Myriad Pictures. Format: Sound, color; theatrical feature film.

Based on the serial *Piccadilly Jim*, published in the United States in the *Saturday Evening Post* (September 16, to November 11, 1916); in book form in the United States (New York: Dodd, Mead, February 24, 1917) and England (London: Herbert Jenkins Limited, May 1918).

Executive producers, Kirk D'Amico, Marion Pilowsky, and Steve Christian; producers, Peter Czernin, Graham Broadbent, and Andrew Hauptman; director, John McKay; screenplay, Julian Fellowes; photography, Andrew Dunn; production design, Amanda McArthur; costume design, Ralph Holes; editor, David Freeman; casting, Jill Trevellick; music, Adrian Johnson.

Cast: Sam Rockwell (Jim Crocker), Frances O'Connor (Ann Chester), Tom Wilkinson (Bingley Crocker), Brenda Blethyn (Nesta Pet), Hugh Bonneville (Reggie Wisbech), Allison Janney (Eugenia Crocker), Austin Pendleton (Peter Pet), Tom Hollander (Willie Partridge), Geoffrey Palmer (Bayliss), Pam Ferris (Trimble), Rupert Simonian (Ogden).

Citations: http://filmcritic.com, May 2005; *Preview Online*, summer 2004, <http://www.preview-online.com/s2004/feature_articles/jim/>.

Notes

Chapter 1

1. PGW, letter to Guy Bolton, April 7, 1958, quoted in Eileen McIlvaine, Louise S. Sherby and James H. Heineman, *P. G. Wodehouse: A Comprehensive Bibliography and Checklist* (New York: James H. Heineman, 1990), 349; Tony Ring, *You Simply Hit Them with an Axe* (London: Porpoise, 1995), 198.

2. Joseph Connolly, *P. G. Wodehouse* (London: Thames and Hudson, 1987), 35.

3. PGW, letters to Leslie Havergal Bradshaw, September 1, 1914 and January 20, 1915, courtesy of Norman Murphy, and quotation in McIlvaine et al., 357.

4. PGW, letter of December 2, 1914, reprinted in "More from Plum's Emsworth Letters," *Wooster Sauce*, no. 24 (December 2002), 9.

5. PGW, letter to Leslie Havergal Bradshaw, October 10, 1914, courtesy of Norman Murphy.

6. PGW, letter of December 2, 1914, reprinted in "More from Plum's Emsworth Letters," *Wooster Sauce*, No. 24 (December 2002), 9. Primary source data for this and similar information on each movie given here is to be found in the Records of Transfers of Film Rights, United States Copyright Office, Library of Congress. See volume 57, pp. 73–77, November 23, 1914. Further citations will refer to these records as "RTFR."

7. Volume 113, pp. 374–376, November 13, 1923, and volume 294, p. 94, October 30, 1925, RTFR. A $5,000 payment from Famous Players that should have been reported on Wodehouse's 1927 income tax is mentioned in Robert McCrum, *Wodehouse: A Life* (London: Penguin, 2004), 459; this is presumably from the same transaction.

8. PGW, letter to Leslie Havergal Bradshaw, January 20, 1915, courtesy of Norman Murphy.

9. *Moving Picture World*, September 11, 1915, 1833.

10. Lee Davis, *Bolton and Wodehouse and Kern* (New York: James H. Heineman, 1993), 179.

11. Davis, 166.

12. Volume 72, pp. 322–324, January 14, 1918, RTFR; Connolly, *P. G. Wodehouse*, 37.

13. Volume 152, pp. 1–19, February 15, 1927, RTFR.

14. Volume 98, pp. 176–179, July 19, 1921, RTFR.

15. Volume 98, pp. 155–159, July 19, 1921, RTFR; Connolly, 38.

16. PGW, letter to Guy Bolton, February 9, 1951, quoted in McIlvaine et al., 345.

17. Davis, 130, 121, 129.

18. Volume 83, p. 262, August 23, 1919, RTFR.

19. Dick Fiddy and Luke McKernan, "Plum Pudding: Christmas with P. G. Wodehouse," *National Film Theater*, November–December 1996, 15.

20. PGW to Paul R. Reynolds, Jr., August 24, 1928, quoted in Barry Phelps, *P. G. Wodehouse: Man and Myth* (London: Constable, 1992), 138–139.

21. Davis, 296.

Chapter 2

1. This may have referred to Frederik Palmer and the Palmer Photoplay Corp., which had been an independent production company, but was best noted for offering the most extensive screenwriting courses in the nation and publishing books on the subject.

2. McCrum, *Wodehouse: A Life*, 186.

3. PGW, letter to William Townend, January 8, 1930, in PGW, *Performing Flea*, chapter 2.

4. Ring, *You Simply Hit Them with an Axe*, 63.

5. Edwin M. Bradley, *The First Hollywood Musicals* (Jefferson, N.C.: McFarland, 1996), 89; Richard Barrios, *A Song in the Dark* (New York: Oxford University Press, 1995), 234.

6. Bradley, 90.

7. Bradley, 89; Barrios, 235.

8. "Leonora Wodehouse and Plum on the Radio," *Wooster Sauce*, no. 6 (June 1998), 9.

9. "Wodehouse Here to Write Movies," *New York Times*, April 23, 1930, p. 31.

10. PGW in Alma Whitaker, "Wodehouse Out and Still Dazed," *Los Angeles Times*, June 7, 1931, p. III-22.

11. PGW, letter to Denis Mackail, June 26, 1930, quoted in Frances Donaldson, ed., *Yours, Plum: The Letters of P. G. Wodehouse* (London: Hutchinson, 1990), 124.

12. PGW, letter to Denis Mackail, April 12, 1931, quoted in Donaldson, ed., *Yours, Plum: The Letters of P. G. Wodehouse*, 114.

13. PGW, letter to Leonora Wodehouse, August 13, 1937, quoted in Donaldson, ed., *Yours, Plum: The Letters of P. G. Wodehouse*, 70.

14. PGW, letter to Denis Mackail, June 26, 1930, quoted in Donaldson, ed., *Yours, Plum: The Letters of P. G. Wodehouse*, 125.

15. PGW in Whitaker, p. III-22.

16. PGW, letter to Denis Mackail, June 26, 1930, quoted in Donaldson, ed., *Yours, Plum: The Letters of P. G. Wodehouse*, 125.

17. PGW, letter to Claude Houghton, January 7, 1937, Harry Ransom Humanities Research Center, University of Texas at Austin, quoted in McCrum, *Wodehouse: A Life*, 465.

18. PGW, letter to Guy Bolton, July 19, 1930, quoted in Donaldson, ed., *Yours, Plum: The Letters of P. G. Wodehouse*, 125, and in McIlvaine et al., 337.

19. PGW, letter to Guy Bolton, July 19, 1930. The pretext of the romantic misadventures of a troika of women would be used in Bolton's play *Three Blind Mice*, using the name Stephen Powys (a pseudonym Wodehouse would later use). The play was purchased by Twentieth Century Fox and made into three films in quick Succession: *Three Blind Mice* (1938), *Moon over Miami* (1941), and *Three Little Girls in Blue* (1946). Seeing its success, Wodehouse in turn created his own version, *French Leave*, published in 1956 (but not in the United States until 1959); he shared a part of the advance with Bolton (McIlvaine, 350). Later, when a handsome sum was offered for the film rights to *French Leave*, the truth of its genesis had to be admitted, although Fox had only paid Bolton $350 for his play (note from Bolton, July 6, 1962, quoted in McIlvaine, 351). For his part, Bolton found the novel far funnier than his own creation (note from Bolton, April 7, 1958, quoted in McIlvaine, 350). However, there were no further plot elements in common between *Those Three French Girls* and *French Leave*.

20. Phelps, 166.

21. Samuel Marx, *Mayer and Thalberg: The Make-believe Saints* (New York: Random House, 1975), 152.

22. "One Hundred Not Out," *Wooster Sauce*, no. 25 (March 2003), 3; Davis, 323.

23. PGW, "The Second Berlin Broadcast," in Iain Sprott, *Wodehouse at War* (London: Ticknor and Fields, 1981), 115.

24. Marx, 152.

25. *Empire Theatre News*, no. 1 (November 21, 1930).

26. PGW in Whitaker, p. III-9.

27. PGW, letter to William Townend, October 28, 1930, in PGW, *Performing Flea*, chapter 2.

28. PGW, *Over Seventy*, chapter 17, in *Wodehouse on Wodehouse*, 622.

29. PGW, letter to Denis Mackail, December 28, 1930, quoted in Donaldson, ed., *Yours, Plum*, 126–127.

30. "Rosalie: A Novelized Version by P. G. Wodehouse," January 30, 1931, p. 91.

31. PGW, letter to Paul Reynolds, November 23, 1930, Reynolds papers, Rare Book and Manuscript Library, Columbia University; quoted in McCrum, *Wodehouse: A Life*, 194.

32. Charles Poore, "Books of the Times," *New York Times*, June 21, 1962, p. 29.

33. PGW, letter to Denis Mackail, December 28, 1930, quoted in Donaldson, ed., *Yours, Plum*, 127.

34. PGW, letter to Peter Schwed, May 20, 1961, Tony Ring Collection.

35. PGW, letter to Denis Mackail, December 28, 1930, quoted in Donaldson, ed., *Yours, Plum*, 127.

36. Marx, 154.

37. PGW in Whitaker, p. III-22.

38. PGW, letter to William Townend, March 14, 1931, in PGW, *Performing Flea*, chapter 2, also quoted in Donaldson, ed., *Yours, Plum*, 127–128.

39. Richard Usborne, *Wodehouse at Work to the End* (London: Barrie and Jenkins, 1976), 242. Renewal of the original June 13, 1931 contract with Loew's was on June 18, 1958. Copyright assignment records indicate the rights to the play along with the novel were purchased. Volume 1011, pp. 56ff, June 18, 1958, and Volume 1019, p. 430, September 30, 1958, RTFR.

40. PGW, letter to Denis Mackail, May 10, 1931, quoted in Donaldson, ed., *Yours, Plum*, 128.

41. PGW, letter to Denis Mackail, June 26, 1930, quoted in Donaldson, ed., *Yours, Plum*, 125.

42. PGW, *Over Seventy*, chapter 17, in *Wodehouse on Wodehouse*, 616.

43. McCrum, *Wodehouse: A Life*, 195.

44. Whitaker, p. III-9, 22.

45. Phelps, 173.

46. William Townend in PGW, *Performing Flea*, chapter 2.

47. "All So Unbelievable," *The New York Herald Tribune*, June 10, 1931, p. 20.

48. PGW, letter to William Townend, March 14, 1931, in PGW, *Performing Flea*, chapter 2.

49. Maureen O'Sullivan, "The Wodehouses of Hollywood," in James H. Heineman, Donald R. Bensen, eds., *P. G. Wodehouse, A Centenary Celebration, 1881–1981* (New York: Pierpont Morgan Library Press, 1981), 17.

50. Marx, 153.

51. "News of the Screen," *New York Times*, August 11, 1936, p. 24.

52. Phelps, 173.

53. PGW, letter to William Townend, June 29, 1931, in PGW, *Performing Flea*, chapter 2; also quoted in Donaldson, ed., *Yours, Plum*, 129.

54. "Wodehouse Faces $259,703 Tax Lien," *New York Times*, August 11, 1934, p. 11.

55. Leonora Wodehouse in *Chums*, excerpted in "What Leonora Said About Plum," *Wooster Sauce*, no. 27 (September 2003), 6.

56. "P. G. Wodehouse Says Farewell," *New York Times*, August 7, 1932, p. X3.

Chapter 3

1. PGW, letter to William Townend, August 24, 1932, Special Collections, P. G. Wodehouse Library, Dulwich College; quoted in McCrum, *Wodehouse: A Life*, 211–212.

2. PGW, *The Luck of the Bodkins*, chapter 11 (British edition), chapter 9 (American edition).

3. PGW, letter to Denis Mackail, May 10, 1931, quoted in Donaldson, ed., *Yours, Plum*, 128.

4. PGW, letter to Paul Reynolds, March 3, 1933, quoted in McIlvaine et al., 377.

5. Beatrice Sherman, "A Wodehouse Packet," *New York Times*, September 22, 1935, p. BR7.

6. Beatrice Sherman, "Typical Wodehouse," *New York Times*, January 12, 1936, p. BR7.

7. J.B. Priestley, *Evening Standard*, August 18, 1932, quoted in McCrum, *Wodehouse: A Life*, 459–460.

8. John Chamberlain, "Books of the Times," *New York Times*, January 6, 1936, p. 15.

9. William Stephenson, "The Wodehouse World of Hollywood," *Film Literature Quarterly* 6 (summer 1978), 191.

10. McCrum, *Wodehouse: A Life*, 235.

11. PGW, *Laughing Gas* (New York: Doubleday Doran and Co., Inc., 1936), 17.

12. PGW, *Laughing Gas*, 16–17.

13. PGW, *Laughing Gas*, 45–46.

14. PGW, *Laughing Gas*, 64.

15. PGW, *Laughing Gas*, 142.

16. PGW, *Laughing Gas*, 250.

17. PGW, *Laughing Gas*, 119.

18. PGW, *Laughing Gas*, 122.

19. PGW, *Laughing Gas*, 115–116.

20. Sherman, BR7; Davis, 331.

21. PGW, *The Luck of the Bodkins*, chapter 14 (British edition), chapter 12 (American edition).

22. PGW, *The Luck of the Bodkins*, chapter 14 (British edition), chapter 12 (American edition).

23. John Chamberlain, "Books of the Times," *New York Times*, January 6, 1936, p. 15; Mordecai Richler, "The Man Who Was Hollywood," *New York Times*, March 26, 1989, p. BR24.

24. PGW, *The Luck of the Bodkins*, chapter 15 (British edition), chapter 14 (American edition).

25. PGW, *The Luck of the Bodkins*, chapter 24 (British edition), chapter 27 (American edition).

26. PGW, *The Luck of the Bodkins*, chapter 14 (British edition), chapter 12 (American edition).

27. PGW, *The Luck of the Bodkins*, chapter 11 (British edition), chapter 9 (American edition).

28. PGW, *The Luck of the Bodkins*, chapter 12 (British edition), chapter 10 (American edition).

29. PGW, *The Luck of the Bodkins*, chapter 15 (British edition).

30. PGW, *The Luck of the Bodkins*, chapter 15 (British edition), chapter 25 (American edition).

31. PGW, *The Luck of the Bodkins*, chapter 11 (British edition), chapter 9 (American edition).

Chapter 4

1. Tom Dardis, *Keaton: The Man Who Wouldn't Lie Down* (New York: Charles Scribner's Sons, 1979), 205; Rudi Blesh, *Keaton* (New York: Macmillan, 1966), 325.

2. *Hollywood Reporter*, May 29, 1935, p. 3.

3. PGW, letter to William Townend, *Performing Flea*, quoted in Davis, 310.

4. McCrum, *Wodehouse: A Life*, 230, 234.

5. McCrum, *Wodehouse: A Life*, 228.

6. Volume 339, pp. 170–199, October 16, 1935, RTFR. The play was registered for copyright on April 30, 1925, as number D71391, but sadly was not retained for the permanent Library collection.

7. Douglas W. Churchill, "How Doth the Busy Little 'B,'" *New York Times*, January 2, 1938.

8. PGW, letter to Guy Bolton, 15 August 1973, quoted in McIlvaine, 66.

9. Jon Lellenberg, "Thank You, Jeeves," *Plum Lines* 14 (spring 1993), 18.

10. PGW in Frank Muir, *A Kentish Lad* (London: Corgi, 1997), 273.

11. PGW, letter to Guy Bolton, 7 August 1965, quoted in McIlvaine, 353.

12. Gerard Garrett, *The Films of David Niven* (London: LSP Books, 1975), 35.

13. David Niven in Tom Hutchinson, *Niven's Hollywood* (Salem, N.H.: Salem House, 1984), 66.

14. "Step Lively, Jeeves," *Film Weekly*, June 12, 1937.

15. Hedda Hopper, "England in Hollywood," page 1, Hedda Hopper Collection, Academy of Motion Picture Arts and Sciences Library.

Chapter 5

1. PGW, letter to William Townend, August 26, 1934, quoted in McIlvaine, 396.

2. PGW, letter to William Townend, June 11, 1934, quoted in McIlvaine, 396.

3. Volume 272, pp. 119–120, June 1, 1931, and volume 324, pp. 28 and 179, June 8, 1933, RTFR; PGW, letter to William Townend, June 3, 1946, quoted in McIlvaine, 407.

4. Paul R. Reynolds, letter to PGW, August 9, 1934; PGW, letter to Reynolds, August 27, 1934; PGW, letter to Guy Bolton, June 8, 1933, quoted in McIlvaine, 337, 379.

5. PGW, letter to Guy Bolton, July 13, 1946, quoted in McIlvaine, 340.

6. McIlvaine, 31.

7. "News of the Screen," *New York Times*, August 11, 1936, p. 24; McCrum, *Wodehouse: A Life*, 465.

8. PGW, letter to William Townend, September 4, 1937, in PGW, *Performing Flea*, chapter 3, and quoted in McIlvaine, 399.

9. PGW, letter to William Townend, November 7, 1936, in PGW, *Performing Flea*, chapter 3.

10. PGW, letter to Guy Bolton, March 8, 1937, quoted in McIlvaine, 338, and in Donaldson, ed., *Yours, Plum*, 130.

11. PGW, letter to William Townend, March 24, 1937, quoted in PGW, *Performing Flea*, chapter 3; McIlvaine, 399; and in Donaldson, ed., *Yours, Plum*, 131.

12. PGW, letter to Leonora Cazalet, July 13, 1937, quoted in Donaldson, ed., *Yours, Plum*, 67.

13. PGW, letter to William Townend, March 24, 1937, in PGW, *Performing Flea*, chapter 3, also quoted in Donaldson, ed., *Yours, Plum*, 131.

14. Walter MacEwen, Inter-office communication to Hal Wallis, April 8, 1937, Warner Bros. Archives, University of Southern California.

15. PGW, letter to William Townend, May 6, 1937, in PGW, *Performing Flea*, chapter 3; also quoted in Donaldson, ed., *Yours, Plum*, 131.

16. PGW, letter to Leonora Cazalet, July 13, 1937, quoted in Donaldson, ed., *Yours, Plum*, 67.

17. PGW, letter to William Townend, June 24, 1937, in PGW, *Performing Flea*, chapter 3; also quoted in Donaldson, ed., *Yours, Plum*, 131–132.

18. PGW, letter to Leonora Cazalet, July 13, 1937, quoted in Donaldson, ed., *Yours, Plum*, 67.

19. PGW, letter to Leonora Cazalet, August 13, 1937, quoted in Donaldson, ed., *Yours, Plum*, 69.

20. Hopper, "England in Hollywood," p. 1.

21. PGW, letter to Leonora Cazalet, July 13, 1937, quoted in Donaldson, ed., *Yours, Plum*, 67.

22. PGW, letter to Leonora Cazalet, July 13, 1937, quoted in Donaldson, ed., *Yours, Plum*, 67.

23. PGW, letter to William Townend, September 4, 1937, in PGW, *Performing Flea*, chapter 3.

24. PGW, letter to William Townend, September 4, 1937, quoted in McIlvaine, 399.

25. PGW, letter to William Townend, June 24, 1937, in PGW, *Performing Flea*, chapter 3.

26. PGW, letter to George Middleton, November 16, 1937, George Middleton Collection, Manuscript Division, Library of Congress.

27. Philip Dunne, *Take Two: A Life in Movies and Politics* (New York: McGraw-Hill, 1980), 50; Nancy Lynn Schwartz, *The Hollywood Writer's Wars* (New York: Knopf, 1982), 105–106. Wodehouse biographers Robert McCrum and David Jasen, the latter a personal friend of Wodehouse, specifically dismisses Dunne's charge of anti-Semitism, considering the many individuals of Jewish faith and background with whom Wodehouse collaborated on stage productions.

28. PGW, letter to Leonora Cazalet, February 12, 1938, quoted in Donaldson, ed., *Yours, Plum*, 71; PGW, letter to William Townend, August 16, 1930, quoted in Donaldson, ed., *Yours, Plum*, 126.

29. PGW, letter to Leonora Cazalet, March 10, 1939, quoted in Donaldson, ed., *Yours, Plum*, 77.

Chapter 6

1. George Cukor in Gene D. Phillips, *George Cukor* (Boston: Twayne, 1982), 46.

2. Paul Reynolds, letter to PGW, June 26, 1941, Reynolds papers, Rare Book and Manuscript Library, Columbia University; quoted in McCrum, *Wodehouse: A Life*, 307.

3. McCrum, *Wodehouse: A Life*, 306–310.

4. PGW, letter to Anga von Bodenhausen, March 30, 1942; Ethel Wodehouse, letter to PGW, August 8, 1942; PGW, letter to Guy Bolton, August 16, 1948; quoted in McIlvaine, 336, 422, 341.

5. PGW, letter to Major E.J.P. Cussen, September 14, 1944, in Sprott, 144.

6. PGW, letter to Major E.J.P. Cussen, September 14, 1944; Financial Statement by P. G. Wodehouse; Further Financial Statement by P.W. Wodehouse, 15 September 1944, in Sprott, 140, 143–144; Phelps, 219.

7. PGW, letter to Major E.J.P. Cussen, 14 September 1944, in Sprott, 143–144; Phelps, 219. My thanks to Chris Horak for helping to clarify the structure of the German industry at the time.

8. PGW, letter to Major E.J.P. Cussen, September 14, 1944, in Sprott, 143–144.

9. Interview with Michael Vermehren, quoted in McCrum, *Wodehouse: A Life*, 333. By contrast, Sprott (73) asserts the Wodehouses did not go to the theater; Wodehouse himself did not know the German language.

10. Ethel Wodehouse, letter to PGW, August 8, 1942, quoted in McIlvaine, 422.

11. PGW, letter to Major E.J.P. Cussen, September 14, 1944, in Sprott, 143–144.

12. PGW, *The Old Reliable*, chapter 4.

13. PGW, *The Old Reliable*, chapter 9.

14. PGW, *The Old Reliable*, chapter 5. A similar idea, for a picture titled *The Vicissitudes of Vera*, had appeared earlier in "A Slice of Life" in the anthology *Meet Mr. Mulliner*.

15. PGW, *The Old Reliable*, chapter 5.

16. PGW, letter to Guy Bolton, December 12, 1951, quoted in McIlvaine, 346. PGW, *The Old Reliable*, chapter 21. Volume 756, p. 212, June 7, 1950, RTFR. PGW, *Barmy in Wonderland*, chapter 20.

Chapter 7

1. PGW, letter to Guy Bolton, February 16, 1957, quoted in McIlvaine, 349.

2. "Television Reviews: Musical Comedy Time," *Variety*, October 4, 1950; "Tele Reviews: Anything Goes," *Daily Variety*, March 1, 1954.

3. PGW, letter to Guy Bolton, January 29, 1950, quoted in McIlvaine, 344; PGW, letter to Guy Bolton, February 9, 1951, quoted in McIlvaine, 345.

4. PGW, letter to Ira Gershwin, December 12, 1948, quoted in McIlvaine, 364.

5. PGW, letter to Denis Mackail, May 6, 1952, quoted in Donaldson, ed., *Yours, Plum*, 210.

6. PGW, letter to Denis Mackail, November 8, 1956, quoted in Donaldson, ed., *Yours, Plum*, 211.

7. PGW, letter to Sheran Hornby, quoted in Frances Donaldson, *P. G. Wodehouse* (New York: Alfred A. Knopf, 1982), 309.

8. PGW, letter to Denis Mackail, June 8, 1957, quoted in Donaldson, ed., *Yours, Plum*, 212.

9. PGW, letter to Guy Bolton, July 2, 1953, quoted in McIlvaine, 348.

10. PGW, letter to William Townend, December 12, 1953, quoted in McIlvaine, 421.

11. Peter Lewis in Philip Purser, "PGW Hits," *Plum Lines* 11 (summer 1990), 2.

12. PGW, letter to Walter McLennan Citrine, July 24, 1965, quoted in McIlvaine, 360; PGW, letter to J. Derek Grimsdick, January 22, 1966, quoted in McIlvaine, 368.

13. PGW, letter to J. Derek Grimsdick, November 10, 1973, quoted in McIlvaine, 369; PGW in Muir, *A Kentish Lad*, 273.

14. PGW, letter to Walter McLennan Citrine, July 24, 1965, quoted in McIlvaine, 360.

15. PGW, letter to Guy Bolton, July 7, 1966, quoted in McIlvaine, 353.

16. Frank Muir, introduction to PGW, *Lord Emsworth Acts for the Best* (London: Penguin, 1992), xiv.

17. PGW, letters to Guy Bolton, May 2, 1967, and March 11, 1968, quoted in McIlvaine, 354.

Chapter 8

1. PGW in Ring, *You Simply Hit Them with an Axe*, 155.

2. McCrum, *Wodehouse: A Life*, 411.

3. PGW, *The Plot That Thickened* (New York: Simon and Schuster, 1973), 75.

4. PGW, *The Plot That Thickened*, 14.

5. PGW, *The Plot That Thickened*, 13.

6. PGW, *The Plot That Thickened*, 112.

7. PGW, *The Plot That Thickened*, 221.

8. PGW, *The Plot That Thickened*, 219.

9. PGW, *The Plot That Thickened*, 7.

10. PGW, *Bachelors Anonymous* (London: Penguin, 1975), chapter 7, p. 56.

11. PGW, *Bachelors Anonymous*, chapter 10, 14, pp. 101, 139.

12. Murray Hedgcock, "Reviews and Previews: Wodehouse Playhouse," *Wooster Sauce*, no. 25 (March 2003), 20.

13. Connolly, 122.

14. PGW, letter to Peter Schwed, October 10, 1971, quoted in McIlvaine, 387; McCrum, *Wodehouse: A Life*, 414–415.

Chapter 9

1. Richard West, "Wodehouse Sahib," *Harpers and Queen*, June 1988, 114–115; "Plum's Indian Summer Is Still Hot," *Wooster Sauce*, no. 23 (September 2002), 1.

2. Hugh Laurie, "Wodehouse Saved My Life," *Sunday Telegraph*, May 23, 1999, reprinted in *Plum Lines* 18 (summer 1999), 9.

3. Stephen Fry, introduction to PGW, *What Ho!* (London: Penguin, 2002), xxiv.

4. Fry, introduction to PGW, *What Ho!*, xv.

5. Stephen Fry in Rhoda Koenig, "'Jeeves and Wooster,'" *Plum Lines* 11 (summer 1990), 2.

6. Curtis Armstrong, interview with the author, August 9, 2003.

7. Tony Ring, "Heavy Weather," *Plum Lines* 15 (winter 1995), 10.

8. John McKay in "PG Tips: Piccadilly Jim," *Preview Online*, summer 2004, <http://www.preview-online.com/s2004/feature_articles/jim/>.

9. McKay in "PG Tips: Piccadilly Jim."

10. McKay in "PG Tips: Piccadilly Jim."

11. Entry on *Piccadilly Jim* at <http://www.cinemovies.fr/fiche_film.php?IDfilm3451>.

12. "PG Tips: Piccadilly Jim."

13. McKay in "PG Tips: Piccadilly Jim."

14. Ronnie Scheib, review of *Piccadilly Jim* posted on Variety.com, April 25, 2005.

15. McKay in "PG Tips: Piccadilly Jim."

16. McKay in "PG Tips: Piccadilly Jim."

17. Philip A. Shreffler, "Piccadilly Jim at It Again," Review for *Plum Lines*, 26 (summer 2005), 5–6.

18. PGW, *Piccadilly Jim* (London: Herbert Jenkins, n.d.), 312.

19. Chris Barsanti, review of *Piccadilly Jim* on <http://filmcritic.com>, May 2005.

20. Scheib, review of *Piccadilly Jim* posted on Variety.com, April 25, 2005.

21. Barsanti, review of *Piccadilly Jim*.

Bibliography

American Film Institute Catalog, Feature Films. Volumes for 1911–1920, 1921–1930, 1931–1940, 1941–1950. Online version at <afi.chadwyck.com>.

Armstrong, Curtis. "Nodders I Have Known: Wodehouse's Hollywood and Mine." *Plum Lines* 24 (autumn 2003), 12–16.

Connolly, Joseph. *P. G. Wodehouse.* London: Thames and Hudson, 1987.

Davis, Lee. *Bolton and Wodehouse and Kern.* New York: James H. Heineman, 1993.

Donaldson, Frances. *P. G. Wodehouse: A Biography.* New York: Alfred A. Knopf, 1982.

_____, ed. *Yours, Plum: The Letters of P. G. Wodehouse.* London: Hutchinson, 1990.

Fiddy, Dick, and Luke McKernan. "Plum Pudding: Christmas with P. G. Wodehouse." *National Film Theater* (November–December 1996), 11–15.

Garrison, Daniel H. *Who's Who in Wodehouse.* 2nd revised edition. New York: International Polygonics, 1989.

Jasen, David A. *P. G. Wodehouse: Portrait of a Master.* New York: Continuum, 1981.

_____. *The Theatre of P. G. Wodehouse.* London: B.T. Batsford, 1979.

Kaufman, Jan Wilson. "Wodehouse in Hollywood." Unpublished speech, 1992 New York convention of the Wodehouse Society.

McCrum, Robert. "A Lotus-Eater at the La-La Land Buffet." *Los Angeles Times,* August 14, 2004.

_____. *Wodehouse: A Life.* London: Penguin, 2004.

McIlvaine, Eileen, Louise S. Sherby, and James H. Heineman. *P. G. Wodehouse: A Comprehensive Bibliography and Checklist.* New York: James H. Heineman, 1990.

Morley, Sheridan. *Tales from the Hollywood Raj.* New York: Viking, 1983.

Ring, Tony. "Wodehouse on the Boards: P. G. Wodehouse's Straight Plays." Unpublished speech, 2003 Toronto convention, the Wodehouse Society.

Sprott, Iain. *Wodehouse at War.* London: Ticknor and Fields, 1981.

Stephenson, William. "The Wodehouse World of Hollywood." *Film Literature Quarterly* 6 (summer 1978).

United States Copyright Office. Library of Congress. Records of Transfers of Film Rights.

Voorhees, Richard J. *P. G. Wodehouse.* New York: Twayne, 1966.

Wodehouse, P. G. *Wodehouse on Wodehouse.* London: Hutchinson, 1980.

Index